VIRTUAL CEO™

STRATEGIC BUSINESS PRINCIPLES

VIRTUAL CEO™
INCORPORATED

STRATEGIC
BUSINESS
PRINCIPLES

Jeffrey A. Rigsby and Guy Greco

Foreword by Richard A. Goodman
The Anderson School at UCLA

Published by Virtual CEO, Inc.

VIRTUAL CEO, INC.
www.virtualceo.com

27128A Paseo Espada, Suite 1521
San Juan Capistrano, California 92675
Telephone —   1-949-248-2404
Fax —   1-949-248-2413
E-Mail —   info@virtualceo.com

ISBN 0-9706032-0-7

First Edition

PRINTED IN THE UNITED STATES OF AMERICA

DEDICATIONS

Lovingly, to my wife, Pam, who has shouldered
the additional responsibilities of home and family
while I have pursued my professional and educational goals.

- JR -

To my mother, Mildred, who has always been
an unconditional supporter of my dreams.

- GG -

ACKNOWLEDGMENTS

We would like to acknowledge some individuals who contributed their time and talents to producing this book.

First and foremost, we'd like to express our deep appreciation to Martine Berreitter, Manager of Product Development at Virtual CEO, Inc. Martine stepped in, pulled all the pieces together, and drove this book to press.

Lynn Lipinski, at UCLA, edited our first draft and made sure that we were actually saying what we intended to say. Thanks very much for helping us create a publication that is consistent in content, message, and intentions.

Richard Bontems devoted many hours to designing a very professional looking publication. Thank you for the attention to detail and your terrific ideas for layout and overall look. We are indebted to you for your ability to takes piles of typewritten sheets and turn them into a very crisp and concise publication.

Scott de Ruyter did extensive literary research to support and elaborate upon the business disciplines contained in this book. His research provided interesting case studies and useful models that effectively illustrate the application of each business discipline. We appreciate his considerable time and effort.

We would also like to extend a special thanks to Dr. Richard A. Goodman, Co-Chair of Management Faculty at the Anderson School at UCLA, for his help and advice in planning the scope and objectives of this book. We appreciate both your counsel and those long drives south.

Lastly and most importantly, we'd like to honor the experts cited in *Strategic Business Principles*. Their decades of research and field work provided us with the fact-based foundation necessary to construct this consolidated body of work.

Thank you all very much.

TABLE OF CONTENTS

VIRTUAL CEO™

STRATEGIC BUSINESS PRINCIPLES

*Radically Transforming the Way
Organizations Evaluate
and Improve
Business Performance*

FOREWORD BY RICHARD A. GOODMAN

Finally, a book for CEOs by a CEO. Jeff Rigsby along with Guy Greco have mined the management literature using their extensive managerial experience as a filter to select concepts and concerns that are critical for the boardroom and senior executive councils. Few executives pause in their career to systematically cull through the management literature. Even fewer focus on the particular needs of the CEO and their top management team.

This book is the result of a three-tiered analysis. The value to the reader increases dramatically with each tier. The foundation tier has been built by researching the vast management literature for issues that determine action steps. This step provides the executive with an immediate, practical window into the literature. Because the management literature is both wide and deep, many of the findings refer to operational concerns with little direct connection to the strategic concerns of the CEO and other top managers. The second tier, which involved narrowing the literature to directly relevant strategic issues, significantly increases the book's value. But a process that stopped at the second tier would be one that delivered great content in a random setting. The final tier of analysis organizes the results into a strategic management framework. The resulting structure of concerns and implications then redoubles the book's value.

In speaking to a conference of management scholars, Mike McCaskey, President of the Chicago Bears, reflected upon his experiences and tested them against theories developed by his audience. The discussion was very stimulating, as management scholars are basically very practical people, and they were pleased to gain insights into the needs of the CEO from someone who has both a doctorate from the Harvard Business School and a World Championship Ring from the National Football League. **Strategic Business Principles** begins at the same place and takes a similar perspective, but it focuses on the CEO audience (rather than the academic audience), probes deeper, and approaches the issues more systematically.

Rigsby and Greco have focused upon the top management concerns of strategy, organization design, and culture — the thrust, structure, and resilience of the firm — the basic leverage points of senior management. They have approached these issues in a unique fashion. After poring through the writings of hundreds of management scholars and puzzling over the substance and the supporting data of each article and book, they have abstracted the pithy material, sharpened the lessons, and provided a concise and focused overview. As they engaged in this review they continuously asked three questions: Which issues are really leverage-points for CEOs and their top management team? What are the basics of the issue? How can these issues be presented in a clear and concise fashion? The ideas were tested through focus groups of CEOs and other top managers and checked against the views of various management educators. This attention to the needs of the reader is extremely important. The result is a tool of great value to the audience of CEOs and other senior executives for whom it was written.

The book was created as a companion to the Virtual CEO™ Organizational Dynamic Model. It provides managers and management consultants who are employing the system with an easy point of reference. But it has larger value as well. The book provides readers with a broad coverage of issues relating to the management of the firm. Structured and focused around the three major concerns and their underlying issues, it provides an effective method with which senior managers can appreciate the insights of the Organizational Dynamic Model. At the same time, it provides better understanding of the work of the management scholars who have discovered and created the fundamentals upon which the book is based.

The structure of the system and thus of the book highlights the question of alignment. Alignment is approached from three complementary angles: internal alignment, communication, and external alignment. The fundamental question of internal alignment is the one of competence matching. Do the various competencies of the firm align with the strategy of the firm? The essence of communication alignment is determining whether all the team members are reading from the same page. Do the firm's members know and understand the firm's strategy and the reasoning behind the firm's strategy? External alignment is essential for determining if strategies align with the marketplace in terms of both customers and competitors. Since the marketplace often changes rapidly, continual realignment is necessary. Thus, the fundamental question here is: Does the firm's strategy line up well with the current and future marketplace? Effectiveness, then, is a combination of internal alignment between competence and strategy, a communication alignment among all the various facets of the firm, and an external alignment between the strategy and the marketplace.

In general, the CEO's greatest challenges arise when the marketplace changes and strategies have to be altered. The challenges begin with the determination of strategic changes. Then the new vision must be communicated. Often, many parts of the organization are insulated from the new executive vision and they continue following the old vision, either slowly changing or becoming points of pain to the new strategy. Thus, the time between re-visioning and the full communication of the new vision is a serious competitive problem. As a companion to the Organizational Dynamic Model, this book provides broad insight into the acceleration of communication alignment and thus the alignment between external and internal strategic needs.

The book is clear and crisp, it is effectively organized, and it serves the companion role to the Organizational Dynamic Model very well. In addition, it is an effective primer for thinking about the three alignment challenges of the CEO and top management: internal alignment, communication, and external alignment. Most executive literature draws upon the author's own experiences and typically describes how successful they were and why. *Not this book.* This is *not* a book about how *they* ran *their* company. It is about running *your* company. It is a book for you.

Richard A. Goodman
Professor of Technology and Strategy
The Anderson School at UCLA
Los Angeles, May 1, 2000

PREFACE

This business primer and reference guide has been prepared to give students, entrepreneurs, and business executives an introductory exposure to strategic business nomenclature and best practice data, processes, and models. References and links to additional resources for each topic, including an academic and popular bibliography, internet sites, and case studies, are listed for further study. This work is not meant to be a comprehensive final authority on any topic, but merely serves as a gateway to exploration of the subject matter in greater detail.

Entries in this primer contain definitions, models, illustrations, worksheets, and case studies to enhance the learning process. Entries parallel the core drivers, key components, and principal elements of the Organization Dynamic Model (shown on the next page) developed by Virtual CEO™, Inc. The model illustrates how an organization's success in achieving its strategic intent is driven through the interdependencies of the three Core Drivers (Figure 1).

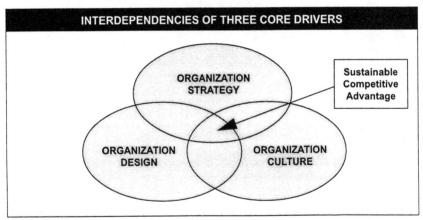

Figure 1

The model expands the three Core Drivers into 12 key components and 49 principal elements of business performance. These components are rooted in best practice statements, models, and processes extracted from a host of academic and business-oriented publications. A complete list of cited best practice sources is listed in the Virtual CEO™ Knowledge Center on the web site.

Virtual CEO™ Organization Dynamic Model

1.0 Organization Strategy		2.0 Organization Design		3.0 Organization Culture	
1.1 Mission, Vision Competitive Advantage	1.1.1 Focused Purpose 1.1.2 Future Perspective 1.1.3 Strategic Advantage 1.1.4 Strategic Integration	**2.1 Basic Structure**	2.1.1 Strategic "Demand Criteria" 2.1.2 Formal Structure 2.1.3 Structure Evolution	**3.1 Values & Beliefs**	3.1.1 Values Integration 3.1.2 Values Communication 3.1.3 Values Durability
1.2 External Assessment	1.2.1 Customer Profile 1.2.2 Industry & Competitive Analysis 1.2.3 Environmental Assessment 1.2.4 Key Success Factors	**2.2 Core Competence**	2.2.1 Identification Core Competence 2.2.2 Application of Core Competence 2.2.3 Leveraging Core Competence	**3.2 Leadership**	3.2.1 Management Modeling 3.2.2 Strategic/Tactical Balance 3.2.3 Empowerment 3.2.4 Developmental Coaching 3.2.5 Building Effective Teams
1.3 Internal Assessment	1.3.1 Market Position 1.3.2 Finance 1.3.3 R & D 1.3.4 Production 1.3.5 Marketing 1.3.6 Sales/Distribution 1.3.7 Customer Service	**2.3 Information, Systems, & Technology**	2.3.1 Organization Communication 2.3.2 Targeted Information 2.3.3 Enterprising Systems 2.3.4 Applied Technology	**3.3 Human Resource Systems**	3.3.1 Selective Recruitment 3.3.2 Employee Orientation 3.3.3 Continuous Learning 3.3.4 Performance Management 3.3.5 Reward Systems
1.4 Objectives, Initiatives, & Goals	1.4.1 Vital Direction 1.4.2 Resource Alignment 1.4.3 Organization Accountabilities 1.4.4 Measurements	**2.4 Organization Efficiency**	2.4.1 Balanced Oversight & Direction 2.4.2 Synthesized Roles & Responsibilities 2.4.3 Managed Outsource & Strategic Alliances	**3.4 Organization Character**	3.4.1 Informal Communication 3.4.2 Organization Feedback 3.4.3 Organizational Credibility 3.4.4 Adaptability to Change

This primer and resource guide is a companion to the references, forums, and links located on the Virtual CEO™ web site at **http://www.virtualceo.com**. The knowledge portal contains additional support services, links, and extensive knowledge management tools designed to radically accelerate organizational performance by capturing elusive intellectual business knowledge and render it tangible, targeted, and actionable.

Together, the Virtual CEO™ suite of knowledge management software tools, the interactive internet resource center, and continuously updated reference materials provide businesses, consultants, and students with a framework to better understand the various influences that impact an organization's culture, effectiveness, and performance.

1.0 ORGANIZATION STRATEGY

"There is no 'perfect' strategic decision. One always has to pay a price. One always has to balance conflicting objectives, conflicting opinions, and conflicting priorities. The best strategic decision is only an approximation — and a risk." — PETER DRUCKER

Key Components
- Mission, Vision, and Competitive Advantage
- External Assessment
- Internal Assessment
- Objectives, Initiatives, and Goals

The task of formulating an organization's strategy in today's dynamic world has become increasingly demanding. The accelerated rate of technological change, increased global competition, and a more sophisticated customer base have combined to challenge managers to rethink their business models, techniques, and tools in favor of faster, more responsive approaches.

Successful strategy formulation is becoming increasingly dependent on how well an organization gathers, manages, and synthesizes vital information into targeted, actionable activities.[1] This information should not only contain hard data from secondary and primary research and analysis, but also the soft views and intuitions of those in key positions throughout the organization.[2]

The chief executive officer of Rockwell International explains, "We expect every business segment head to be responsible for the strategic direction of the business and the business team to be very knowledgeable about their business in the worldwide marketplace, to know where they are taking the business long term; and how they are going to position the business."[3] Strategic dialogue and debate among key employees and managers is a vital component of a successful strategic planning process.

Michael Porter captured the essence of the assessment process by identifying the key questions that need to be answered in order to advance a company's strategic intent (Figure 1).

PROCESS FOR FORMULATING A COMPETITIVE STRATEGY [4]	

A. What is the business doing now?	1. Identification
	   What is the implicit or explicit current strategy?
	2. Implied Assumptions
	   What assumptions about the company's relative position, strengths and weaknesses, competitors, and industry trends must be made for the current strategy to make sense?

B. What is happening in the environment?	1. Industry Analysis
	   What are the key factors for competitive success and the important industry opportunities and threats?
	2. Competitor Analysis
	   What are the capabilities and limitations of existing and potential competitors, and their probable future moves?
	3. Societal Analysis
	   What important governmental, social, and political factors will present opportunities or threats?
	4. Strengths and Weaknesses
	   Given an analysis of industry competitors, what are the company's strengths and weaknesses relative to present and future competitors?

C. What should the business be doing?	1. Test of Assumptions and Strategy
	   How do the assumptions embodied in the current strategy compare with B above? Is the strategy consistent or does it fit with your core competence, your capital, people, and technology resource. Does your design and culture support your strategy?
	2. Strategic Alternatives
	   What are the feasible strategic alternatives given the analysis above? (Is the current strategy one of these?)
	3. Strategic Choice
	   Which alternative best relates the company's situation to external opportunities and threats?

Figure 1

Involving strategic team members in prioritizing and validating significant issues is critical to empowering employees to respond in ways consistent with the overall objectives of the organization.

Empowered work teams, upon execution of their plans, may self-assess their effectiveness in light of their understanding of and commitment to the organization's strategic intent and respond with tactical adjustments as necessary.

A summary of the organizational process and phases is shown in Figure 2 on the following page.

Assess
- Determine senior management's perception of the direction and performance of the organization.
- Identify the impediments to achieving the company's strategic intent.
- Invite cross-functional input from the executive team.

Relate
- Align management thinking to a common understanding.
- Identify and prioritize critical issues based on their impact on strategic success.
- Benchmark performance against relevant standards.

Respond
- Develop targeted solutions for each identified area needing improvement.
- Integrate action items with the organization's values and beliefs.
- Align the necessary resources.
- Synthesize roles and responsibilities.
- Establish clear measurements for success.

Execute
- Implement targeted action plans.
- Communicate execution and progress.
- Encourage feedback.
- Remain flexible to seize emerging opportunities.
- Support and sustain competitive advantage.

Figure 2

This organization strategy process can ensure employee participation, contribution, and most importantly commitment to sustaining the strategic intent of the company.

Footnotes for Section 1.0 —

[1] Bill Gates. *Business at the Speed of Thought.* Warner Books, 1999, p. 3.

[2] Henry Mintzberg. *The Fall and Rise of Strategic Planning.* The Free Press, 1994, p. 324.

[3] Donald Beal, Former Chairman and CEO. "Internal Report." Rockwell International, 1990.

[4] Michael E. Porter. *Competitive Strategy.* Free Press, 1980, p. xix-xx.

1.1.0 MISSION, VISION, AND COMPETITIVE ADVANTAGE

"The general who wins the battle makes many calculations in his temple before the battle is fought. The general who loses makes but few calculations beforehand." — SUN-TZU

Description

A company's mission, vision, and competitive advantage describe the business it is in, its short- and long-term market position, and the manner in which it will differentiate itself from the competition.

Principal Elements

- Mission: Focused Purpose
- Vision: Future Perspective
- Strategic Advantage
- Strategic Integration

The concepts of mission, vision, and competitive advantage are the foundations of the organizational strategy process. Together and separately, these concepts describe a company's business, its short- and long-term market position, and its points of differentiation from its competitors.

Simply stated, a company's mission should reflect who they are, what they do, to whom they offer products and services, and how they will be offering those products and services in terms of basic philosophy and technology. A vision statement takes the long view, expressing where the organization should ultimately develop.

Before defining a mission, a vision, or a competitive advantage, a company first describes the arena in which it will compete. In other words, what industry is this company in?

Defining the industry may seem like a basic exercise, but it is helpful in establishing a general overview of the environment the business competes in, the customers it serves and the industry dynamics that establish the rules of engagement. These definitions tend to be very broad descriptions of the industry and about what product or service the industry provides. For example, United Airlines is in the transportation business, Wells Fargo Bank is in the banking or financial service business, Pfizer is in the pharmaceutical business, Oracle is in the information technology business, and K-Mart is in the retail/general merchandise business.

Industry descriptions also clearly identify activities in which a company does not participate. This can be helpful in separating direct competitors (those that provide the same product or service to the same market) from companies that are substitutes, (those that provide a different product or service that meets the same consumer need).

Understanding the nature of an industry can also help determine the need for diversification of risk from business cycles or the need to focus on a limited business arena. McDonald's, for example, has concentrated primarily on the fast food business, while firms such as Allied Signal have minimized their cycle risk by operating business in several related and unrelated industries.

King and Cleland recommend that organizations carefully develop a written mission statement for the following reasons:

REASONS TO DEVELOP A MISSION STATEMENT [1]

1. To ensure unanimity of purpose within the organization.
2. To provide a basis, or standard, for allocating organizational resources.
3. To establish a general tone or organizational climate.
4. To serve as a focal point for individuals to identify with the organization's purpose and direction and to deter those who cannot from participating further in the organization's activities.
5. To facilitate the translation of objectives into a work structure involving the assignment of tasks to responsible elements within the organization.
6. To specify organizational purposes and the translation of these purposes into objectives in such a way that cost, time, and performance parameters can be assessed and controlled.

Some organizations develop separate vision and mission statements. Separate statements more clearly illustrate the company's overall direction for the near term and provide a clearer understanding of the organization's future direction of evolution. However, it is not unusual for the mission and vision to be combined into a single statement.

Footnote for Section 1.1.0 —

[1] W. R. King and D. I. Cleland. *Strategic Planning and Policy.* McGraw-Hill, 1979, p. 124-125.

1.1.1 MISSION: THE FOCUSED PURPOSE

"He who wishes to fulfill his mission in the world must be a man of one idea, that is, of one great overmastering purpose, overshadowing all his aims, and guiding and controlling his entire life."

— JULIUS BATE

Definition

Effectively mapping a course of action for the near term. Understanding the needs of a company's primary stakeholders. Stating a clear point of differentiation from the competition.

Areas of Focus

- Clearly defined short-term purpose.
- Realistic approach.
- Serves the best interests of all stakeholders.
- Clearly defined point of differentiation.

The mission and vision statements are maps to a company's future — the mission provides short-term guidance; while the vision statement provides a broader, longer-term view of the company's desired destination. Peter Drucker described a mission this way:

> The mission statement is the foundation for priorities, strategies, plans, and work assignments. It is the starting point for the design of managerial jobs and, above all, for the design of managerial structures. Nothing may seem simpler or more obvious than to know what a company's business is...Actually, "What is our business?" is almost always a difficult question and the right answer is usually anything but obvious.[1]

Derek F. Abell's approach to the question "What is our business?" takes the form of three customer-oriented questions: "Who is being satisfied?" (*customer groups*); "What is being satisfied?" (*customer needs*); and "How are these needs being satisfied?" (*distinctive competencies*).[2]

Caution should be taken when crafting a mission statement to avoid financial or other goal-related language. "Creating profit" for example is why a company is in business; therefore, the mission statement should speak to "how" to create profit.

The following examples illustrate the nine essential components of a mission statement:

NINE ESSENTIAL COMPONENTS OF A MISSION STATEMENT [3]		
Component	**Test/Question**	**Example**
1. Customers	Who are our firm's customers?	"We believe our first responsibility is to the doctors, nurses, and patients, to mothers and all others who use our products and services..." — Johnson & Johnson
2. Products and Services	What are the firm's major products or services?	"AMAX's principal products are molybdenum, coals, iron ore, lead, and magnesium." — AMAX
3. Markets	Geographically, where does the firm compete?	"We are dedicated to the total success of Corning Glass Works as a worldwide competitor ..." — Corning Glass Works
4. Technology	Is the firm technologically current?	"Control Data is in the business of applying micro-electronics and computer technology in two general areas: computer-related hardware and computer-enhancing services." — Control Data
5. Concern for Survival, Growth, and Profitability	Is the firm committed to growth and financial soundness?	"In this respect, the company will conduct its operations prudently and will provide the profits and growth which will assure Hoover's ultimate success." — Hoover Universal
6. Philosophy	What are the basic beliefs, values, aspirations, and ethical priorities of the firm?	"We believe human development to be the worthiest of goals of civilization and independence to be the superior condition for nurturing growth in the capabilities of people." — Sun Company
7. Self-Concept	What is the firm's distinctive competence or major competitive advantage?	"Crown Zellerbach is committed to leapfrogging competition within 1,000 days by unleashing the constructive and creative abilities and energies of each of its employees." — Crown Zellerbach
8. Concern for Public Image	Is the firm responsive to social, community, and environmental concerns?	" . . . To share the world's obligation for the protection of the environment." — Dow Chemical
9. Concern for Employees	Are employees a valuable asset of the firm?	"To recruit, develop, motivate, reward, and retain personnel of exceptional ability, character, and dedication by providing good working conditions, superior leadership, performance based compensation . . . and a high degree of employment security." — The Wachovia Corporation

In summary, a mission should:

- Contain realistic and obtainable concepts and define the benefits to stakeholders, e.g., customers, employees, shareholders, and the community.

- Differentiate the company from its competitors.

- Empower and enable everyone within an organization to align his or her efforts.

Footnotes for Section 1.1.1 —

[1] Peter Drucker. *Management: Tasks, Responsibilities and Practices.* Harper & Row, 1974, p. 61.

[2] Derek F. Abell. *Defining the Business: The Starting Point of Strategic Planning.* Prentice-Hall, 1980, p. 17.

[3] Fred R. David. *Strategic Management, 7th Edition.* Prentice-Hall, 1998, p. 91.

1.1.2 Vision: The Future Perspective

"A strategist's job is to see the company not as it is...but as it can become."

— John W. Teets

Definition

Having a clear long-term vision for the organization. Having a clear projection of the company's market position for the future. The long-term needs of stakeholders respected. Evolutionary in nature, responsive to evolving opportunities.

Areas of Focus

- Clearly defined long-term outlook.
- Appeals to long-term interests of the company's stakeholders.
- Provides foundation for all decisions.
- Flexible; allows for meeting evolving opportunities.
- Clear understanding of long-term financial requirements.

The vision statement, as noted in the previous chapter, presents an organization's long-term ideals while the mission statement maps a course of action in the near term. However, both the vision and the mission statements serve as a reference point for strategic decisions, conveying benefits to stakeholders, and articulating competitive advantages.

A vision must be evolutionary in nature, creating an organization that is flexible and responsive to a constantly changing environment. Such an organization needs strong leadership and a forward-thinking culture. John Kotter, in his book, *Leading Change*, outlined what his research uncovered as "vision characteristics," shown in Figure 1.

Vision statements are often articulated within a documented mission statement, yet their purpose can be clearly distinguished from a short-term mission. Visionary CEOs will postulate on the future, consider where the trends of technology, society, and economics are going, and match their definition of their company to the emerging opportunities within that future perspective. The vision statement is used to

1. Imaginable	Conveys a picture of what the future will look like
2. Desirable	Appeals to the long-term interest of employees, customers, stock-holders, and others who have a stake in the enterprise
3. Feasible	Comprises realistic, attainable goals
4. Focused	Is clear enough to provide guidance in decision making
5. Flexible	Is general enough to allow individual initiative and alternative responses in light of changing conditions
6. Communicable	Is easy to communicate; can be successfully explained within five minutes

Figure 1

prepare the company for the future. Resource alignment, including financial requirements for the future, can only be determined with a firm future perspective on the company's destination.

Although motivating in its description, the vision should remain flexible enough to take advantage of any new emerging opportunities as well. To illustrate the differences in a vision statement and a near-term mission statement, we have included both from Harley-Davidson, Incorporated, as Figures 2 and 3:

HARLEY-DAVIDSON MISSION STATEMENT [2]

Stay true to the things that make a Harley-Davidson a Harley-Davidson. Keep the heritage alive. From the people in the front office to the craftsmen on our factory floor, that is what we do. And it's why each new generation of Harley-Davidson motorcycles, well refined, contain the best of the ones before it. We have a passion for our product few companies understand. But when you see the result, it all becomes clear. We're not just building motorcycles. We're carrying on a legend. Ask anyone who's ever owned a Harley-Davidson. It gets in your blood. Becomes part of your life. And once it does, it never leaves. It's something you can't compare with anything else. We know because we've been there. That's why, for 90 years, we've remained firm in our commitment to building the kind of motorcycles that deserve the intense loyalty that Harley-Davidson enjoys. The styling is still pure. The engines rumble. It's also why you'll see us at major rallies and rides throughout the year, listening and talking to our customers. Staying close to riders and to the sport is how we've kept alive the things that make a Harley-Davidson a Harley-Davidson. Our approach has always been different. But, again, so has owning a Harley-Davidson. We wouldn't have it any other way.

Figure 2

Harley-Davidson, Inc., is an action-oriented, international company — a leader in its commitment to continuously improve the quality of profitable relationships with stakeholders (customers, employees, suppliers, shareholders, governments, and society). Harley-Davidson believes the key to success is to balance stakeholder interests through the empowerment of all employees to focus on value-added activities. Our vision is our corporate conscience and helps us to eliminate short-term thinking, such as cashing in on demand for our new motorcycles by giving quantity precedence over quality or cutting corners in recreational or commercial vehicles to save a few dollars per unit. It also encourages every employee in our organization to be acutely aware of his or her role in satisfying our stakeholders.

Equally important to our Vision, we live by a Code of Business Conduct that is driven by a value system that promotes honesty, integrity, and personal growth in all our dealings with stakeholders. Our values are the rules by which we operate: Tell the truth; be fair; keep your promises; respect the individual; and encourage intellectual curiosity. In addition, we never lose sight of the issues we feel must be addressed in order for us to be successful in the future: Quality, participation, productivity, and cash flow. As a shareholder, you should expect no less from us.

Figure 3

In the case of both the mission and vision statements, to be truly effective, look for them to instill a sense of urgency, direction, and success throughout the organization. Porsche CEO Peter Schultz relates this illustration of how an effective vision can motivate others and increase their productivity:

> Three people were at work on a construction site. All three were doing the same job, but when each was asked what his job was, the answers varied. "Breaking rocks," the first replied. "Earning a living," responded the second. "Helping to build a cathedral," said the third. Few of us can build cathedrals. But to the extent we can see the cathedral in whatever cause we are following, the job seems more worthwhile. Good strategists and a clear mission help us find those cathedrals in what otherwise could be dismal issues and empty causes.[3]

Footnotes for Section 1.1.2 —

[1] John P. Kotter. *Leading Change*. Harvard Business School Press, 1996, p. 72.

[2] Quoted from www.harley-davidson.com.

[3] Peter Schultz. Business Week. September 14, 1987, p. 120.

1.1.3 STRATEGIC ADVANTAGE

"The secret to business is to know something that nobody else knows."
— ARISTOTLE ONASSIS

Definition

Identifying what a company perceives to be its competitive advantage. Initiating specific activities that support the company's point of differentiation within their industry. Employees understand how their performance supports the strategic advantage.

Areas of Focus

- Competitive advantage is the key driver to forming strategy.
- Competitive advantage is clearly understood by all stakeholders.
- Employees clearly understand how their role supports the company's strategy.

A company's strategic intent conveys a sense of direction about the long-term market or competitive position that a firm hopes to build over the coming decade or so — it conveys a sense of direction. A company's strategic intent should hold a competitively unique point of view about the future, offer to employees the promise of exploring new competitive territory. At the same time, strategic intent must be perceived by employees as inherently worthwhile. In summary, strategic intent should offer an organization and its employees a sense of direction, a sense of discovery, and a sense of destiny.

J. Liedtka puts it this way:

> Strategic intent provides the focus that allows individuals within an organization to marshal and leverage their energy, to focus attention, to resist distraction, and to concentrate for as long as it takes to achieve a goal. In the disorienting swirl of change, such psychic energy may well be the most scarce resource an organization has, and only those who utilize it will succeed.[1]

Hamel and Prahalad describe strategic intent to include "...focusing the organization's attention on the essence of winning; motivating people by communicating the value of the target; leaving room for individual and team contributions; sustaining enthusiasm by providing new operational definitions as circumstances change, and using intent consistently to guide resource allocations."[2]

Eastman Kodak defines its strategic intent as being "the world leader in imaging." To this end, Kodak identified several skill sets that they would need to build a competitive advantage in the world markets. The competitive skills that Kodak identified are as follows (Figure 1):

KODAK-IDENTIFIED COMPETITIVE SKILLS [3]	
Customer focus	The ability to identify and serve customer needs
Cycle time	The ability to rapidly develop new products the serve customer needs
Manufacturing	The ability to raise manufacturing quality and lower manufacturing costs
Alliances	The ability to gain access to critical technology through strategic alliances
Benchmarking	The ability to measure Kodak's skills against those of other competitors

Figure 1

Strategic intent is most influential when personnel believe fervently in their product and industry and when they are focused entirely on their firm's ability to outdo its competitors.[4] Some would argue that strategic intent provides employees with the only goal worthy of personal effort and commitment — to unseat the best or remain the best, worldwide.[5]

In order for a company to define its strategic intent, it must have a clear understanding of its competitive advantage, or the bundle of skills, knowledge, and special abilities that help the company outperform its competitors. Michael Treacy and Fred Wiersema have defined three areas into which competitive advantages usually fall (Figure 2). Although they are usually mutually exclusive, the advent of cutting-edge technology has led some companies to excel in more than one area.

COMPETITIVE ADVANTAGE AREAS [6]	
Low-Cost Provider	Does the company emphasize cost control and containment in producing goods or services at the best cost for the quality delivered?
Product or Innovation Leader	Are the company's products and services innovative and consistently first-to-market?
Service Leader – High "Customer Intimacy"	Does the company's customer service consistently exceed customer expectations and lead the industry for personalized attention?

Figure 2

These three competitive advantage areas leverage a distinctive segment of customer demand: the elastic demand for lower prices, the inelastic demand for highly innovative products, or the inelastic demand for the extraordinary personalized service.

A company's ability to articulate its competitive advantage to its stakeholders will launch the organization towards achieving its strategic intent.

Wal-Mart Stores, Inc.,[7] provides an excellent example of a company defining its strategic intent and relentlessly pursuing its fulfillment. Wal-Mart, as a "low-cost" provider of goods, developed an organizational push and market outreach that supported their "Every Day Low-Price" policy.

As a low-cost provider, Wal-Mart sought to dominate share per market by driving down costs at every opportunity. Without sacrificing quality, Wal-Mart emphasized best price and good selection, while instilling a sense of family in the members of its highly-motivated family.

From 1980 to 1993, Wal-Mart grew in sales from $1.6 billion to $67 billion. (See Figure 3.) During the same period, Sears, considered the industry leader, went from $18.6 billion to $29.5 billion (Merchandise Group Operations only). While Sears and K-Mart struggled to define their market position going forward, Wal-Mart had

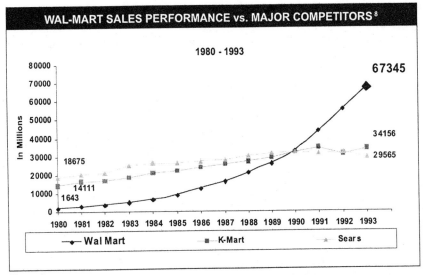

Figure 3

clearly defined its market position and had aligned human capabilities and organizational resources, and had met financial and physical requirements to achieve their overall strategic intent.

Footnotes for Section 1.1.3 —

[1] J. Liedtka. "Strategic Thinking; Can It Be Taught?" Long Range Planning, 31, (1), 1998, p. 120-129.

[2] Gary Hamel and C. K. Prahalad. "Strategic Intent." Harvard Business Review, May-June 1989, p. 64.

[3] J. B. Barney. "Firm Resources and Sustained Competitive Advantage." Journal of Management, 17, p. 99-120.

[4] E. P. Przybyowicz and T. W. Fulkner. "Kodak Applies Strategic Intent to the Management of Technology." Research Technology Management, Jan-Feb 1993, p. 31-38.

[5] Stratford P. Sherman. "The Secret to Intel's Success." Fortune, 1994, p. 14.

[6] Michael Treacy and Frederik D. Wiersema. *Disciplines of Market Leaders.* Addison-Wesley, 1995.

[7] A. A. Thompson, Kem Pinegar, and Tracy Robertson Kramer. *Wal-Mart Stores,* Irwin McGraw-Hill, 1994.

[8] A. A. Thompson and A. J. Strickland. *Strategic Management, 10th Edition.* Irwin McGraw-Hill, 1998, p. 923.

1.1.4 STRATEGIC INTEGRATION

"What is especially difficult is getting different departments working together in the best interest of customers, yet managers at all levels are the critical link to aligning the entire organization toward the customer." — RICHARD WHITELEY

Definition

Synthesizing the strategic formulation process and the implementation planning process. Ensuring that managers who are responsible for implementation plans participate in or receive detailed information relating to the company's strategy. Making sure that implementation plans are uniform and that they reflect the company's strategic intent.

Areas of Focus

- Strategy and tactics aligned.
- Implementers participate in the strategic formulation process.
- Units and divisions effectively plan together.
- Plans specify how divisions, departments, or groups will contribute.
- Plans reflect a universal approach.

Because most strategic plans are the accumulated efforts of various decision-makers at different levels in the organization, how a firm integrates the various functions and disciplines into achieving the strategic intent is critical to the organization's strategic success. Trying to keep managers and their departments focused on doing what is best strategically for the company instead of what is best for them can often result in heated debate as the organization seeks strategic consensus.

Thompson and Strickland[1] illustrate the networking of objectives and strategies down through the organization's managerial hierarchy (Figure 1). The vertical linkages representing two-way influences on mission, objectives, and strategies at each level can help unify the activities of many managers into a mutually reinforcing pattern, when properly managed to promote coordination.

Thompson and Strickland go on to compare the disarray that occurs in an orga-

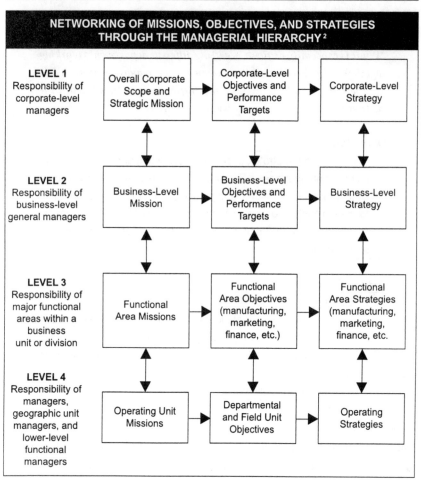

NETWORKING OF MISSIONS, OBJECTIVES, AND STRATEGIES THROUGH THE MANAGERIAL HIERARCHY [2]

LEVEL 1 Responsibility of corporate-level managers	Overall Corporate Scope and Strategic Mission	Corporate-Level Objectives and Performance Targets	Corporate-Level Strategy
LEVEL 2 Responsibility of business-level general managers	Business-Level Mission	Business-Level Objectives and Performance Targets	Business-Level Strategy
LEVEL 3 Responsibility of major functional areas within a business unit or division	Functional Area Missions	Functional Area Objectives (manufacturing, marketing, finance, etc.)	Functional Area Strategies (manufacturing, marketing, finance, etc.
LEVEL 4 Responsibility of managers, geographic unit managers, and lower-level functional managers	Operating Unit Missions	Departmental and Field Unit Objectives	Operating Strategies

Figure 1

nization when management does not exhibit strong strategic leadership to a football team whose quarterback doesn't call a play, but instead leaves the play selection up to each individual to take advantage of his own position.

A company's chances of realizing its strategic intent increases when everyone in the organization understands the interdependencies within the organization and commits to the steps necessary to integrate strategically. The following model (Figure 2) illustrates the steps and tasks that the management team must accomplish in order to fully integrate their business units.

MANAGEMENT STEPS TO STRATEGIC INTEGRATION [3]	
Connecting the silos	1. Achieving synergistic results from the behavior of empowered functional employees, who are intimately involved from the beginning. 2. Understand which market signals can improve the customer value of the enterprise's offerings.
Ensure the free flow of information	Resolve: 1. Inadequate or passive research capabilities. 2. Intermediaries that stand between the customer and the entire enterprise. 3. Lack of direct feedback mechanisms between customers, suppliers, distributors, and the enterprise. 4. Information systems that fail to detect and properly classify data coming from the marketplace.
Preserve the independence of the "voice of the market"	If information flow is owned by an individual or unit, management must ensure: Every function, team, and individual employee should have access to market information and the ability to develop an independent view of what the market is saying. When this happens, the enterprise develops a richer set of insights about products, services, competitors, pricing, and workflow.
Orchestrate the many voices within the company	The role of leadership is not to impose a vision or the leader's own "voice" but to draw out the best of the many visions and voices that already exist in scattered parts of the organization.
Change the decision-making process and cultural change will follow	The decision-making process is what really defines the enterprise. Change it by adopting a process that embodies the principles of the dialogue decision process or Senge's five disciplines or Ackoff's circular organization, for instance, and the rest will follow. If you want the cultural change to come about – and to stick – stop fiddling with the organizational chart and start changing the decision-making process.
Move the enterprise from data to decisions	The job of management is to create a sense of urgency, making it clear that the only point of these data-gathering and learning activities is to provide the intellectual content for effective decision-making. The enterprise cannot wait until the nth degree of uncertainty is eliminated before making a decision.
Move from marketing as a function to marketing as a state of mind	Just as war is too important to be left to the generals, marketing is too important and too universal to be left to the marketing organization – indeed, to any single function. The communication link that defines marketing must be seen as everyone's responsibility.
Develop a knowledge-use network	The knowledge-use, in whatever form, should act as the binding agent for the activities of listening, learning, and leading – ensuring that each is done well, that each informs the other, and that every operating unit of the enterprise follows these processes in a systematic way.

Figure 2

Robert S. Kaplan and David P. Norton, in their work *The Balanced Scorecard*, describe how the CEO of the Kenyon Company developed a strategic agenda for each of his retail business units. The purpose was to underscore the guiding principles for their implementation plans and the manner in which they should be measuring their units' performance. This agenda (Figure 3) captures ten key items or themes that underscore the organization's strategic intent and the key success factors to be measured:

KENYON STRATEGIC AGENDA [4]			
Financial	**Customer**	**Internal Business Process**	**Learning and Growth**
1. Aggressive growth 2. Maintain overall margins	3. Customer loyalty 4. Complete product-line offering	5. Build the brand 6. Fashion leader 7. Quality product 8. Superior shopping experience	9. Strategic skills 10. Personal growth
Assessed through: • EVA • Profitability • Growth	Assessed through: • Differentiation • Cost • Quick response	Assessed through: • Product development • Demand management • Order fulfillment	Assessed through: • Leadership • Organizational learning • Ability to change

Figure 3

Implementation plans should support key elements in achieving a company's strategic intent. They should serve as guides to fulfilling objectives, initiative, and goals down through the organization. For example, 3M Corporation has a personnel policy, called the 15 percent rule, that allows virtually any employee to spend up to 15 percent of the workweek on anything that he or she wants to, as long as it is product related. 3M, which defines itself as a highly innovative manufacturer, requires each division to have a quarter of its annual sales come from products introduced within the past five years. This policy gives employees the room to be innovative and creative.

By coordinating multi-level tactical and strategic plans, successful companies ensure that strategic decisions made at the executive level will be implemented throughout the organization.

Footnotes for Section 1.1.4 —

[1] A. A. Thompson and A. J. Strickland. *Strategic Management, 10th Edition.* Irwin McGraw-Hill, 1999, p. 46.

[2] A. A. Thompson and A. J. Strickland. *Crafting and Implementing Strategy.* Irwin, 1995, p. 48.

[3] Vincent P. Barabba. *Meeting of the Minds.* Harvard Business School Press, 1995, p. 214-222.

[4] Robert S. Kaplan and David P. Norton. *The Balanced Scorecard.* Harvard Business School Press, 1996, p. 169-171.

1.2.0 EXTERNAL ASSESSMENT

"Awareness of the environment is not a special project to be undertaken only when warning of change becomes deafening."
— KENNETH R. ANDREWS

Description

Reflects an organization's approach to gathering and analyzing essential market data. Included in this data are competition profiles, macro and micro economic studies, industry opportunities and threats, and key success factors.

Principal Elements

- Customer Profile
- Industry and Competitive Analysis
- Environmental Assessment
- Key Success Factors

Successful strategies and organizational performance are often dictated or at least influenced by the attractiveness of the environment in which the firm competes. Attractiveness of the environment is linked to a number of interrelated factors that shape the organization's effectiveness.

It is the combination of these factors that present opportunities and threats to the organization as it competes in the environment. Understanding these factors, such as relative benchmarks for performance, the strategic intents of competitors,

Figure 1

and customer preferences, is essential to crafting and implementing a viable strategy. Without a frame of reference, strategy would have no durability and no influence.

There is an oft-told story about the executive team who, while in the middle of congratulating themselves on obtaining their goal of 12% growth, discovered that their industry had grown 20 percent in the same period, leaving them 8 percent behind.

The goal of employing an effective market research and analysis approach is not to develop a comprehensive list of every potentially influential factor, but rather to identify key trends and market opportunities, avoid environmental pitfalls, and gain an ability to expand market presence, operate more efficiently, and enjoy a longer harvest period than key competitors.

The sophistication of computer technology has made data relatively inexpensive to obtain. The following partial list of websites contains links to other useful sources of data:

USEFUL WEBSITES	
American Management Association	www.amanet.org
American Stock Exchange	www.amex.com
Better Business Bureau	www.bbb.org
Census Bureau	www.census.gov
Competitive Intelligence Guide	www.fuld.com
DBC online	www.dbc.com
Federal Trade Commission	www.ftc.gov
Hoover's Online	www.hoover.com
Investor's Guide	www.investorguide.com
NASDAQ	www.nasdaq.com
New York Stock Exchange	www.nyse.com/public/home.htm
PC Financial Network	www.dljdirect.com
Small Business Administration	www.sba.gov
Strategic Leadership Forum	www.slfnet.org
Strategic Management Society	www.virtual-indiana.com/sms/
Thomas Publishing Co.	www.thomaspublishing.com
US Business Advisor	www.business.gov/business.htm
US Department of Commerce	www.doc.gov
Wall Street Research Net	www.wsrn.com

Footnote for Section 1.2.0 —

[1] John A. Pearce II and Richard B. Robinson. *Strategic Management: Formulation, Implementation, and Control.* Irwin, 1997, p. 62.

1.2.1 CUSTOMER PROFILE

"We started thinking about a lifetime value of customers as opposed to their transactional value."

— HENRY JOYNER

Definition

A company's efforts to fully explore the multiple dimensions of its customers. Having a clear understanding of the needs of its customers, including specific benefits sought by the customer, their resistance points to purchase, shifts in habit, bargaining power, specific buying characteristics, and choice of distribution channels.

Areas of Focus

- Clearly defined reasons why customers buy company products/ services.
- Clearly defined benefits that customers seek.
- Clearly defined reasons why customers would not buy company products or services.
- Assessed customer bargaining power.
- Knowing customer-preferred choice of distribution channel.

The old adage for successful entrepreneurs, "Determine what your customer wants; and then give it to them," is still an effective guideline for strategic success. An organization cannot respond to customer needs until it identifies them.

Understanding the benefits customers seeks, their buying habits, their choice of channel, and their points of resisitance, is essential to sound product design and development, customized production, and employee orientation.

Standard approaches to profiling customers usually come in one of three forms, as shown in Figure 1.

Profiling a customer involves more than employees empathizing with a customer. The challenge becomes to solicit customer feedback while having the organizational systems necessary to route that feedback to the appropriate personnel. Customer feedback was a major influencer in Land's End's decision to convert

STANDARD CUSTOMER PROFILE APPROACH [1]
Demographics — Generally consisting of specific statistics: age, sex, marital status, family size and make up, residence status (own or rent), ethnicity, education level, employment, and other census based data.
Psychographics — Generally reflect lifestyle or desired lifestyle characteristics. Where the person lives, what they drive, what they wear, where they vacation, where their children are educated, where they retire, and other self-image related information make up a psychographic profile.
Psychodemographics — Generally a hybrid of life stages and corresponding life style choices. Attitudes toward saving, gender roles, leisure time, product quality, and service are among psychodemographics.

Figure 1

from a sailboat equipment company to an outdoor clothing organization.[2] Customer feedback taken by mail-order operators urged them to include the clothing as part of their catalog offering. Soon the offerings migrated away from equipment and solely to clothing. Today, the company still solicits customer feedback, printing and distributing customer requests and comments on a monthly basis.

The following table (Figure 2) represents one approach to clearly defining the primary characteristics of a targeted customer.

VIRTUAL CEO™ CUSTOMER PROFILE MODEL				
Data Requirements	Target Customer A	Target Customer B	Target Customer C	Target Customer D
Buying Characteristics/ Nature of Demand				
Primary Benefits Sought				
Resistance Points to Purchase				
Trends in Buying Patterns, Needs, and Shifts in Habit				
Substitute Products				
Desired buying Channel or Method of Purchase				

Figure 2

A good example of responding to a changing customer profile is Yamaha's strategy in the piano industry.[2] With a decline in sales approaching 10 percent annually,

Yamaha discovered that most pianos in American, European, and Japanese homes were not being played often. In most cases, the reasons for the piano's purchase had expired. Children had left home, opportunities were seldom. Yamaha also uncovered that most pianos were being used as fine furniture and that most purchasers had incomes well above average.

In response to this market opportunity, Yamaha released a converter that would play prerecorded tunes on the pianos. They followed the release of the piano converter with an upright that could play and record tunes on a floppy disk. The sales revived a maturing market and Yamaha enjoyed renewed profitability.

Trend analysis, such as that performed by Yamaha, positions an organization to anticipate the future needs of its customers, thereby strengthening its customer relationships and impeding the threats posed by the competition.

Footnotes for Section 1.2.1 —

[1] A. B. Blankenship and George E. Breen. *State of the Art Marketing Research.* American Marketing Association, 1995, p. 389-390.

[2] A. A. Thompson and A. J. Strickland. *Crafting and Implementing Strategy.* Irwin, 1995, p. 154.

1.2.2 Industry and Competitive Analysis

"Competitive strategy must grow out of a sophisticated understanding of the rules of competition that determine an industry's attractiveness." — Michael Porter

Definition

Applying the necessary resources to put critical industry and competitive data at a company's disposal. Assessing the outlook for industry growth, the rising sales of substitute products, the impact of new entrants into the marketplace, and the industry's key market drivers. Maintaining sufficient data relating to specific direct and indirect competitors, their strengths, weaknesses, and strategic intent.

Areas of Focus

- Clearly defined primary competitors.
- Identified potential or indirect competitors.
- Clearly defined strengths, weaknesses, and strategies of direct/indirect competitors.
- Assessing the threat of substitute products or services and new entrants into the marketplace.
- Defined key market drivers.
- Ongoing market evaluation process.

Harvard Professor Michael E. Porter, in his book *Competitive Strategies*, introduced the notion of industry environment and the influences the five forces within the industry have on competition.[1] Porter's model (Figure 1) examines the five forces that influence and challenge competition within an industry and how to strive for a sustainable competitive advantage.

Porter submits that by identifying and assessing the key structural features of industries, you can determine the strength of the competitive forces and, hence, potential industry profitability.

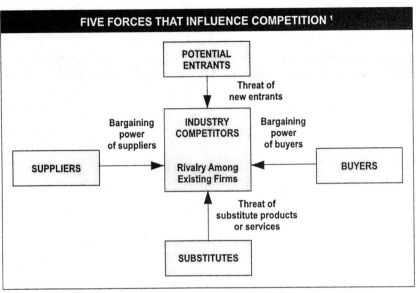

FIVE FORCES THAT INFLUENCE COMPETITION [1]

POTENTIAL ENTRANTS

Threat of new entrants

Bargaining power of suppliers

INDUSTRY COMPETITORS

Bargaining power of buyers

SUPPLIERS

Rivalry Among Existing Firms

BUYERS

Threat of substitute products or services

SUBSTITUTES

Figure 1

Utilizing Porter's model, or a variation that accomplishes the same intent, you should find yourself in a position to make the following assessments:

1. Identify the main structural features of an industry that influence competitive behavior and profitability and analyze relationships between industry structure, competition, and the level of profitability.

2. Assess the attractiveness of an industry in terms of the industry's potential for generating above- or below-average returns.

3. Use evidence on structural trends within industries to forecast changes in industry profitability in the future.

4. Identify the opportunities available to a firm to influence industry structure in order to moderate the intensity of competition and improve industry profitability.

5. Analyze competition and customer requirements in an industry in order to identify key success factors — opportunities for competitive advantage within an industry.

The following table (Figure 2) is a simplified example of an approach to assessing your competition, and evaluating competitive positioning.

MARKET SHARE LEADERS AND COMPETITIVE ADVANTAGES™					
Rank	Competitor	Market Share %	Competitive Advantage	Weaknesses	Impact on Your Company
1	Company A				
2	Company B				
3	Company C				
4	Company D				

Figure 2

Successful companies continuously monitor changes in the environment, competitive conditions, and emerging trends and respond to opportunities in a rapid and timely fashion.

The following table (Figure 3) contains a summary profile of the analysis:

INDUSTRY AND COMPETITIVE ANALYSIS SUMMARY PROFILE [2]	
Dominant Economic Characteristics of the Industry Environment	• Market growth • Geographic scope • Industry structure • Scale economies • Experience curve effects
Competition Analysis	• Competitive rivalry • Threat of potential entrants • Competition from substitutes • Supplier power • Customer power
Driving Forces	• Based on industry being analyzed
Competitive Position of Major Companies/ Strategic Groups	• Favorably positioned and why • Unfavorably positioned and why
Competitor Analysis	• Strategic approaches/predicted moves of key competitors • Who to watch and why
Key Success Factors	• Specific to targeted industry
Industry Prospects and Overall Attractiveness	• Factors making the industry attractive • Factors making the industry unattractive • Special industry issues/problems • Profit outlook (favorable/unfavorable)

Figure 3

An example of one of the forces' influence on a company's strategy is the story of NutraSweet's rise and fall as a powerful supplier of aspartame.[3] While holding the patent for NutraSweet, Monsanto could dictate terms to its customers such as pricing and displaying the NutraSweet logo. After the patent expired, Monsanto was forced to lower their prices and support their customers' promotional efforts due to the advent of new aspartame suppliers. Monsanto was successful in differentiating NutraSweet among the new entrants by focusing on customers who had high stakes in their customer's brand and taste loyalty. The switching costs for two important customers, Coke and Pepsi, were too high for them to risk replacing a vital ingredient of their products' image and reputation. Monsanto then focused its efforts on producing still another super-sweet, no calorie sweetener to continue its direction in differentiated products.

Footnotes for Section 1.2.2 —

[1] Michael E. Porter. *Competitive Strategy.* Free Press, 1980, p. 4.

[2] A. A. Thompson and A. J. Strickland. *Crafting and Implementing Strategy.* Irwin, 1995, p. 90.

[3] M. Wilke, "Sweetener Battle Could Fizz Up." Advertising Age, 1 May 1995, p. 39 — "America's Most Valuable Companies." Business Week, 28 March 1994, p. 72 — Therrien, P. Oster, and C. Hawkins, "How Sweet It Isn't at NutraSweet." Business Week, 14 Dec 1992, p. 42 — M. J. McCarthy. "Pepsi, Coke Say They're Loyal to NutraSweet." Wall Street Journal, 22 April 1992.

1.2.3 ENVIRONMENTAL ASSESSMENT

"Positive trends in the environment breed complacency. That underscores a basic point: In change, there is both opportunity and challenge." — CLIFTON GARVIN

Definition

Assessing and understanding the critical environmental conditions that face a company's industry. This includes assessing economic conditions, technology shifts, demographic shifts, socio-cultural values and institutions, regulatory infringement, and vulnerability to unidentified business cycle influences.

Areas of Focus

- Defined and clarified regulatory requirements.
- Assessing vulnerability to adverse business cycles.
- Summarized opportunities and threats due to:
  - Economic conditions
  - New technology
  - Demographic structure
  - Legal or political events
  - The natural environment
  - Socio-cultural conditions

A company must have a thorough understanding of the environmental issues that influence its industry in order to sustain optimal performance. The best products or services can be seriously hampered if the company has not taken into consideration the external factors of the industry and markets in which it competes.

These broad environmental issues include industry and business cycles, specific industry regulatory issues, economic conditions, technological capability, demographic shifts in structure, political and legal reforms, ecological concerns, and socio-cultural developments.

Although some of these environmental indicators are somewhat subtle in their direct influence, others are quite easy to observe. The seasonal and cyclical natures of some industries can leave a business vulnerable to fluctuations in buyer demand and economic up- and down-turns.

Another easily identified environmental consideration is regulation. Businesses should be aware of current regulations that affect their operations, as well as the outlook for increased or decreased demand as a result of regulatory actions. Taxation and operating parameters of the local environment can also affect organization performance. Economic data provides the foundation for running realistic "what if" scenarios. Understanding how local, national, and global economic conditions — such as unemployment, consumer confidence, interest rates, and gross domestic product — influence business is the key to designing successful approaches to production, distribution, and promotion.

The following model (Figure 1) is one example of how critical data can be compressed into a comprehensive, easy to review format:

BLUE CHIP CONSENSUS - EXTERNAL FORECASTS [1]											
	Actual								Forecast		
Indices	1995				1996				1997		
	1Q	2Q	3Q	4Q	1Q	2Q	3Q	4Q	1Q	2Q	3Q
Fed Funds	5.79	6.03	5.78	5.72	5.39	5.27	5.40	5.50	5.60	5.50	5.50
3 Mo. T-Bill	5.96	5.79	5.54	5.43	5.07	5.16	5.30	5.40	5.50	5.40	5.40
30 Yr. Treasury	7.64	6.96	6.72	6.23	6.30	7.06	7.10	7.00	6.80	6.80	6.70
Home Mtg. Rate	8.82	7.95	7.70	7.34	7.26	8.11	8.20	8.10	8.10	7.90	7.80
GDP	0.6	0.5	3.6	0.5	2.2	4.2	2.6	2.1	1.9	1.8	2.0
CPI	3.2	3.2	2.1	2.1	2.8	3.9	2.7	2.8	3.1	3.0	3.0
Unemployment	5.5	5.6	5.7	5.6	5.5	5.4	5.5	5.6	5.6	5.6	5.6

Figure 1

The pace of technology has rapidly accelerated since World War II. Technological advancement can make products and processes obsolete literally overnight. On the other hand, it can offer new opportunities for business commerce. Organizations monitoring technology should address the issues discussed in the table (Figure 2) on the next page.

ORGANIZATION'S TECHNOLOGY MONITORING PROCESS™
1. What forms of technology are forming, shaping, or influencing the industry?
2. What are the specific threats or opportunities that technology presents to the growth aspects of the business?
3. How do these technologies support or impair the company's competitive advantage?
4. How does technology support and influence the buying patterns and needs of target customers?

Figure 2

Similarly, the aging of the population, along with a host of other changing demographics, has created threats and opportunities for organizations. Companies catering to senior needs have experienced increased demand, while others have been affected by changing spending habits, income levels, and attitudes.

Another emerging external variable that can have profound influence on organization performance is ecological concern. More and more resources are being put into green initiatives such as air and water pollution, ozone depletion, and waste management. (See Figure 3.)

SOME ADDITIONAL MACROENVIRONMENTAL FORCES [2]			
Political/Legal	**Economic**	**Technological**	**Socio-Cultural**
Tax laws	Money supply	R&D expenditures	Attitudes toward
International trade	Monetary policy	Rate of new product	lifestyles,
regulations	Unemployment rate	introductions	innovations,
Consumer lending	Energy costs	Automation	careers, and
regulations	Disposable personal	Robotics	consumer activism
Environmental	income	Focus of R&D	Life expectancies
protection laws	Stage of economic	expenditures	Concern with quality
Antitrust regula-	cycle		of life
tions and			Birth rates
enforcement			Population shifts
Hiring, firing,			Shifts in the
promotion, and			presence of
pay laws			women in the
Wage/price			workforce
controls			

Figure 3

Environmental analysis can also help a company take advantage of socio-cultural forces. Miami-based Knight-Ridder, originally a newspaper company and now a $2.3 billion information industry player, is a good example. Taking advantage of technology's impact on how its customers gather information, Knight-Ridder owns an on-line newswire service, a cable television channel, and an electronic information retrieval service. Aware of changing social and demographic changes in Miami, Knight-Ridder launched a Spanish-language daily newspaper that became the largest of its kind in the U.S.[3]

The following chart (Figure 4) presents the relative utility of data-gathering and forecasting techniques for analyzing these various environmental segments:

ENVIRONMENTAL ANALYSIS TECHNIQUES [4]							
	Social			**Political**			
Data Gathering Methods	**Demographics**	**Life-styles**	**Social Values**	**Political Milieu**	**Regulatory**	**Economic**	**Techno-logical**
Type of sources	Primarily quantitative Secondary sources	Quantitative & qualitative Secondary & primary	Inferential/ qualitative Primary & secondary	Real-time personal Qualitative	Historical/ real-time Primary & secondary Qualitative	Historical/ real-time Secondary Quantitative	Mostly primary/ qualitative Secondary sources for later stages
Techniques	Market research techniques	Focus groups In-depth interviews Panels	In-depth interviews Panels Content analysis	Content analysis of speeches Lobbying Opinion leaders	Content analysis of legislation Regulatory opinions Expert opinion	Outputs of model	Expert panels Interviews with experts
Forecasting Methods	Simulation (A) Logistics equation models (M) Transition matrices (M) Geographic mobility models (A-M)	Life-style (M) profiling Probability-diffusion matrices (A)	Analytical (A) Value profile Social pressures, priority analysis (A)	Event history analysis Political risk analysis (M) Networks (M)	Network analysis (M)	World & historical dynamics (A-M) Econometric models (A-M) Input-output analysis (M) Simulation models (A) Trend extrapol-ation (M) Time-series analysis (M)	Historical analysis (M) Probability-diffusion matrices (A-M) Morpho-logical methods (I) Delphi (A) Relevance trees (I) Logistical curves
Character-istics	Generally robust	Variable in robustness	Very variable	Weak in robustness	Moderately robust	Robust in terms of direction of change	Variable/ inventive

M = mechanistic   A = adaptive   I = inventive

Figure 4

A powerful example of a company who failed to capitalize on its key environmental assessment strengths was Wang Laboratories, Inc.[5] Founded in 1951, the company managed in the early 1970s to find a niche in the word processing industry. By carefully outmaneuvering IBM, the software/hardware manufacturer grew to generate over $92.7 million in after-tax profits on revenues of over $3 billion by 1988. However, by 1992, the company had filed for bankruptcy. The company had lost a total of $1.9 billion since 1988 and its stock market value had fallen from $5.6 billion and had slumped to $70 million. Once trading at $42.50 per share in 1982, 1992 share price was around $0.37 per share.

One observation is that Wang had allowed the talents that had brought them so much success to lay dormant. By overlooking the changes in the marketplace, the growing sophistication of the buyer, and competitor encroachment, Wang had failed to respond to emerging opportunities to stay ahead of their rivals.

When offered a chance to align with Apple in early 1984, Wang declined, saying Apple was too young and unpredictable a partner. They also failed to take notice of small start-up software competitors such as WordPerfect and WordStar. By assuming that $2 billion was enough of a head start, Wang underestimated the value of routine analysis and response. Consequently, unwatched, unimpeded distant rivals, very much like Wang at their start, have endured and have far surpassed Wang in sales.

Footnotes for Section 1.2.3 —

[1] Economic forecast as of August 10, 1996 and financial forecast as of August 1, 1996.

[2] Peter Wright, Mark J. Kroll, and John Parnell. *Strategic Management, 4th Edition*. Prentice-Hall, 1998, p. 31.

[3] Mary Gentile, Jeffrey F. Rayport, and Sara B. Gant. Harvard Business School 9-395-022, Rev. Feb. 23, 1995. The Miami Herald Publishing Company.

[4] Liam Fahey and V. K. Narayanan. *Macroenvironmental Analysis for Strategic Management*. West, 1986, p. 212.

[5] P. Andrews, "Wrong Turns on the Road to PCdom Come Back to Haunt Wang." Seattle Times, 25 August 1992, p. D3 — W. M. Bulkeley and J.R. Wilkes. "Steep Slide: Filing in Chapter 11, Wang Sends Warning to High Tech Circles." Wall Street Journal, 19 August, 1992, p. A1.

1.2.4 KEY SUCCESS FACTORS

"To swim a fast 100 meters, it's better to swim with the tide than to work on your stroke."

— WARREN BUFFETT

Definition

Applying a critical thinking process when evaluating market data. Determining which factors drive success and influence business within a particular sector of commerce. Utilizing a "key success factor" approach to identify opportunities within a given industry.

Areas of Focus

- Implementing critical thinking process.
- Understanding the ease or complexity of new entrants entering the marketplace.
- Measuring product or service demand within a market.
- Clearly defined drivers of success within an industry.
- Having a system that consistently monitors key influences within the industry.

Many industries have characteristics that, although minor when looked at singularly, are extremely important when taken together in terms of gaining and maintaining competitive advantages. Key or critical success factors are those areas in which all firms must be competent at performing or achieving in order to be successful in their industry. Most of these success factors have a direct bearing on a company's profitability. A sound strategy will usually incorporate the intent to excel in one or more of these critical success factors.

Many typical entrepreneurial companies find that in order to maintain their momentum and strengthen their market position, they need to balance their intuitive understanding and implementation of key success factors with certain structural disciplines that must also be adopted.

Robert M. Grant, in *Contemporary Strategy Analysis*, introduces an effective model to follow in an organization's approach to identifying industry "key success" factors. (See Figure 1.)

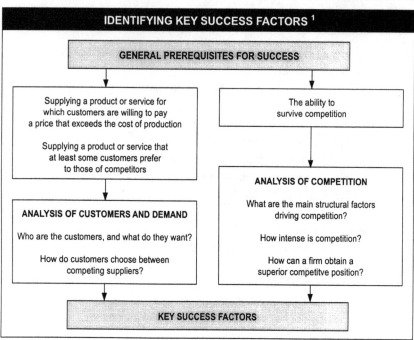

IDENTIFYING KEY SUCCESS FACTORS [1]

GENERAL PREREQUISITES FOR SUCCESS

Supplying a product or service for which customers are willing to pay a price that exceeds the cost of production

Supplying a product or service that at least some customers prefer to those of competitors

The ability to survive competition

ANALYSIS OF CUSTOMERS AND DEMAND

Who are the customers, and what do they want?

How do customers choose between competing suppliers?

ANALYSIS OF COMPETITION

What are the main structural factors driving competition?

How intense is competition?

How can a firm obtain a superior competitve position?

KEY SUCCESS FACTORS

Figure 1

Determining an organization's industry success factors should be a top priority in light of today's technology-influenced and rapidly changing environment. Prioritizing initiatives and aligning resources on issues that truly influence success is the key to a winning strategy.

Microsoft's efforts to turn "positive feedback" of its operating system into a winning strategy is described in Chairman Bill Gates' book *The Road Ahead*.[2] By focusing on its core technology of operating systems and languages, Microsoft encourages other software application developers to compete with them by developing applications for their operating systems. The key success factor in their business is installed customer base. By encouraging applications expansion, more businesses will install Microsoft's operating system, and with a growing installed base, more software developers will make applications. This positive feedback spiral is a cornerstone of Microsoft's rapid growth strategy.

The following table (Figure 2) illustrates types of Key Success Factors.

TYPES OF KEY SUCCESS FACTORS [3]

Technology-related KSFs
- Scientific research expertise.
- Production process innovation capability.
- Product innovation capability.
- Expertise in a given technology.

Manufacturing-related KSFs
- Low-cost production efficiency.
- Quality of manufacture.
- High utilization of fixed assets.
- Low-cost plant locations.
- Access to adequate supplies of skilled labor.
- High labor productivity.
- Low-cost product design and engineering.
- Flexibility to manufacture a range of models and sizes/customization.

Distribution-related KSFs
- A strong network of wholesale distributors/dealers.
- Gaining ample space on retailer shelves.
- Having company-owned retail outlets.
- Low distribution costs.
- Fast delivery.

Marketing-related KSFs
- A well-trained, effective sales force.
- Available, dependable service and technical assistance.
- Accurate filling of buyer orders.
- Breadth of product line and product selection.
- Merchandising skills.
- Attractive styling/packaging.
- Customer guarantees and warranties.

Skills-related KSFs
- Superior talent.
- Quality know-how.
- Design expertise.
- Expertise in a particular technology.
- Ability to come up with clever, catchy ads.
- Ability to get newly developed products out of the R&D phase and into the market very quickly.

Organizational capability KSFs
- Superior information systems.
- Ability to respond quickly to shifting market conditions.
- More experience and managerial know-how.

Figure 2

Footnotes for Section 1.2.4 —

[1] Robert M. Grant. *Contemporary Strategy Analysis.* Blackwell, 1995, p. 76.

[2] Bill Gates. *The Road Ahead.* Penguin, 1996, p. 50-52.

[3] A. A. Thompson and A. J. Strickland. *Crafting and Implementing Strategy.* Irwin, 1995, p. 87.

1.3.0 INTERNAL ASSESSMENT

"If a company is not 'best in world' at a critical activity, it is sacrificing competitive advantage by performing that activity with its existing technique." — JAMES BRIAN QUINN

Description

Reflects the company's ability to objectively evaluate its strengths and weaknesses. This would include defining its market position, its management processes, and how effectively it utilizes a "value-chain" analysis approach.

Principal Elements

- Market Position
- Finance
- Research, Development, and Design
- Production
- Marketing
- Sales and Distribution
- Customer Service

Internal assessment is the organization's moment of truth within the scope of the strategic planning process. A thorough audit of an organization comes only through an objective and painfully honest approach to internal issues. All areas, from finance to R&D to production to marketing, must be put under the microscope, in order to identify gaps and inconsistencies as well as distinctive competencies early in the planning process. This enables the organization to mitigate weaknesses while leveraging its strengths.

One popular approach to evaluating a company's capabilities and performance is through the use of complementary perspectives. Authors Kaplan and Norton use flying an airplane to illustrate a need to focus on a broad range of issues when evaluating performance. Just as a pilot would not rely upon a single instrument to monitor his flight, so should managers utilize a variety of perspectives and information sources to develop a successful strategy. The Balanced Scorecard approach emphasizes the need to balance each perspective and not allow any one perspective to out-influence any other in evaluating performance. A summary of the four perspectives appears below in Figure 1:

BALANCED SCORECARD PERSPECTIVES [1]

Financial Perspective
Does the firm's strategic response and execution contribute to improvement of the bottom-line? Most measurements include traditional business financial performance ratios and economic valuation models.

Customer Perspective
Does the firm provide the customer with superior value defined on the customer's terms. Measurements may include, depending on industry, satisfaction, new customer acquisition, retention, profitability, and market share.

Internal Business (Operations) Perspective
Does the firm efficiently and profitably produce the products and/or services that its customers value? Measurements may include time to market, new product innovations, and cost of goods.

Learning and Growth Perspective
Does the firm readily adapt to shifts in strategy? Does its culture support change? Are the employees committed to its strategic intent? Measurements include employee satisfaction, retention, training, and skill sets.

Figure 1

Understanding an organization from these interrelated perspectives gives a clearer understanding of the functional areas for improvement, as well as areas of expertise to leverage for competitive advantage.

Robert Grant relates a good example of this type of analysis. The Walt Disney Company traditionally identified its strengths in its assets and resources, and leveraged them to gain an advantage in their industry. In 1984, under their new CEO's direction, Disney aggressively licensed their classic film library beyond their traditional periodic rereleases. They revitalized their movie studio and heavily recruited top talent to quickly double their movie title output, in four short years becoming America's leading studio in terms of box office receipts.

But Disney's number one strength was always the love of millions of adoring fans for Disney characters and the Disney name. The company exploited this extraordinary resource by deploying aggressively developing theme parks and pushing into cable and network TV.

Grant also proposes identifying strengths or weaknesses by mapping a company's profile by resource (Figure 2).

ASSESSING A FIRM'S RESOURCES [2]		
Resource	**Main Characteristics**	**Key Indicators**
Financial Resources	The firm's borrowing capacity and its internal funds generation determine its investment capacity and its cyclical resilience.	• Debt/equity ratio. • Ratio of net cash to capital expenditure. • Credit rating.
Physical Resources	The size, location, technical sophistication, and flexibility of plant and equipment; location and alternative uses for land and buildings, reserves of raw materials constrain the firm's set of production possibilities and determine the potential for cost and quality advantage.	• Resale values of fixed assets. • Vintage of capital equipment. • Scale of plants. • Alternative uses of fixed assets.
Human Resources	The training and expertise of employees determine the skills available to the firm. The adaptability of employees determines the strategic flexibility of the firm. The commitment and loyalty of the employees determines the firm's ability to maintain competitive advantage.	• Educational, technical, professional qualifications of employees. • Pay rates relative to industry average.
Technological Resources	Stock of technology including proprietary technology (patents, copyrights, trade secrets) and expertise in its application of know-how. Resources for innovation: research facilities, technical and scientific employees.	• Number and significance of patents. • Revenue from patent licenses. • R&D staff as a percentage of total employees.
Reputation	Reputation with customers through the ownership of brands, established relationships with customers, the association of the firm's products with quality, reliability, etc. The reputation of the company with the suppliers of components, finance, labor services, and other inputs.	• Brand recognition. • Price-premium over competing brands. • Percentage of repeat buying. • Objective measures of product performance. • Level and consistency of company performance.

Figure 2

Footnotes for Section 1.3.0 —

[1] Robert S. Kaplan and David P. Norton. *The Balanced Scorecard.* Harvard Business School Press, 1996, p. 2.

[2] Robert M. Grant. *Contemporary Strategy Analysis.* Blackwell, 1995, p. 120-122.

1.3.1 Market Position

"Competing in the marketplace is like war. You have injuries and casualties, and the best strategy wins." — JOHN COLLINS

Definition

Maintaining a consistent awareness of a company's specific market position. Understanding its proprietary position, market share, and the outlook for a growing customer base. Growing at a rate that meets or exceeds industry rate.

Areas of Focus

- Maintaining or sharing a position of dominance within a market.
- Competitors viewing company as a market leader.
- Possessing a proprietary position in:
  - Patents
  - Technology
  - Innovations
  - Distribution
- Growing at a rate that meets or exceeds the industry.
- Having a higher degree of customer retention than competitors.

How a company positions itself in the marketplace —with regard to its product offerings, proprietary technology, innovations, channel selection, pricing, or promotional strategies — generally will determine their magnitude for success.

Understanding where competitor strengths lay, which market segments are being exploited, and what customer needs are being met (and by what means they are being met) can improve an organization's market position. (See Figure 1.) By selecting a market that is void of leadership, has an underserved customer base, and invites innovation can lead to significant customer acquisition and long-term retention.

Southwest Airlines[1] is an example of an airline that thoughtfully considered its market position before opening its doors to commuter passenger traffic over 30 years ago. The company launched operations in the midst of a rather closed, highly regulatory environment. By positioning itself as a high-frequency, no-frills airline,

QUESTIONS FOR DETERMINING MARKET POSITION™
Who is buying our products?
Is this market increasing?
Are there promising markets not being served?
Why will these customers buy our product/service?
How do our customers buy our product/service?
How do we reach these customers with our messages?
What is our market share overall?
Are customers satisfied with our product?
How do our competitors view our company?
How do our customers perceive our company?

Figure 1

specializing in short-hop flights of less than two hours, or connecting passengers with other long-distance carriers, Southwest obtained a unique market position.

The company quickly became a dominant player in their market and, with the coming of deregulation, it leveraged a brilliantly aligned low-cost strategy by implementing fast turnarounds at their gates (producing more on time flights per day with less aircraft), no meals, assigned seating, baggage transfer to connecting airlines, and automated ticketing.

In addition to price, reliability, and service, Southwest supported their position by fostering an innovative work environment, only recruiting personnel who reflected the innovative, upbeat, people-oriented culture that bred so much success.

Southwest positioned themselves in the market by delivering low cost, frequent service, and on-time flights to their customers. They kept their cost per passenger mile well below that of their next competitor. Their competitors have made several attempts to emulate the Southwest strategy with limited success. It is fair to state, based on market share, company performance, and perceived customer loyalty, that Southwest possesses a position of dominance within their industry.

By matching their customers' needs with their unique set of benefits, Southwest positioned itself for success. They proved a company can revolutionize an industry that was perceived to be mature and established.

Some companies find that market positioning is done so well that it is difficult to change. Harley-Davidson enjoys a distinctive definition related to its motorcycle image in the movie, *The Wild One*. Its reputation was deliberately cultivated among riders as being rebellious and tough. Its definition contrasts sharply with that of Honda's image. In its early motorcycle advertisements, Honda proclaimed, "You meet the nicest people on a Honda." This image persists today, and it has been difficult for Honda to penetrate the "tough guy" market.[2]

Coors Beer once enjoyed the mystique that came from its distribution strategy being limited to the West Coast. Beer drinkers from the eastern and midwestern states would travel back from Colorado with loads of the brew in their trunks. When Coors achieved national distribution, however, some of its distinctiveness and Rocky Mountain image was lost.

Footnotes for Section 1.3.1 —

[1] Charlotte Thompson. "Southwest Airlines." Case Study, University of Virginia, 1993.

[2] Henry Mintzberg, James Brian Quinn, and John Voyer. *The Strategy Process.* Prentice Hall, 1995, p. 120-121.

1.3.2 FINANCE

"Remember that time is money."   — BENJAMIN FRANKLIN

Definition

Effective alignment of financial resources. Adequate funding of key initiatives. Utilizing cost/benefit models. Employing "If/Then" scenario techniques. Ensuring accurate financial and economic forecasting as well as long-term financial planning. Overseeing effective financial controls.

Areas of Focus

- Consistently performing within a range of financial goals.
- Adequate funding of key initiatives.
- Employing a "cost/benefit" approach to resource allocation.
- Having a targeted long-term financial plan.
- Employing an "If/Then" model when forming strategy.
- Establishing realistic goals based on past performance.
- Resources are aligned well.
- Financial plan allows for economic or environmental disruption.

The financial condition of a firm is often considered the single best measure of its competitive potential and its attractiveness to investors. Whether a sole proprietorship, a privately held enterprise, or a publicly traded corporation, the integrity of an organization's financial performance is critical in the achievement of the firm's strategic intent. A firm's profitability, cash flow, liquidity, working capital, leverage, and asset utilization can limit some strategic options.

Without effective financial management, the ability to raise capital, attract investors, or satisfy regulators can be seriously impaired. The *Wall Street Journal* reports that 38.4% of all business failures are financially related. (See Figure 1.)

Simply stated, the financial manager's task is to acquire and use funds to maximize the value of the firm. Brigham and Gapenski attack the challenge of the finance paradigm and point out four key responsibilities of the financial function within the organization (Figure 2).

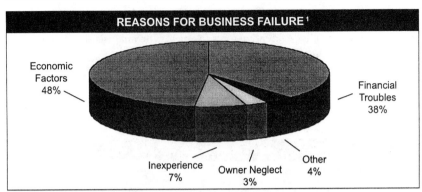

Figure 1

FOUR KEY RESPONSIBILITIES OF THE FINANCIAL FUNCTION [2]	
1. **Forecasting and Planning**	The financial manager must interact with other executives as they look ahead and lay the plans which will shape the firm's future.
2. **Major Investments and Financial Decisions**	A successful firm usually has rapid growth in sales, which requires investments in plant, equipment, and inventory. The company must determine the optimal sales growth rate, they must decide on the specific assets to acquire and the best way to finance those assets.
3. **Coordination and Control**	Under normal circumstances it is the responsibility of the financial group to insure that the firm is operating as efficiently as possible. All business decisions have financial implications, and all managers — financial and otherwise — need to take this into account. For example, marketing decisions affect sales growth, which in turn influence investment requirements. Thus, marketing decision-makers must take account of how their actions affect (and are affected by) such factors as the availability of funds, inventory policies, and plant capacity utilization.
4. **Capital Position and Capital Markets**	If your organization deals with the capital markets as a financial resource, you are well aware of the impact the markets can have on your ability to raise capital, how your stock may trade, and whether your investors make or lose money.

Figure 2

Financial ratio analysis is probably the most commonly used method for assessing an organization's financial strengths and weaknesses. Because financial decisions impact all functional areas of an organization, weak ratios can often indicate issues in management, marketing, production, and information systems.

Ratio analysis has some limitations, as the ratios are based on accounting data that can differ in treatment of inventory valuation, depreciation, taxes, etc., from firm to firm. Also, like any comparative exercise, industry norms can be affected by seasonal demand, aggressive competition, and the firm's own innovative practices. Like all other evaluative tools financial ratio analysis should be used in conjunction with other assessment tools and with a holistic view of the organization.

The following (Figure 3, through page 60) is a summary of some key financial ratios, how to calculate them, and what they indicate:

KEY FINANCIAL RATIOS [3]		
Profitability Ratios		
	Formula	**Definition**
Gross profit margin	$$\frac{\text{Sales–Cost of Goods Sold}}{\text{Sales}}$$	An indication of the total margin available to cover operating expenses and yield a profit.
Operating profit margin (or return on sales)	$$\frac{\text{Profits before taxes and before interest}}{\text{Sales}}$$	An indication of the firm's profitability from current operations without regard to the interest charges accruing from the capital structure.
Net profit margin (net return on sales)	$$\frac{\text{Profits after taxes}}{\text{Sales}}$$	Shows after-tax profits per dollar of sales. Sub par profit margins indicate that the firm's sales prices are relatively low or that costs are relatively high, or both.
Return on total assets	$$\frac{\text{Profits after taxes}}{\text{Total assets}}$$ *or* $$\frac{\text{Profits after taxes + interest}}{\text{Total assets}}$$	A measure of the return on total investment in the enterprise. It is sometimes desirable to add interest to after-tax profits to form the numerator of the ratio since total assets are financed by creditors as well as by stockholders; hence, it is accurate to measure the productivity of assets by the returns provided to both classes of investors.
Return on stockholders' equity (return on net worth)	$$\frac{\text{Profits after taxes}}{\text{Total stockholders' equity}}$$	A measure of the rate of return on stockholders' investment in the enterprise.
Return on common equity	$$\frac{\text{Profits after taxes – preferred stock dividends}}{\text{Total stockholders' equity – par value of preferred stock}}$$	A measure of the rate of return on the investment the owners of the common stock have made in the enterprise.
Earnings per share	$$\frac{\text{Profits after taxes – preferred stock dividends}}{\text{Number of shares of common stock outstanding}}$$	Shows the earnings available to the owners of each share of common stock.

Figure 3

Liquidity Ratios		
	Formula	**Definition**
Current ratio	Current assets / Current liabilities	Indicates the extent to which the claims of short-term creditors are covered by assets expected to be converted to cash in a period roughly corresponding to the maturity of the liabilities.
Quick ratio	Current assets − Inventory / Current liabilities	A measure of the firm's ability to pay off short-term obligations without relying on the sale of its inventories.
Inventory to net working capital	Inventory / Current assets − current liabilities	A measure of the extent to which the firm's working capital is tied up in inventory.

Leverage Ratios		
	Formula	**Definition**
Debt-to-asset ratio	Total debt / Total assets	Measures the extent to which borrowed funds have been used to finance the firm's operations.
Debt-to-equity ratio	Total debt / Total stockholders' equity	Provides another measure of the funds provided by creditors versus the funds provided by owners.
Long-term debt-to-equity ratio	Long-term debt / Total stockholders' equity	A widely used measure of the balance between debt and equity in the firm's long-term capital structure.
Times-interest-earned (or coverage) ratio	Profits before interest & taxes / Total interest charges	Measures the extent to which earnings can decline without the firm becoming unable to meet its annual interest costs.
Fixed-charge coverage	Profits before interest & taxes + lease obligations / Total interest charges + lease obligations	A more inclusive indication of the firm's ability to meet all of its fixed-charge obligations.

Activity Ratios		
	Formula	**Definition**
Inventory turnover	Sales / Inventory of finished goods	When compared to industry averages, it provides an indication of whether a company has excessive of perhaps inadequate finished goods inventory.
Fixed assets turnover	Sales / Fixed assets	A measure of the sales productivity and utilization of plant and equipment.
Total assets turnover	Sales / Total assets	A measure of the utilization of all of the firm's assets; a ratio below the industry average indicates the company is not generating a sufficient volume of business, given the size of its asset investment.
Accounts receivable turnover	Annual credit sales / Accounts receivable	A measure of the average length of time it takes the firm to collect the sales made on credit
Average collection period	Annual credit sales / Total sales ÷ 365 *or* Accounts receivable / Average daily sales	Indicates the average length of time the firm must wait after making a sale before it receives payment.

Other Ratios		
	Formula	**Definition**
Dividend yield on common stock	Annual dividends per share / Current market price per share	A measure of the return to owners of stock received in the form of dividends.
Price-earnings ratio	Current market price per share / After-tax earnings per share	Faster growing or less risky firms tend to have higher price-earnings ratios than slower growing or more risky firms traditionally.
Dividend payout ratio	Annual dividends per share / After-tax earnings per share	Indicates the percentage of profits paid out as dividends.
Cash flow per share	After-tax profits + depreciation / Number of common shares outstanding	A measure of the discretionary funds over and above the expenses that are available for use by the firm.

One of the biggest factors that can impact the financial performance of an organization is its pricing policy. A comprehensive approach to pricing can serve as an economic benchmark for how your product performs and what ongoing decisions have to be made in order to optimize profitability. The following model (Figure 4) captures the essence of a comprehensive pricing approach:

A GENERAL PRICING MODEL [4]	
1. **Define Market Targets**	All marketing decision-making should begin with a definition of segmentation strategy and the identification of potential customers.
2. **Estimate Market Potential**	The maximum size of the available market determines what is possible and helps define competitive opportunities.
3. **Develop Product Positioning**	The brand image and the desired niche in the competitive marketplace provide important constraints on the pricing decision as the firm attempts to obtain a unique competitive advantage by differentiating its product offering from that of competitors.
4. **Design the Marketing Mix**	Elements of mix are product, promotion, pricing, and distribution. Design of the marketing mix defines the role to be played by pricing in relation to and in support of their marketing variables, especially distribution and promotional policies.
5. **Estimate Price Elasticity of Demand**	The sensitivity of the level of demand to differences in price can be estimated by either from past experience or through market tests.
6. **Estimate All Relevant Costs**	While straight cost-plus pricing is to be avoided because it is insensitive to demand, pricing decisions must take into account necessary plant investment, investment in R&D, and investment in market development, as well as variable costs of production and marketing.
7. **Analyze Environmental Factors**	Pricing decisions are further constrained by industry practices, likely competitive response to alternative pricing strategies, and legal requirements.
8. **Set Pricing Objectives**	Pricing decisions must be guided by a clear statement of objectives that recognizes environmental constraints and defines the role of pricing in the marketing strategy while at the same time relating pricing to the firm's financial objectives.
9. **Develop the Price Structure**	The price structure for a given product can now be determined and will define selling prices for the product (perhaps in a variety of styles and sizes) and the discounts from list price to be offered to various kinds of intermediaries and various types of buyers.

Figure 4

It is important to recognize that a firm's financial condition may be impacted not only by functional issues, but by market conditions, environmental issues, and other factors affecting all firms within the industry as well.

Allied Signal is a good example of an organization that put emphasis on the right measurement of financial performance. Allied, like many organizations, had traditionally relied upon cutting costs through labor reductions. However, since Allied Signal's operations tend to be capital-intensive, labor amounted to only 25 percent of their total costs. One manager pointed out that cutting costs through labor reduction would ultimately lead to a plant with no one in it. Instead, they focused on "total cost productivity" calculated as sales:

- Discounted for price increases due to inflation and not value-added.

- Divided by all costs, including plant, materials, equipment, and labor.

Managers were thus encouraged to look over the broad spectrum of operations for increased productivity.[5]

Footnotes for Section 1.3.2 —

[1] Wall Street Journal. 16 October 1992, p. R7.

[2] Eugene F. Brigham and Louis C. Gapenski. *Financial Management — Theory and Practice*, Dryden, 1994, p. 9-10.

[3] A. A. Thompson and A. J. Strickland. *Strategic Management, 10th Edition*. Irwin McGraw-Hill, 1998, p. 36.

[4] Fredrick E. Webster. *Marketing for Managers*. 1974, p. 178-179.

[5] Thomas A. Stewart. "Allied Signal's Turnaround Blitz." Fortune, 30 Nov 1992, p. 72-75.

1.3.3 Research, Development, and Design

"As market windows open and close more quickly, it is important that R&D be tied more closely to corporate strategy."

— William Spenser

Definition

Maintaining an aggressive attitude toward discovery, creativity, and innovation. Resource allocation reflects a commitment to the R&D function.

Areas of Focus

- R&D has all required resources to successfully fulfill its function.
- Maintaining a creative and innovative process.
- Performance reflects robust R&D contribution.

With expenditures in Research and Development (R&D) for all U.S. firms exceeding $200 billion in 1997, there is an ever-increasing need for organizations to focus their attention on productive R&D operations. Organizations invest in research and development in order to improve their competitive advantage either through product innovation or process improvement.

Effective R&D requires integration between all other functions of the organization and the R&D function. The best managed firms today incorporate a cross-functional approach to the R&D process. This has required once-isolated R&D managers to work with other functional managers to prioritize tasks and align resources.

The model on the next page (Figure 1) reflects key considerations of an effective R&D process.

While most firms have little choice but to invest in R&D due to the dynamics of technology and changing tastes of consumers, some firms are content to follow market innovations with lower-cost imitations. In this time of technology shifts and strong global competition, the task of innovation is increasingly more difficult. The pharmaceutical industry, for example, enjoys only one successful launch out of

EVALUATING INTELLECTUAL OUTPUT: RESEARCH AND DEVELOPMENT AS AN OUTPUT SYSTEM [1]					
R&D Activities	Direct Outputs: Technologies	Opportuni-ties to Exploit	Indirect Outputs: Value Actually Exploited	Goals	Value Created
Fundamental Research Applied Research Development Engineering	Ideas Theories Understanding Consulting Timing advantages Designs Software Processes Products Materials Devices Services	Present value as oppor-tunities to exploit (Net of costs)	New products or services Improved products or services Patent position or saleable intelligence Cost reducing materials, processes or software Flexibility and responsiveness Image building Bases for further knowledge building	Assets Profits Jobs Community contribu-tions Image Customer service Share-holder value	
The sources of intellectual output...	...produce technology as an output...	...which has value as opportunities to exploit, if taken,...	...which the company may exploit in different forms...	...to support its multiple goals...	...which have value.

Figure 1

10,000 drugs created. Noted strategists Scarpello, Boulton, and Hofer explain that different strategies require different R&D capabilities.[2] For market leaders and in-novators, new product launches and innovations are the driving force behind their strategy. R&D must play an integral part in terms of new ideas, technology, and service. Market followers need to focus on making current products in a cost-effec-tive way. Process-oriented R&D must be the driving force.

An organization's understanding of the nature of its product types, its life cycle, and its industry position is a key driver of product improvement. The model on the following page illustrates several product types.

Intel Corporation is the world leader in the development of microprocessing chips that play a key role in the computer industry. Competition for controlling the technology is very tight, as competitors such as Motorola, Digital Equipment, NEC, and others race to introduce the latest improved performance chip to the market.

DEFINING THE PRODUCT OR SERVICE TYPE [3]	
Breakthrough	Breakthrough products, as the name implies, depart significantly and fundamentally from existing practice. They may introduce highly innovative product or process technology, open up a new market segment, or take the business into a totally new arena.
Platform	Platform products form the base of a product "family" that can be leveraged over several years and often across multiple market segments. Though not as radically different as a breakthrough, a new platform usually provides a substantial boost in value to customers and to the firm's competitive position. Thus, it may enable the business to address a new distribution channel or may involve a new manufacturing process.
Derivative	Derivative products are derived from other products – usually platforms. They may offer lower cost, enhanced features, or modifications in packaging. They usually extend the product line, fill in gaps in the offerings, exploit a niche, and otherwise leverage investment in a platform.
Support	Support products lie at the very end of the change spectrum, and entail only minor changes in technology, marketing, or processing to support the product line. These minor modifications support the product line by extending the range of its application, correcting a problem in an existing product, keeping it fresh in customers' minds, giving the sales force something "new" to discuss during regular customer visits, or customizing it for a specific customer.

Figure 2

In order to stay ahead of these competitors, Intel has organized its R&D department into work teams. The company has six different teams working on the next generation of chip technology simultaneously. Each team's innovations are often synthesized to make the final product, such as the successful Pentium-generation chip unveiled in 1993.

Intel, however, has six other teams working on its successor, as well as six more teams on the generations of chip design to follow. To ensure its market leadership, Intel has focused its efforts on R&D, where it hopes to control the technology of not only today but tomorrow as well.[4]

Footnotes for Section 1.3.3 —

[1] James Brian Quinn. *Intelligent Enterprise.* Free Press, 1992, p. 250.

[2] Vida Scarpello, William Boulton, and Charles Hofer. "Reintegrating R&D into Business Strategy." Journal of Business Strategy, 6:4 Sp, 1986, p. 50.

[3] Steven C. Wheelwright and Kim B. Clark. *Leading Product Development.* Free Press, 1995, p. 51-52.

[4] V. Kasturi Rangan, Benson P. Shapiro, and Rowland T. Moriarty. *Business Marketing Strategy: Cases, Concepts and Application.* Irwin, 1995, p. 244.

1.3.4 PRODUCTION

*"The benefits attained by improving product development can be
strategically significant, including increased revenue, improved
development productivity, and operational efficiencies."*
— MICHAEL E. MCGRATH

Definition

The ability to manufacture goods and provide services to the marketplace. Consistently demonstrating operating efficiency, speed, flexibility, and a capacity for continual improvement.

Areas of Focus

- Fully integrating all departments to support production.
- Production process is fast and cost-efficient.
- Evolves to reflect changes within company and within industry.
- Process contributes to competitive advantage.
- Strategic partners consistently fulfill production commitments.

The production process within the value chain, following the concept and design created in the R&D system, transforms inputs (such as raw materials, labor,
capital, plant, and equipment) into products and services deliverable to the
company's targeted customer. Often utilizing the largest portion of an organization's
human and capital assets, production and operations activities affect strategic choices
in achieving a company's strategic intent. Indeed, limited production capabilities
and policies may even dictate corporate strategies if not first considered by management in formulating their strategic intent.

Roger Schroeder suggests that production/operations management has five basic
functions, as shown in Figure 1 on the following page.

In a highly competitive marketplace, production often holds the key to sustaining an organization's competitive edge or losing it. Slow cycle times have often
been to blame for a dominant player to lose ground to competitors.

General Motors is a classic example of a large firm that has been traditionally
mired in bureaucracy. The company's five-year product development cycle was a

FIVE FUNCTIONS OF PRODUCTION/OPERATIONS MANAGEMENT[1]	
1. Process	Process decisions concern the design of the physical production system. Specific decisions include choice of technology, facility layout, process flow analysis, facility location, line balancing, process control, and transportation analysis.
2. Capacity	Capacity decisions concern determination of optimal output levels for the organization — not too much and not too little. Specific decisions include forecasting, facilities planning, aggregate planning, scheduling, capacity planning, and queuing analysis.
3. Inventory	Inventory decisions involve managing the level of raw materials, work in progress, and finished goods. Specific decisions include what to order, when to order, how much to order, and materials handling.
4. Workforce	Workforce decisions are concerned with managing the skilled, unskilled, clerical, and managerial employees. Specific decisions include job design, work measurement, job enrichment, work standards, and motivation techniques.
5. Quality	Quality decisions are aimed at ensuring that high-quality goods and services are produced. Specific decisions include quality control, sampling, testing, quality assurance, and cost control.

Figure 1

severe handicap in its struggle to compete with faster, more innovative companies, like Ford, Mazda, Toyota, and Honda, each of which with cycle times of less than four years.

In 1980, Apollo Computer created the market for engineering computer workstations. Experiencing rapid growth and a virtual monopoly for nearly two years, Apollo failed to accelerate their technology capabilities. Unable to adapt their design and production function to keep pace with Sun Microsystems' encroachment, Apollo eventually lost their market lead, and their market share dwindled to less than 20 percent by 1988. Facing mounting problems brought on by outdated systems, Apollo was acquired by Hewlett-Packard in 1989.[2]

The model shown on pages 68 and 69 (at the end of this section) illustrates the different strategic concerns a firm will have, depending on its stage of development. Being mindful of an organization's evolution in today's dynamic environment is also a hallmark of good operations management.

A good production system can have a significant impact on sustaining a strategy. Bose Corporation is known for manufacturing some of the best speakers in the world, and their products are best sellers in the United States and Japan. Bose maintains its speaker manufacturing facilities in Massachusetts, while most of its materials come from the Far East. Strategically committed to meeting the changing demands of its customers, Bose materials managers have the challenge of maintaining a just-in-time inventory strategy while fulfilling customer demands accurately and on time.

The way they accomplish this is by tracking their inventory, using a strategic partnership with a local freight forwarding company. Using technology to handle their inventory as easily as if it were housed in their facilities, Bose works in tandem with their shipping agent to bring in the needed parts on time. Bose is even electronically tied to U.S. Customs and can often clear their goods electronically, five days before the shipment enters the harbor.

Proof of their success in their materials-handling program came when a large Japanese customer doubled their order for a popular speaker system. Bose geared up their facility and, by using the technology of the forwarder/partner, was able to reroute needed parts out of their normal delivery channel and airfreight them in time to meet the customer's delivery date. The system may cost more, but speed plays a vital role in maintaining Bose's image and reputation in the marketplace.

Bose facilities represent the new age of flexible manufacturing. When polled by *Business Week*, production and operations managers agreed on the following characteristics of the responsive factory of the future (Figure 2):

CHARACTERISTICS OF THE TRULY RESPONSIVE FACTORY [3]	
Concurrent everything	Enterprise-wide computer integration, with electronic links to customers and suppliers, means that transactions occur mostly between computers, which will automatically route information to all proper departments or operations.
Fast development cycles	A real-time database will unite the distributed processing computers used by design, engineering, production, logistics, marketing, and customer service—whether the work is done in-house or is outsourced. All parties will have instant access to the latest information, eliminating the rework now caused by delays in shuffling paper.
Flexible production	Flexibility will be built into all levels of manufacturing, from the controls on each machine to the computers that coordinate work cells and factory-wide systems. Products can thus be turned out in greater variety and customized easily, with no cost penalty for small production runs.
Quick response	Dynamic factory-scheduling systems will put production "on call" and thus pare inventories to the bone. Production will begin only after a customer places an order.
Commitment to lifelong quality	Ongoing quality programs will lead to continuous improvement of both processes and products. A primary focus will be to make products easier to recycle or dispose of in environmentally sound ways.

Figure 2

PRODUCT AND CYCLE-TIME EXCELLENCE EVOLUTION [4]		
Characteristics	**Stage 0**	**Stage 1**
Product Development Process (Structure and Definition)	None – Concern about just getting the product out overwhelms any consideration of process. Weak project management discipline.	Distinct functional process. Hard to coordinate. Adherence to process varies widely.
Project Team Orientation	Ad hoc. Firefighters often more highly regarded than project managers.	Inconsistent team membership. Functional policies strong. Leadership shifts or is indeterminate.
Management Decision Process	Informal and highly reactive. Resources flow to whatever catches management's attention.	Priorities are set through annual budgeting. Project status reporting is initiated but is time consuming. Functional managers set de facto, often conflicting priorities. Resource allocation is very difficult.
Continuous Improvement	Individual learning takes place, but is not captured in a process.	Process elements are owned by individual functions, key skills often known only to certain individuals. It's hard to learn from failed projects because of fear of being blamed.
Target-Setting/ Metrics	No process targets. Focus is often on survival or financial turnaround.	Overall process targets not set or set by management flat. Currently performance is hard to measure.
Product Strategy Process	No process in place, only the de facto implications of past decisions. Tendency to follow inconsistent strategies.	Strategic visions inconsistent and not linked with product strategy. Tendency to attempt too much to be all things to all customers.
Technology Management Process	No distinction between technology and product development .	This is a functional responsibility. Finger pointing between marketing and technical functions is common. Large resource swings year- to-year are common.
Pipeline Management	Pipeline not managed or balanced. Fire fighting gets disproportionate share of resources.	Project proliferation is common. Chronic bottlenecks occur in certain functions.
Time-to-Market Performance	Not measured or managed. May be infinite.	Inconsistent and unpredictable. Very hard to measure. Tendency to bring many products to market before they are fully debugged, so manufacturing problems or high levels of engineering changes are common.
Development Productivity	Not measured or managed. Typically very low.	Many projects are cancelled late or never brought to market. Slow time to market limits productivity. Revenues from new products lag behind industry leaders.

Characteristics	Stage 2	Stage 3
Product Development Process (Structure and Definition)	The process is structured and clearly but simply defined. A single overall process integrates all functions. Used on all projects.	Process is integrated in the culture. Product development process is formally linked to product strategy and technologies processes.
Project Team Orientation	Small dedicated cross-functional teams similar to Core Team model. Strong project management.	Experienced Core Teams often develop multiple generations of products. Core Teams are used for platform and technology development.
Management Decision Process	Efficient, event-based Phase Review process is used by a decisive cross-functional management team (e.g., PAC) to set priorities. Priorities are accompanied by resources.	Decisions are based on fully developed product and technology strategies. Priorities set within context of overall pipeline and skill mix plans. Product platform decisions get an increased focus of attention.
Continuous Improvement	Full-time process owner in place. Process is evaluated regularly and updated. Opportunities to advance to next stage identified.	Process is "owned" by all who used it. There is a history of process upgrades and extensions. Opportunities to advance the state of the art regularly identified.
Target-Setting/ Metrics	Process targets are routinely set and measured against. These include cycle time and quality measures.	Process targets are set based on quantitative benchmarking of world-class companies. 5%-15% in all major metrics routinely planned.
Product Strategy Process	Focus is on individual products, not platforms. Product strategy is done in annual planning, if at all. Product strategy issues raised in phase reviews tend to be dealt with informally.	Focus is on product platforms, current and new. Product strategy is a formal process. It is linked to technology planning and executed through efficient product development process.
Technology Management Process	Typically no formal process for technology planning. Distinction between technology and product development becomes clearer, but not managed.	Technology strategy is linked to product strategy. Technology development is more deliberately managed. Technology transfer to product development process is well defined.
Pipeline Management	Distribution of projects by phase is known. Fewer projects staffed. Skill mix problems still common.	The strategic distribution of projects is known and managed. Skill mix management is long term.
Time-to-Market Performance	40% - 60% of Stage 1 Cycle times are based on completing development of a quality product, which is manufacturable in volume and at acceptable yields.	Best in industry and declining. Combined with product strategy advantages, which focus effort on right products, the advantage is very hard for competitors to overcome.
Development Productivity	Reduced time to market greatly increase productivity. Greatly reduced wasted R&D since phase reviews lead to earlier cancellation. Revenues from new products increasing.	Little wasted R&D. All efforts highly focused by platform, technology, and product. High percentage of sales generated by new products and new platforms.

Footnotes for Section 1.3.4 —

[1] R. Schroeder. *Operations Management.* McGraw-Hill, 1981, p. 12.

[2] B. Buell and R. D. Hof. "Hewlett-Packard Rethinks Itself." Business Week, 1 April 1991, p. 76-79.

[3] John A. Pearce II and Richard B. Robinson. *Strategic Management: Formulation, Implementation, and Control.* Irwin, 1997, p. 313; originally appeared in Busi ᵔess Week, 22 Oct 1993.

[4] Michael E. McGrath. *Setting the PACE in Product Development.* Butterworth-Heinemann, 1996, p. 150-151.

1.3.5 MARKETING

"Marketing is not the art of finding clever ways to dispose of what you Make. Marketing is the art of creating genuine customer value. It is the art of helping your customers become better off." — PHIL KOTLER

Definition

Creating a targeted marketing plan. Maintaining a constant awareness of the company's branding approach or competitive advantage when developing promotional strategies. Using available targeted information to support marketing decisions. Clearly determining the "return-on-investment" on all marketing campaigns.

Areas of Focus

- Having a clearly defined marketing plan.
- Coordinating all departs to support marketing.
- Monitoring the ROI of all marketing campaigns.
- Branding plays a critical role.
- Utilizing a marketing system or database to track customer and market information.
- Marketing department contributes to product or service development.
- "Competitive advantage" is a key driver for all marketing decisions.

At its root, marketing is "the analysis, planning, implementation, and control of programs designed to bring about desired exchanges with target markets for the purpose of achieving organizational objectives. It relies heavily on designing the organization's offering in terms of the target market's needs and desires and on using effective pricing, communication, and distribution to inform, motivate, and service the market."[1]

In other words, marketing is the activity that bridges the gap between buyer and seller — a very important activity in today's crowded and individualized marketplace. Marketing as a cross-functional discipline integrates with all other areas of organizational performance.

Since the objective of marketing is to satisfy customer needs now and in the future, marketing activities integrate many of the concepts introduced in this book.

TRADITIONAL MARKETING MIX™			
Product	**Price**	**Promotion**	**Place**

• Quality
• Features and
  benefits
• Style
• Brand name
• Packaging
• Product line
• Warranty
• Service level
• Supporting
  services
	• Level
	• Discounts
	• Allowances
	• Payment
	  terms
	• Returns
		• Advertising
		• Personal
		  selling
		• Sales
		  promotion
		• Publicity
		• Investor
		  relations
		• Tradeshows
			• Distribution channels
			• Distribution coverage
			• Outlet locations
			• Sales territories
			• Inventory locations
			• Transportation
			  centers

Figure 1

The framework for marketing activities is provided by the "marketing mix" (Figure 1), or the blending of the four "P's" of marketing — Product, Price, Promotion, and Place (or distribution). Elements of each are outlined below:

Product — In marketing, a product is more than just a good offered for sale. A product is a bundle of satisfactions sold to a customer. A product can be a good or it can be a service — or it can be a combination of the two. A product is not what the seller sells, it is what the buyer buys. For example, a realtor knows that a new home buyer is looking to buy more than just shelter. He or she may be making an investment in financial security, hoping to gain higher social status, and access to better school districts.

A product has multiple dimensions. Packaging, warranty, brand name, product image, and the level of customer service offered all play a role in driving a customer's purchase.

Promotion — The objectives of promotion are to inform the consumer, differentiate the product, increase demand, accentuate a product's value, and stabilize sales. Promotional campaigns are first used to develop primary demand for a product, and then later to build the brand to create selectivity. Promotion can be used to communicate basic facts (necessary early in the product life cycle); to persuade customer to choose one product over another; and finally, to remind existing customers of its existence and spur repeat purchases.

Types of promotional campaigns include advertising, personal selling, public relations, and sales promotion.

Pricing — Product pricing can be set using either a cost-based approach or a market-based one. Cost-based is tied to the actual cost of production; and market-based reflects what consumers are willing and able to pay. Pricing can be set to maintain a percent of the market; to avoid competition; and to position the product.

Consider Saturn Corporation. The company wants to let consumers know that it is friendly and easy to do business with. Part of this message is conveyed through initiatives such as inviting customers to the factory to see where the cars are made; others include sponsoring evenings at the dealership or reunion picnics. Saturn's pricing policy also sends a strong message. They have a "no hassle, no haggle" policy (one price, no negotiations) which removes the possibility of adversarial discussions between dealer and potential customer. Customers have an easier time buying a car knowing that the next person in the door won't negotiate a better deal.

The pricing policy for Swatch watches illustrates the same point. Swatch's pricing policy sends the message that a watch can be more than just functional; it can be fun as well — so much fun, that a customer ought to own several. The price for a basic model has not changed in ten years. As Franco Bosisio, the head of Swatch design lab noted, "Price has become a mirror for the other attributes we try to communicate...A Swatch is not just affordable, it's approachable. Buying a Swatch is an easy decision to make, an easy decision to live with. It's provocative, but it doesn't make you think too much."[2]

Place (Distribution) — Distribution channels provide the means for delivery of a product to a consumer. Channels can be direct or indirect, either going straight from the company to the consumer or from the company to a middleman (or middlemen) to a consumer. Products distributed through conventional channels go from one independent company to another until finally reaching the end customer. Packaged goods, such as food items, are often sold through conventional channels. Vertical channels are linked together, either as part of the same corporate entity or on a contractual basis.

As in a company's other functional areas, activities in marketing should be guided by a strategic plan based on the company's mission and objectives. The plan should also be subject to ROI measurements. Just as with overall organizational strategy, creation of the marketing strategy should begin with an examination of the company's situational analysis, both internally and externally. At what stage is the firm's development? What is the corporate culture? What is the competitive situation? What external factors must be considered?

Next, the marketing plan should choose its target market; and determine its positioning within that market. The marketing mix should then be developed using these criteria (Figure 2).

KEY ELEMENTS IN THE MARKETING PLAN [2]	
People	What is the target market for the firm's product(s)? What is its size and growth potential?
Profit	What is the expected profit from implementing the marketing plan? What are other objectives of the marketing plan, and how will their achievement be evaluated?
Personnel	What personnel will be involved in implementing the marketing plan? Will only intrafirm personnel be involved, or will other firms, such as advertising agencies or marketing research firms, also be employed?
Product	What product(s) will be offered? What variations in the product will be offered in terms of style, features, quality, branding, packaging, and terms of sale and service, how should products be positioned in the marketplace?
Price	What price or prices will products be sold for?
Promotion	How will information about the firm's offerings be communicated to the target market?
Place	How, when, and where will the firm's offerings be delivered for sale to the target market?
Policy	What is the overall marketing policy for dealing with anticipated problems in the marketing plan? How will unanticipated problems be handled?
Period	For how long a time is the marketing plan to be in effect? When should the plan be implemented, and what is the schedule for executing and evaluating marketing activities?

Figure 2

Figure 3 illustrates ten key principles for marketing success.

For emphasis in this reference guide, many marketing subjects are addressed specifically on their own. These include: industry and competitive analysis (section 1.2.2), environmental assessment (section 1.2.3), customer profile (section 1.2.1), market position (section 1.3.1), sales and distribution (section 1.3.6), and customer service (section 1.3.7) Areas within other principal elements will encompass tradi-

TEN KEY PRINCIPLES OF MARKETING [3]	
Principle 1	Create Customer Want Satisfaction
Principle 2	Know Your Buyer Characteristics
Principle 3	Divide the Market into Segments
Principle 4	Strive for Higher Market Share
Principle 5	Develop Deep and Wide Product Lines
Principle 6	Price Position Products and Upgrade Markets
Principle 7	Treat Channels as Intermediate Buyers
Principle 8	Coordinate Elements of Physical Distribution
Principle 9	Promote Performance Features
Principle 10	Use Information to Improve Decisions

Figure 3

tional marketing areas such as targeted information (section 2.3.2) and organization communication (section 2.3.1).

While volumes have been written on any of these marketing issues, common themes are cross-functional integration and the use of ROI-based benchmarks for success, that is, monitoring marketing activities for their impact on profitability.

Footnotes for Section 1.3.5 —

[1] Philip Kotler. *Marketing Management*. Prentice-Hall, 1984, p. 14.

[2] Robert J. Dolan. "How Do You Know When the Price Is Right?" Harvard Business Review, Sep/Oct 1995, p. 4.

[3] John J. Peter and James H. Donnelly, Jr. *A Preface to Marketing Management, 6th Edition*. Irwin, 1994, p. 24.

[4] Fred C. Allvine. *Marketing: Principles and Practices*. Harcourt Brace Jovanovich, 1987, p. viii.

1.3.6 SALES AND DISTRIBUTION

"Through direct contact with the customer, the salesperson is able to identify solutions to the customer's problems that unlock the customer's enthusiasm, budgets, and loyalty."   — ANONYMOUS

Definition

Developing and executing an effective sales management process. Achieving sales goals. Rewarding the sales organization for the correct skills and behaviors. Consistently demonstrating efficiency or speed of distribution. Having the means to track sales activity from lead generation through close.

Areas of Focus

- Employing a fully integrated sales management process.
- Coordinating all departments to support sales process.
- Consistently achieving sales goals.
- Sales teams/channels possess all required skills to achieve plan.
- Sales teams/channels are provided with the necessary information to achieve their goals.
- Sales channels are quick and responsive.
- Tracking sales activity from lead generation through close.
- Competitors recognize sales process as "Best-in-Class."

In a growing global economy — with fewer barriers to entry, non-traditional channels, quality wars, price wars, and substitute products — the sales management function has never been more challenging. Many companies have acknowledged this difficulty and have opted to obtain growth through merger or acquisition. At times, it would appear that it is more cost efficient, more reliable, and much less risky for certain industries to buy market share rather than to capture it. Yet, it still remains true that, in general, successful long-term strategy implementation rests upon the ability of an organization to sell and deliver their product or service.

The sales process includes sales promotion, personal selling, sales force management, and customer relations. The traditional approach to selling is based on a step-by-step process:

- Getting the customer's attention.
- Arousing the customer's interest.
- Stimulating the customer's desire for the product.
- Getting the customer to buy.
- Building satisfaction into the transaction.

In his book *Customer Centered Selling*, Robert Jolles outlines the sales process from the customer's perspective.

CUSTOMER DECISION CYCLE [1]	
Satisfaction	Customer is unaware of any need
Acknowledgement	Customer admits pain, but takes no action
Decision	Customer decides pain is big enough
Criteria	Customer problem's define criteria for remedy
Measurement	Customer criteria is specific
Investigation	Customer initiates search for remedy providers
Selection	Customer commits to remedy
Reconsideration	Customer questions process and decision

Figure 1

Whether an organization's sales process involves personal selling or mass communication, it is important that messages are congruent with the firm's overall strategic intent. Consistent messages will build durability, market position, and brand identity among potential customers. As companies refocus on more effective sales and customer service the following ingredients have been identified as keys to selling success:

1. *Rethink training* — Salespeople now require new skills. They must be taught to be advocates of their customers with detailed knowledge of their customers' businesses to enable them to target sales opportunities as service problems. High-pressure selling tactics and one-time slam-dunk sales will not be effective.

2. *Total involvement* — Effective salespeople no longer act alone. The efforts of product designers, plant managers, and financial officers must be a part of selling and serving customers.

3. *Top management support* — CEOs and other top managers must be visibly and frequently involved in any change effort. This often includes regularly making sales calls and leading sales training meetings.

4. *Relating objectives to motivation* — Discourage incentives that encourage quick hit sales. Include measures of long-term customer satisfaction in compensation plans.

5. *Use technology* — Increase responsiveness with marketing and distribution technology. Technology can be used to track customer relationships, to insure the right products get to the right place at the right time, and to simplify order taking.

6. *Stay close to the customer* — Pay attention to customers. Call them often or send notes to frequent shoppers. Assign an employee to good customers.

In summary, sales management crosses functional lines. Having trained personnel understand the relationship between their job function and customer service is key to transforming a production-oriented company into a sales-oriented one. The following are fundamentals for all sales-oriented personnel to have:

1. A thorough knowledge of the company, including its past history, the management philosophy, and its basic operating policies.

2. A thorough technical and commercial knowledge of products and product lines.

3. A good working knowledge of competitors' products, including their costs and benefits, strengths and weaknesses.

4. An in-depth knowledge of the market, including economic and other external issues that may affect demand.

5. A thorough understanding of methods used to locate and qualify prospects. A consistent method of evaluating potential customers' needs, financial resources, and willingness to be approached.

6. An accurate knowledge of the customer's buying profile, including product applications and customer requirements. Be able to describe product benefits as well as understand how the customer makes a buying decision.

Nordstrom has proven that department stores can survive in the competitive world of retailing by implementing a good sales process. Its intense personalized service and attention to the customer has resulted in high customer loyalty and steady growth. General Electric has also achieved success by training their salespeople to work long-term with customers, experimenting with team-based compensation, assigning staff full-time to customers' facilities, and nurturing deep relationships with their own suppliers.

Well-trained, sales-oriented employees are only one part of the equation. An organization also must evaluate its sales and distribution channels for alignment with its strategic intent. These channels are the paths a product or service takes as it moves from the originating company to the ultimate consumer (Figures 2 and 3). Channels can be direct or indirect, either going straight from the company to the consumer or from the company to a middleman (or middlemen) to a consumer. Whether an organization selects an indirect channel such as Compaq's distribution through CompUSA, Costco, Staples, et al., or a direct channel such as Dell Computer's e-commerce or direct mail catalog process, channel selection is vital to reaching a firm's customer base profitably and efficiently.

The number of indirect and direct channels has increased dramatically, aided by technology, and innovative companies continue to find new ways to reach customers.

CATEGORIES OF DIRECT AND INDIRECT CHANNELS [2]		
Direct	Indirect	
Product Ownership	Product Ownership	Product Nonownership
Direct sales force	Distributor	Manufacturer sales representative
National account sales	Private label	Broker
Direct Mail	Stocking manufacturer sales representative	Independent sales agent
Telemarketing	Original equipment manufacturer (OEM)	Export management company (EMC)
Manufacturer's catalog	Catalog house	Synthetic channel of distribution
Internet	Telemarketing company	Fulfillment channel
	Wholesaler	
	Master distributor	
	Reseller	
	Retailer	
	Dealer	
	Value-added reseller	
	System integrator	
	Phantom channel of distribution	

Figure 2

1. Identify the new market you want to penetrate or new product you need to launch.

2. Verify the need for a new channel or distribution or some form of channel reorganization.

3. Evaluate all macro market conditions.

4. Conduct a competitive channel analysis.

5. Research and rank customers/end user satisfaction requirements.

6. Specify and rank the tasks you want your channel partner to perform.

7. Investigate all possible channels of distribution structures.

8. Decide upon the best channel partners.

9. Obtain internal corporate recommitment.

10. Approach and sign the selected distributors.

11. Monitor and evaluate the channel structure.

Figure 3

For years, IBM had relied upon a direct sales force to sell its large mainframes. But using this type of distribution channel to sell its new microcomputers was costly and quite simply, inadequate. Instead, Big Blue turned to new indirect channels to sell its microcomputer products directly to consumers and small businesses. Rubbermaid has made big inroads into Tupperware's market share by selling similar products through efficient channels such as Wal-Mart, while Tupperware continues to sell through much more costly multilevel distribution.

Although a difficult task to master, sales and distribution in today's marketplace offer firms a greater number of options than ever before. Organizations that are customer-driven, technology-savvy, and congruent in their positioning can restructure their channel design to reach their customer base with increasingly more efficient methods.

Footnotes for Section 1.3.6 —

[1] Adapted from Robert Jolles. *Customer Centered Selling*. Free Press, 1998, p. 40-60.

[2] Kenneth Rolnicki. "Channels of Distribution," AMACOM, 1998, p. 11.

[3] Kenneth Rolnicki. "Channels of Distribution," AMACOM, 1998, p. 11.

1.3.7 CUSTOMER SERVICE

"People expect a certain reaction from a business and when you pleasantly exceed those expectations you've somehow passed an important psychological threshold."

— RICHARD THALHEIMER

Definition

Clearly defining service standards and maintaining an effective customer service management system. Ensuring that customer expectations are consistently met or exceeded. Tracking and measuring service strengths, such as customer loyalty, repeat business, and minimal complaints.

Areas of Focus

- Meeting or exceeding customer expectations.
- Measuring customer satisfaction by routinely obtaining direct customer feedback.
- Managers and employees share a high commitment to achieving customer loyalty.
- Maintaining a customer relationship management system that provides critical service information to make the best decision.

Sustaining customer value is an important key to strategic management. Successful strategy implementation involves measuring customer value in order to understand potential problems and emphasize customer service and satisfaction. Meeting customer expectations is the key to satisfaction, but exceeding expectations is the key to customer loyalty.

There are literally hundreds of good examples of outstanding customer service in business journals and in best practice literature. Companies like Nordstrom, Tiffany's, FAO Schwartz, and American Express have legendary customer service. But these stories of excellent customer service are most noteworthy because of their infrequency. After all, extraordinary levels of customer service are difficult to sustain.

However, organizations have much to learn from these stories of exceptional customer service. At the crux of each are systemic approaches that can transform

TOP TEN BEST PRACTICE CUSTOMER SERVICE DIAGNOSTIC QUESTIONS[1]

1. What is your customer retention? Does it indicate any trends you can act upon?
2. What is the level of cross-functional communication between your company and its customers?
3. Do you train employees throughout the organization in various tasks so that any of them can handle any problem that arises during the customer cycle?
4. What financial empowerment do you provide to your frontline employees to solve customer problems? Do you give them additional authority to make decisions on the spot?
5. Do those frontline employees have access to executive groups such as IBM's customer action councils where they can receive additional assistance and powers of authority?
6. Do you have in place a cross-functional database to track and analyze customer service highlights and lowlights?
7. How do you explicitly gauge your customers' satisfaction? Do focus groups play a role?
8. Is any portion of your company's merit system based on customer service?
9. Do you have a client advisory board? How often does it meet? What does it accomplish?
10. Do you surprise your customers with great customer service? Do your customers experience a level of service that is beyond their expectations?

an organization into a more customer-focused enterprise. Metro Bank defined three key elements of excellent customer relations in their industry:

1. *Knowledgeable people:* Differentiate ourselves through employees capable of recognizing customer needs and possessing the knowledge to proactively satisfy them.

2. *Convenient access:* Give customers access to banking services or information 24 hours a day.

3. *Responsiveness:* Service customers expediently. The timeliness of the response could meet the customer's perceived sense of urgency.

Although marketing plays a critical role in meeting customer expectations before, during, and after a sales transaction, other functions within the organization also contribute to superior customer responsiveness.

A young boy entered a drugstore phone booth, and the owner overheard the following conversation: "Hello, is this the Smith residence? I am looking for work as a gardener...What's that, you already have a gardener? Is he good...Are you satisfied with his work?...Do you plan on keeping him?...Is he not doing anything that you would like him to do?...I see...Well, thanks anyway. I'm glad you are

PRIMARY ROLES OF DIFFERENT FUNCTIONS IN ACHIEVING SUPERIOR CUSTOMER RESPONSIVENESS [2]	
Value-Creation Function	**Primary Role**
Infrastructure	Through leadership by example, build a company-wide commitment to customer responsiveness.
Manufacturing	Achieve customization by implementing flexible manufacturing.
Marketing	Know the customer. Communicate customer feedback to appropriate functions.
Materials Management	Develop logistics systems capable of responding quickly to unanticipated customer demands.
R&D	Bring customers into the product development process.
Human Resources	Develop training programs that make employees think of themselves as customers.

getting such excellent service. Bye." As he left the booth, the owner remarked, "Johnny, I couldn't help overhearing. I know it's none of my business, but aren't you the Smith's gardener?" To which Johnny replied, "Yes, I am. I just called to see how I was doing."

In 1994, USAA designed, built, and installed its own computer technology that captures any customer query, complaint, or comment, while that person speaks to a USAA representative. The "ECHO" system, an acronym for "Every Contact Has Opportunity," has transformed the way USAA provides customer service.[3]

Footnotes for Section 1.3.7 —

[1] Robert Hiebler, Thomas B. Kelly, and Charles Ketteman. *Best Practices: Building Your Business with Customer-Focused Solutions.* Simon & Schuster, 1998, p. 199-200.

[2] Charles W. L. Hill and Gareth R. Jones. *Strategic Management Theory: An Integrated Approach.* Houghton Mifflin, 1995, p. 162.

[3] Robert Hiebler, Thomas B. Kelly, and Charles Ketteman. *Best Practices: Building Your Business with Customer-Focused Solutions.* Simon & Schuster, 1998, p. 170.

1.4.0 Objectives, Initiatives, and Goals

"Objectives are not fate; they are direction. They are not commands; they are commitments. They do not determine the future; they are means to mobilize the resources and energies of the business for the making of the future." — PETER DRUCKER

Description

Reflects the company's ability to articulate what it wants to accomplish, how it will do it, and when it will be achieved. The company's process of defining its direction, aligning financial and human resources, while instilling accountability and critical measurements.

Principal Elements

- Vital Direction
- Resource Alignment
- Organization Accountabilities
- Measurement

Goals, objectives, and initiatives provide a framework for strategic planners to articulate a company's future plans in concrete terms. Goals are stated outcomes of the strategic planning process, and are long-term in nature. Goals can address both financial and non-financial issues, and cut across functional boundaries.

Figure 1 is a basic example of a strategic decision to increase sales.

STRATEGIC OBJECTIVES, INITIATIVES, AND GOALS SUMMARY™				
Objective	**Initiatives**	**Goals**		
Increase product sales volume through the introduction of a new delivery channel	• Create customer direct delivery channel • Expand website support • install "e-commerce" software • Expand database capabilities to support initiatives	*Fiscal Year* 1998 1999 2000	*% of Total Sales* 5% 12.5% 18%	*ROI* -.65 .75 2.75

Figure 1

Though a basic example, the table above illustrates the intent and expectation of the sales objective. This organization made the decision to increase sales by creating a new delivery channel that leverages their customers' comfort with the internet. The initiative calls out the technology and resources necessary to meet the objective. The goals reflect a desired increase in sales performance, the return-on-investment, and when the company intends to realize the increases.

Within your objectives, initiatives, and goals, you are developing the communication vehicle that will summarize the critical elements that support your strategic intent, as well as an explicit timeline in which these expectations are to be achieved.

In larger or diversified companies, these may be broad-stroked descriptions, allowing business units or divisions the ability to build their operating plans in a manner that specifically identifies their contribution and role in achieving the organizations' strategic intent. These are the tactical plans that provide the muscle necessary for the company to successfully fulfill its plan and are captured in the fourth and final leg of the strategic planning model.

The management challenge in setting objectives, initiatives, and goals is to align the organization's resources, and to ensure that the plans are prioritized and consistent with the overall strategic intent of the organization. And, upon implementation, management should show leadership in communicating roles and responsibilities throughout the organization, assuring that the organization has efficient structure and skills to achieve the overall intent.

1.4.1 Vital Direction

"We strategize beautifully, we implement pathetically."
— Executive of an Auto Parts Firm

Definition

Effectively converting strategic intent into clearly defined, actionable activities. Prioritizing critical objectives by their strategic importance, aligning these objectives with the company's values and beliefs, and remaining poised to integrate dynamic emerging opportunities.

Areas of Focus

- Identifying key strategic objectives.
- Actions fully integrated into values and beliefs.
- Action items clearly prioritized by importance and magnitude.
- Having quantifiable and measurable actions.
- Remaining flexible to respond to new opportunities.

Once an organization's management team has crafted a strategy, the next priority is to convert the strategy into complementary actions and aligned results. While successful strategy formulation relies on analysis, assessment, and creativity, establishing and furthering the vital direction of the firm requires leadership and motivation, as well as the ability to successfully execute. Often, implementation is carried out by a manager.

Successful implementation starts with a close examination of the current organization, in light of the new strategy. A manager should ask the following questions:

1. Does the organization possess the necessary skill sets to implement our new strategy? If not, how shall we get them?

2. Does the structure of the organization support the new strategy? Are the proper reporting responsibilities, policies, information systems, communication, and operating efficiencies in place?

3. Is the culture and rewards systems of the organization aligned with the new strategy? Do we have a nurturing supportive environment? Are our performance measurements appropriate?

The next page contains an example of an action planning report that outlines several initiatives that have been distilled from a strategic planning exercise. Additional reports may be found at the Virtual CEO™ web site: **http://www. virtualceo.com**.

The management validation and action plan illustrates the intent and expectation of the sales and distribution priorities of the organization. To meet its objective of increasing sales, this organization formed initiatives to formalize the sales process, train its staff, and review potential channels for new potential clients. These initiatives call out the technology and resources necessary to meet the objective. The goals reflect a desired increase in sales performance and return-on-investment, and an objective defines when the company intends to realize the increases.

This description of the organization's strategic intent in terms of sales and distribution provides a solid framework to communicate the vital direction the organization will take during the short term. With communication of the strategy enhanced by this documentation, the necessary resources, personnel training, and organizational processes may be put into play more quickly.

In larger or more diversified companies, these initiatives may be broad-stroked descriptions, allowing business units or divisions the ability to build operating plans in a manner that specifically identifies their contribution and role in achieving the organization's strategic intent. These tactical plans provide the muscle necessary for firms to successfully implement their strategies.

EnergyCo is a closely-held fuel distribution company. Founder Sam Rutledge has led an outstanding management team that has made EnergyCo a major player in eastern Virginia. Credit for the firm's success is given to an emphasis on action plans and annual objectives. During the process, priorities are weighed, resources aligned, and ownership assigned. Such clarity of purpose and the assignment of allocation helps to formalize the organization's vital direction.

Management Validation & Action Planning

VIRTUAL CEO

Priority	Objectives	Resource Allocation	Ownership	Milestones	Due Date	Measurements
Customer Profile	Build profile database	Internal/External Resource	Simone Charles - Director Market Research <charles@linear.com>	Organize project IPT	10/02/2000	30% increase in cross-sell products
				Set up necessary connectivity for group members	10/05/2000	
	Conduct research/focus groups	Internal Resource	Simone Charles - Director Market Research <charles@linear.com>	Select research company	10/02/2000	75% or better favorable response to new product offerings
				Set up focus group schedule	10/09/2000	
				Compile data from focus groups	10/27/2000	
				Create reports and recommendations	10/30/2000	
	Link key learnings to marketing plan	Internal Resource	Martin Langley - EVP Marketing <langley@linear.com>	Analyze focus group impact on marketing plan	11/03/2000	5% increase in direct mail responses
				Modify marketing plan to reflect impact	11/10/2000	
Applied Technology	Inventory current company technological environment	Internal Resource	Donald Chang - EVP Information Systems <chang@linear.com>	Select project team	10/06/2000	10% minimum save with redundant systems
				Complete inventory	10/30/2000	
				Create summary report	11/03/2000	
	Research advancements in mainframe/PC technology	External Resource	Richard Monahan - Director of Info Services <monahan@linear.com>	Hire Tech consultant	10/16/2000	35% reduction in hardware/software costs
				Attend Comdex trade show	10/25/2000	
	Research advancements in Internet technology	External Resource	Richard Monahan - Director of Info Services <monahan@linear.com>	Hire Internet consultant	10/16/2000	25% increase in website hit rate
				Attend Comdex trade show	10/25/2000	
	Make recommendations to Executive Committee	Internal Resource	Donald Chang - EVP Information Systems <chang@linear.com>	Compile data from trade show/consultant research	11/09/2000	Acceptance and approval of Exec Committee
				Make presentation to Executive Committee	11/14/2000	Overall cost reduction of not less than 10% in annual IT costs
Building Effective Teams	Select top performing managers as mentors	Internal Resource	Jane Thomason - Director of Training and Development <thomason@linear.com>	Send e-mail to regional VP's to nominate mentors	10/04/2000	Substantial increase in Leadership 360 results on the part of the candidates
				Mentor candidate nominations due	10/13/2000	Favorable response from candidate staff interviews
				Mentors selected	10/20/2000	Successful completion of action items on candidate personal development plan

1.4.2 Resource Alignment

"No company can afford everything it would like to do. Resources have to be allocated. The essence of strategic planning is to allocate resources to those areas that have the greatest future potential."

— Reginald Jones

Definition

Committing the necessary capital, human, or technological resources to achieve key strategic objectives. Evaluating individual or group capacity when planning resource allocations.

Areas of Focus

- Resources are clearly aligned for each action item.
- Resource alignment is linked to competitive advantage.
- Individual or group capacity plays a critical role in assigned workload.

One barrier to implementing strategy is the failure to link action plans and resource allocation to short, and long-term strategic priorities.[1] Organizational business units need enough resources to contribute to the strategic intent of the firm. The most critical resources are sufficient budget funding, and the appropriate and trained people to perform the tasks. Too often, financial budgets are established through methods that are totally separate from the strategic planning process. Actual budgets and expenses are often reviewed for variances against budgeted targets, without regard for accomplishing the firm's intent.

How well a firm redirects its assets can make or break a strategy. Too little funding can slow or stop any progress made in achieving a firm's strategic intent, while too much funding can waste precious resources and reduce financial returns. Careful attention must be paid to linking strategic goals with adequate resources.

Some strategic initiatives require substantial redirection of investment on the part of the firm. Whirlpool Corporation's "Quality Express" initiatives outlined on-time, prompt delivery of product to 90 percent of Whirlpool's dealers network within 24 hours and the rest within 48 hours. This initiative to provide superior customer service and maintain customer satisfaction required a huge logistics effort and a shift in capital and resources.[2]

When supporting an increased budget to implement a new initiative, management ought to be prepared to justify any budget allocations in terms of contribution to the overall strategy. A cash flow budget can anticipate any cash short falls during the period of the initiative. A sample budget (Figure 1) follows:

SAMPLE SIX-MONTH CASH BUDGET™							
Cash Budget (in $000's)							
Desired Level of Cash Balance: 5,000							
	Month 1	**Month 2**	**Month 3**	**Month 4**	**Month 5**	**Month 6**	**Total**
Income							
Receipts	12,000	21,000	15,000	14,000	9,000	18,000	89,000
Other Income							0
Total Income	12,000	21,000	15,000	14,000	9,000	18,000	89,000
Expenses							
Purchases	10,500	18,000	13,500	12,000	7,000	12,000	73,000
Wages & Salaries	1,500	1,500	1,500	1,500	1,500	1,500	9,000
Rent	500	500	500	500	500	500	3,000
Other Expenses	250	300	350	200	450	125	1,675
Interest	100	100	100	100	100	100	600
Taxes		6				377	383
Total Expenses	12,850	20,406	15,950	14,300	9,550	14,602	87,658
Net Cash Gain (Loss)	(850)	594	(950)	(300)	550)	3,398	1,342
Beginning Cash Balance	6,000	5,150	5,744	4,794	4,494	3,944	6,000
Cumulative Cash Balance	5,150	5,744	4,794	4,494	3,944	7,342	7,342
Cash Available (Required)	150	744	(206)	(506)	(1,056)	2,342	2,342

Figure 1

In the above example, the unit forecasting the cash flow based on its strategic implementation of the initiatives needs to allocate an additional $1 million to cover its projected cash shortage during months 3, 4, and 5. At the end of the period, there will be a surplus of cash available to repay the cash investment with a small return. If this unit contributes to the overall intent of the company, then the investment is well worth the effort.

Other resources often overlooked are the people and skill sets required to fulfill the strategic initiative. Too often, rewards and incentives are geared away or in direct opposition to the strategic intent. No matter how well conceived a strategy may be, without incentives and career consequences linked to its accomplishment, employees will have difficulty implementing initiatives successfully. Assembling, motivating, and managing human resources is just as critical to a firm as crafting a targeted strategy.

Finally, successful implementation requires the appropriate systems support. For example, in order to carry out its mission of next-day delivery, FedEx has a communication system that tracks every package in its transit delivery system. It can report instantly the last known whereabouts of any package. The system allows FedEx to coordinate its 21,000 vans nationwide who make an average of 720,000 stops per day.[3] Proctor & Gamble codes more than 900,000 phone calls it receives annually as an early warning indicator of product problems and changing consumer tastes.[4] No company can expect to execute its strategic intent without sufficient support systems already in place. Moreover, unusually good support systems can strengthen a firm enough to give it a competitive advantage in the marketplace.

Footnotes for Section 1.4.2 —

[1] Robert S. Kaplan and David P. Norton. *The Balanced Scorecard*. Harvard Business School Press, 1996, p. 196.

[2] A. A. Thompson and A. J. Strickland. *Strategic Management: Concepts and Cases*, 10th Edition. 1998.

[3] James Brian Quinn. *Intelligent Enterprise*. Free Press, 1992, p. 114-115.

[4] James Brian Quinn. *Intelligent Enterprise*. Free Press, 1992, p. 181.

1.4.3 ORGANIZATION ACCOUNTABILITIES

"I have a duty to the soldiers, their parents, and the country to re-move immediately any commander who does not satisfy the highest performance demands. It is a mistake to put a person in a command that is not the right command. It is therefore my job to think through where that person belongs." — GENERAL GEORGE C. MARSHALL

Definition

Ensuring that individuals and groups within the company have a clear understanding of management's expectations, and that they understand their specific roles in accomplishing critical objectives, initiatives, and goals. Communicating progress against key objectives.

Areas of Focus

- Ensuring that employees understand how their roles and responsibilities relate to strategic objectives.
- Employing a standardized vehicle and format to track and report performance.
- Having an internal system that routinely communicates status of key objectives.

Individual and group accountability holds the key to successful achievement of an organization's goals, objectives, and initiatives. Managers must clearly define each strategic role, then communicate the intent of the organization as well as each role and responsibility.

These roles may be filled either by existing staff, or by recruiting people with the correct mix of experience, expertise, values, and management style.

Training and retraining are additional options that can reinforce a strategy requiring new skill sets or operating methods. Training budgets, programs, and schedules should be part of the strategic plan for execution. Training needs to begin early in the execution phase and should be a priority initiative.

Once employees are trained and completely understand their roles and responsibilities, especially in terms of contribution to the overall strategic intent of the company, management and employee performance should be tracked against milestones, timeframes, and initiatives established in the planning process (Figure 1).

BASIC ACCOUNTABILITY MODEL™					
Goal or Task	Priority	Person(s) or Group Responsible	Begin Date	Milestones or Due Date	Outcome or Results

Figure 1

1.4.4 MEASUREMENT

"Complicated controls do not work. They confuse. They misdirect attention from what is to be controlled to the mechanics and methodology of the control." — SEYMOUR TILLES

Definition

Demonstrating consistency when tracking or reporting performance. Using an effective and uniform measurement process for financial reporting, project management, third party performance, and operating standards.

Areas of Focus

Effectively measuring key performance indicators, such as:
- Financial ratios
- Project phases and milestones
- Qualitative processes
- Individual, group, or partner performance
- Technology

Performance measurement is critical to the achievement of a company's strategic intent. However, the biggest challenge in evaluating performance is ensuring that what is being measured is drawn specifically from the critical success factors of the organization. Many factors can be measured — financial ratios, production quality, customer satisfaction, employee retention — but it is up to the company to determine and prioritize what its critical success factors are. At the same time, dependence on only a few measures should be avoided. Such one-sided metrics can allow a business to show good progress in the measured activity while drifting away from the overall strategy.

Kaplan and Norton[1] give a good example of the dangers of measurement myopia. A company, in attempting to increase customer satisfaction, decided to use on-time delivery as the primary measure of its success. Its focus on on-time delivery encouraged the firm to invest large amounts of capital in producing enough goods to always meet customer demand. However, while pleasing the customer, the firm also encountered higher shipping, storage, and handling expenses, as well as the threat of obsolete inventory. Hardly good business practice.

The following table (Figure 1) illustrates one method of summarizing the key items to measure against one's strategy.

MEASURING BUSINESS STRATEGY [2]	
Perspective	**Generic Measures**
Financial	• Revenue growth and mix • Cost reduction/productivity improvement • Asset utilization/investment strategy
Customer	• Share • Customer retention • Customer acquisition • Customer satisfaction • Profitability
Internal	• Quality • Response time • Cost • New product introductions
Learning and Growth	• Employee satisfaction • Employee retention • Employee productivity

Figure 1

There are multiple subsets that fall under each of the above bullet points. However, a company must review these areas and determine whether they are meeting minimum standards of strategic performance measurement.

The table on the next page illustrates a simplified report that tracks the current status of performance indicators to a firm's strategy.[3] These indicators show progress after two years of a five-year strategy intended to differentiate the firm as a customer service-oriented provider of high quality products. When evaluating performance, management should compare expected results with actual progress. Any negative deviations should form the basis of additional action planning or adjustments to the overall initiative.

Key Success Factors	Objective, Assumption, or Budget	Forecast Performance at This Time	Current Performance	Current Deviation	Analysis
SAMPLE MONITORING AND PERFORMANCE EVALUATION FOR A DIFFERENTIATED FIRM					
Cost Control: Ratio of indirect overhead costs to direct field and labor costs	10%	15%	12%	+ 3% (ahead)	Are we moving too fast, or is there more unnecessary overhead than was originally thought?
Gross Profit	39%	40%	40%	0%	
Customer Service: Installation cycle in days	2.5 days	3.2 days	2.7 days	+ 0.5 days (ahead)	Can this progress be maintained?
Ratio of service to sales personnel	3.2	2.7	2.1	- 0.6 (behind)	Why are we behind here? How can we maintain the installation-cycle progress?
Product Quality: Percentage of products returned	1.0%	2.0%	2.1%	- 0.1% (behind)	Why are we behind here? What are the ramifications for other operations?
Product performance versus specification	100%	92%	80%	- 12% (behind)	
Marketing: Monthly sales per employee	$12,500	$11,500	$12,100	+ $600 (ahead)	Good progress. Is it creating any problems to support?
Expansion of product line	6	3	5	+ 2 products (ahead)	Are the products ready? Are the perfect standards met?
Employee Morale in Service Area: Absenteeism	2.5%	3.0%	3.0%	On target	
Turnover	5%	10%	15%	- 5% (behind)	Looks like a problem! Why are we so far behind?
Competition: New product introductions (average number)	6	3	6	- 3 (behind)	Did we underestimate timing? What are the implications for our basic assumptions?

Measurement

Footnotes for Section 1.4.4 —

[1] Robert S. Kaplan and David P. Norton. *The Balanced Scorecard*. Harvard Business School Press, 1996, p. 164.

[2] Robert S. Kaplan and David P. Norton. *The Balanced Scorecard*. Harvard Business School Press, 1996, p. 43-44.

[3] John A. Pearce II and Richard B. Robinson. *Strategic Management: Formulation, Implementation, and Control*. Irwin, 1997, p. 391.

2.0 ORGANIZATION DESIGN

"The single biggest problem in business is staying with your previously successful business model...one year too long." — LEW PLATT

Key Components

- Basic Structure
- Core Competence
- Information, Systems, and Technology
- Organization Efficiency

Management's challenge in designing an organization is to effectively combine hierarchical reporting relationships, policies, procedures, control systems, and information flow into an efficient responsive structure.

Design issues include basic structural decisions, such as committing to a formal hierarchy while still maintaining the flexibility to meet emerging requirements of a new chosen strategy. Organizational design processes go beyond structure, encompassing the organizational systems of the firm, such as how the firm communicates, what processes need to be built to support the information requirements of the strategy, and what capacities need to be built or outsourced to secure an advantage in the marketplace.

An established or mature company faces the challenge of modifying its existing structure, staff, and systems in order to adapt and succeed within its evolving industry. **An emerging company** must commit to a course of action that allows the firm to align its strategic plan with its organization structure, its human resources, its information, systems, and technology applications and systems. Regardless of the company's age, size, or industry, its ability to consistently evaluate and modify its organizational design will determine its success in achieving its strategic intent.

The organizational design of a company is a work in progress. In today's dynamic operating environment, industry changes, new competitive pressures, and technology innovations keep savvy managers constantly monitoring the design assumptions of their firms. Management must remain poised and willing to make targeted design changes that support the long-term success of the enterprise.

Hewlett-Packard is an excellent example of a company who modified their organizational design to support their strategic initiatives.[1] In 1985, HP began to reverse its long-standing practice of allowing its units to operate as independent companies, each having its own manufacturing, marketing, finance and other functional departments. By having control at the local level, unit managers could set their own product volume and quality levels. But the downward pressure on prices as the PC market matured made this costly design strategy inappropriate. HP consolidated manufacturing into a few sites and put the entire production department under control of a single manager.

Under their previous organizational design, HP manufactured three different computers that were incompatible with one another, although they were marketed to the same target customer. The three business units acted as if they were competitors. In 1987, HP consolidated these divisions and mandated that all products should share technology and be cross-compatible.

The following four guidelines can be helpful in fitting design to strategy:[2]

1. Pinpoint the activities and tasks in the value chain that are pivotal to successful strategy execution, and make them the main building blocks in the organizational structure.

2. Whenever it doesn't make organizational sense to group all facets of a strategy-related activity under a single manager, establish ways to bridge departmental lines and achieve the necessary coordination.

3. Determine the degrees of authority needed to manage each organizational unit, endeavoring to strike an effective balance between capturing the advantages of both centralization and decentralization.

4. Determine whether noncritical activities can be outsourced more efficiently or effectively than they can be performed internally.

Without a specific strategic reference, designing the organization would be a difficult venture. Structure and everything that goes with it should be designed to facilitate the strategic pursuit of a firm. Understanding the dynamics of the relationship between design and strategy is key to achieving a firm's strategic intent.

---

[1] "IBM's Plan to Decentralize May Set a Trend—But Imitation Has a Price." Wall Street Journal, 19 Feb 1988, p. 17.

[2] A. A. Thompson and A. J. Strickland. *Crafting and Implementing Strategy.* Irwin, 1995, p. 239.

2.1.0 Basic Structure

"The ideal organizational structure is a place where ideas filter up as well as down, where the merit of the idea carries more weight than their source, and where participation and shared objectives are valued more than executive orders." — Edson Spencer

Description

Evaluates an organization's hierarchy and design in relation to the "Demand Criteria" indicated in the strategic plan. Evaluates whether or not the company is structurally poised to achieve its strategic intent. Basic structure also pertains to an organization's ability to adjust to an evolving environment.

Principal Elements

- Strategic "Demand Criteria"
- Formal Structure
- Structure Evolution

After formulating an organization's strategy, management must look toward designing the organizational structure so that the strategy can be implemented in an efficient manner. Strategy-related activities, along with the overall strategic intent behind them, need to be coordinated between often-myopic functional departments.

The goals of the Research and Development department, for example, focus on innovation and product design, whereas the production department is traditionally more concerned about efficiencies. Functionally isolated in their respective silos, these two departments would find very little synergy between themselves. If coordinated through effective communication and reporting systems along lines of authority, however, Research and Development efforts could produce products that were both innovative and cost-efficient, meeting both departmental goals. Effectively managing the flow of resources and capacities is management's top priority when designing the organization to achieve its strategic intent.

There is no one correct way to structure an organization. In business, organizational charts are as different as the companies they describe. They are a product of the company's established pattern for doing business and reflect past and current management's bias toward reporting relationships, personnel politics, and internal circumstances. In addition, since every strategy is conceived amidst its own set of key success factors and own value-chain activities, company structures that support them will be different as well.

Organizational structures take many forms. They may be organic, evolving without formal design or planning, or they may reflect a well-planned architecture. In either case, structures contain the mechanisms that facilitate the development and execution of the firm's strategic intent and the means in which the enterprise develops, supports, and coordinates the business of marketing its products or services. These mechanisms[1] include:

1. Hierarchical reporting relationships.
2. Policies, standard operating procedures, and control systems.
3. Information systems and flow of information moving through the organization.

Depending on the size of the organization, the structural map or organizational chart can illustrate the functional roles of individuals and departments. The structure in Figure 1 reflects a basic organization chart:

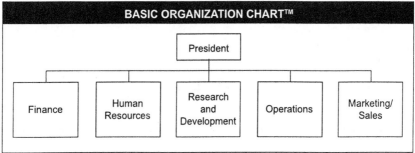

Figure 1

Regardless of the size of the enterprise, these basic components are represented in every company. In smaller companies, all of these functional responsibilities may reside with a single individual or a small number of individuals. As the organization evolves into a larger one, these functions would be assigned individually. As the organization grows even larger, additional functional roles such as Production,

Purchasing, etc., would be added. Those responsible for these key functions would in most cases constitute the executive team in the organization. The table (Figure 2) below highlights some of the basic strategy-related activities that fall within the traditional functional areas of a firm:

BASIC ORGANIZATION STRUCTURE — FUNCTIONAL COMPONENTS™					
Executive Team	Finance	Human Resources	Research & Development	Operations	Marketing/ Sales
Business Planning Capital Structure Resource Allocation Corporate Strategy	General Accounting Accounts Payable & Rreceivable Payroll	Business Planning Reward Systems Recruitment Training	Market Research Competitor Analysis Environ-mental Assessment Product & Process Design	Production Fulfillment Customer Service Purchasing Information Systems	Marketing Plan Collateral Develop-ment Direct Sales Customer Relations Channel Manage-ment

Figure 2

Appropriate structure design will prioritize these strategy-related activities and support them through the structure of the firm. The structure should be flexible enough to yield to new strategic influences, along with changes in the operating environment. If managers choose the right structure to coordinate strategy-related activities, this will enhance the efficiency of the firm, create added value, reduce costs, and contribute more to the firm's profitability. In today's competitive environment, more and more companies are restructuring to follow their strategy, improve efficiencies, and increase their bottom-line performance.

Footnote for Section 2.1.0 —

[1] L. J. Bourgeois, Irene M. Duhaime, and J. L. Stimpert. *Strategic Management: A Managerial Perspective.* Dryden, 1999, p. 260.

2.1.1 STRATEGIC "DEMAND CRITERIA"

"A management truism says structure follows strategy. However, this
truism is often ignored. Too many organizations attempt to carry out
a new strategy with an old structure." — DALE MCCONKEY

Definition

Assessing the organization structure prior to making a strategic commitment. Being willing to reorganize to advance a strategy. Not allowing political or departmental influence to shape design decisions.

Areas of Focus

- Structure is conducive strategy.
- Company willing to reorganize, if necessary.
- Structure is based on strategic need, not "in-house" politics.

Changes in a firm's overall strategy often call for modifications in the way the
firm is structured for two reasons. First, resource allocation most often is dictated
by the organization's structure. For example, if the organization is structured along
functional lines, resources will be deployed along those functional areas. Similarly,
if new strategic initiatives require more customer focus, then the firm will tend to
reorganize based on targeted customer groups, allocating resources in a more efficient manner. Unless the revised strategy utilizes resources in the identical way as
the old strategy, some structure adjustment will probably be required.

The other reason for structure to follow strategy is that the development of goals,
objectives, and initiatives normally follow organizational lines. That is, for firms
having a customer- or product-focused structure, most goals and objectives would
be established in product or customer terms. This method would not be efficient
for a firm whose intent was to respond to their markets more geographically.

Matching structure to strategy requires that strategy-critical activities and strategy-critical operational units be the cornerstones of the new organizational structure. Most company structures are difficult to assess, with their various nuances
and idiosyncrasies. But the key to good organizational structure is how well it supports the organization in achieving its strategic intent. The questions in Figure 1
can at least assist in assessing the strategic appropriateness of a firm's structure.

| CHECKLIST FOR DETERMINING APPROPRIATENESS |
| OF ORGANIZATIONAL STRUCTURE [1] |

1. *Is the structure compatible with the corporate profile and the corporate strategy?*
   A single business company can easily adopt a functional structure. As it grows, however, the functional nature of its structure may become limiting. A product or divisional structure would be more appropriate. A discussion of these types of formal structures appears in section 2.1.2.

2. *At the corporate level, is the structure compatible with the outputs of the firm's business units?*
   The outputs of a firm influence structure depending on how customers purchase them. Culturally dependent items such as shoes and clothing would respond to a geographic structure while more universal products such as screws, bolts, and tools could be more suited to a product structure.

3. *Are there too few or too many hierarchical levels at either the corporate or business unit level of analysis?*
   Flat organizations tend to favor dynamic, fast growing or changing environments and strategies, while more traditionally tall, multi-level organizations offer more stability and tighter spans of control. For larger corporations, not all divisions need have the same substructure. Managers should understand that business units need to respond to their own environments.

4. *Does the structure promote coordination among its parts?*
   Depending on how an organization supports its core competencies, a firm may need to coordinate most of its strategy-related activities across functions and divisions. If the company is a small or single business enterprise, then cross-functional coordination may simply involve good information systems. For synergistic conglomerates whose businesses are all related to their core business, a matrix or team-oriented structure may be appropriate.

5. *Does the structure allow for appropriate centralization or decentralization of authority?*
   The traditional evolution of a company is from a centralized organization to a decentralized one. Smaller companies tend to make decisions for the entire enterprise from one source, while large corporations with multidivisional or business unit structures tend to leave control at the local level. The relative stability of the environment also plays a role in this decision. Stable environments favor centralized structures, while dynamic ones usually require faster decisions facilitated by a decentralized structure.

6. *Does the structure permit the appropriate grouping of activities?*
   The nature of products may affect how a company groups activities. If the firm sells closely related products such as computer products, then it might serve the customer best by grouping the activities around sets of related products. Some would argue that groups should control the entire value chain related to a set of products, claiming it is difficult to hold a product manager responsible if he or she does not control production and design as well.

Figure 1

In addition to the traditional forms of structure, it is important to note that other options exist for flexible companies. Outsourcing may blur traditional organizational charts, as competencies normally assigned in-house are transferred to vendors to allow the firm to focus on core value-added activities. Dell Computers and Nike are good examples of firms who outsource key activities.

Finally, structures should be crafted to maximize the firm's potential to achieve its strategic intent. Too often, politics influence personnel assignments and departmental divisions, much to the detriment of the firm's performance. In the early 1990s, IBM had to overcome political and culture obstacles in order to regain some of its performance luster.

The large and successful firm recorded its first loss ever — $2.8 billion, in 1991. In the years following, IBM[2] continued to stick to its tried and tested structure, while the competitive landscape changed dramatically. Technological discoveries and innovation altered the marketplace, and suddenly IBM was faced with a slew of competitors that were more flexible, aggressive, and customer-oriented. While these young start-ups enjoyed the high margins common to first-to-market innovators, IBM was consistently shut out at the gate.

IBM's traditional culture and structure combined to slow the giant down. All major decisions were made at headquarters in New York, which had, as its number one policy, forbidden internal competition with its flagship mainframe business. As a result of this political and culturally inspired policy, IBM was four years late behind Apple with their personal computers, five years behind Toshiba in the laptop market, and eleven years behind Digital Equipment in breaking into the minicomputer market.

To turn the company around, top management restructured the company into semiautonomous profit centers. For the first time in its 70-year history, IBM reduced its workforce by 160,000 and its payroll by 40 percent, with most of the cuts coming in managerial and staff positions. Finally, IBM streamlined its research and development department, reducing the organization's time to market.

Footnotes for Section 2.1.1 —

[1] Peter Wright, Mark J. Kroll, and John Parnell. *Strategic Management, 4th Edition*. Prentice-Hall, 1998, p. 218.

[2] B. Ziegler. "IBM is Growing Again; 'Fires Are Out', Chief Says." Wall Street Journal Interactive, 1 May 1996 — L. Hayes. "Gerstner Is Struggling as He Tries to Change Ingrained IBM Culture." Wall Street Journal, 13 May 1994, p. A1, A8 — D. Moreau. "From Big Bust to Big Blue: IBM and Its Vigorous Rebirth." Kiplinger's Personal Finance Magazine, July 1995, p. 34-35.

2.1.2 FORMAL STRUCTURE

"Winning companies know how to do their work better."
— MICHAEL HAMMER AND JAMES CHAMPY

Definition

Ensuring that the current structure optimizes the company's value-chain approach (Research, Development, Design, Production, Marketing, Sales, Distribution, and Service). Creating a structure that provides for interaction across departmental lines. Designing sensible and effective reporting relationships and lines of authority.

Areas of Focus

- Structure optimizes execution of the "value-chain."
- Structure supports inter-department effectiveness.
- Current structure is optimal for current strategy.

There are five formal approaches to designing an organizational structure:

FIVE FORMAL ORGANIZATION STRUCTURES [1]	
Type	**Description**
Functional Structure	Small-size, single-product line Undifferentiated market Scale or expertise within the function Long product development and life cycles Common standards Hybrids in large organizations may follow structure by division or business unit
Geographical Structures	Low value-to-transport cost ratio Service delivery on-site Closeness to customer for delivery or support Perception of the organization as local Geographical market segments needed
Product or Line of Business Structure	Product focused Multiple products for separate customers Short product development and life cycle Minimum efficient scale for functions or outsourcing
Business Unit Structure	Important market segments Product or service unique to segment Buyer strength Customer knowledge advantage Rapid customer service and product cycles Minimum efficient scale in functions or outsourcing
Matrix Structure	Alternative to the functional structure Potential for new processes and radical change to processes Reduced working capital Need for reducing process cycle times

Figure 1

Companies can also be centralized or decentralized along the traditional lines shown.

As mentioned in Section 2.1.1, certain structures are more appropriate because of different characteristics of the industry or the firm's strategic intent. Most firms evolve from one structure to the next through natural growth. Depending on the new strategic intent or changes in the environment, these formal structures can be adopted whenever strategically necessary.

By understanding the potential relationship of these structures to the firm's strategic intent, management can select the format that will optimize their potential for strategic success. The table on pages 110 through 112 (Figure 2) illustrates the five structures and their advantages and disadvantages.

It is important to recognize that these structures are rarely implemented in their purest form. Organizational structures are the product of past and current management's bias toward reporting hierarchies, past strategic needs, politics, and other internal circumstances. In practice each company should adjust, expand, and combine structures to optimize its efficiency.

As the organization evolves, growth in the structure can come horizontally or vertically. Horizontal growth is a result of adding and promoting additional functional or divisional responsibilities to the executive level. Vertical growth comes from establishing additional levels in the organizational hierarchy. Organizations with a relatively large number of reporting levels are described as being relatively tall, and those with fewer levels as relatively flat. Flat organizations traditionally have wide spans of control, are decentralized, and have lower administrative costs. Tall organizations generally have better communication and coordination and are typically centrally directed.

ADVANTAGES AND DISADVANTAGES OF FIVE FORMAL ORGANIZATION STRUCTURES [2]

Functional Organization

STRATEGIC ADVANTAGES	STRATEGIC DISADVANTAGES
Centralized control of strategic results. Very well suited for structuring a single business. Structure is linked tightly to strategy by designating key activities as functional departments. Promotes in-depth functional expertise. Well suited to developing functional skills and functional based competencies. Conducive to exploiting learning/experience curve effects associated with functional specialization. Enhances operating efficiency where tasks are routine and repetitive.	Excessive fragmentation of strategy-critical processes. Can lead to inter-functional rivalry and conflict, rather than team-play and cooperation – GM must referee. Multi-layered management bureaucracies and centralized decision-making slow response time. Hinders development of managers with cross-functional experience because the ladder of advancement is up the ranks within the same functional area. Forces profit responsibility to the top. Functional specialists often attach more importance to what's best for the functional area than to what's best for the whole business – can lead to functional empire-building. Functional myopia often inhibits creative entrepreneurship, adapting to change, and attempts to create cross-functional core –functional core competencies.

Geographic Organization

STRATEGIC ADVANTAGES	STRATEGIC DISADVANTAGES
Allows tailoring of strategy to needs of each geographical market. Delegates profit/loss responsibility to lowest strategic level. Improves functional coordination within target market. Takes advantage of economies of local operations. Area units make an excellent training ground for higher-level general managers.	Poses a problem of how much geographic uniformity headquarters should impose versus how much geographic diversity should be allowed. Greater difficulty in maintaining consistent company image/reputation from area to area when area managers exercise much strategic freedom. Adds another layer of management to run geographic units. Can result in duplication of staff services at headquarters and district levels, creating cost disadvantages.

Figure 2

Decentralized Line of Business (Product or Service)

STRATEGIC ADVANTAGES	STRATEGIC DISADVANTAGES
Offers a logical and workable means of decentralizing responsibility and delegating authority in diversified organizations. Puts responsibility for business strategy in closer proximity to each business' unique environment. Allows each business unit to organize around its own value chain system, key activities, and functional requirements. Frees CEO to handle corporate strategy issues. Puts clear profit/loss accountability on shoulders of business-unit managers.	May lead to costly duplication of staff functions at corporate and business-unit levels, thus raising administrative overhead costs. Poses a problem of what decisions to centralize and what decisions to decentralize (business managers need enough authority to get the job done, but not so much that corporate management loses control of key business-level decisions). May lead to excessive division rivalry for corporate resources and attention. Business/division autonomy works against achieving coordination of related activities in different business units, thus blocking to some extent the capture of strategic-fit benefits. Corporate management becomes heavily dependent on business unit managers. Corporate managers can lose touch with business-unit situations, end up surprised when problems arise, and not know much about how to fix such problems.

Strategic Business Units

STRATEGIC ADVANTAGES	STRATEGIC DISADVANTAGES
Provides a strategically relevant way to organize the business-unit portfolio of a broadly diversified company. Facilitates the coordination of related activities within a SBU, thus helping to capture the benefits of strategic fits in the SBU. Promotes more cohesiveness among the new initiatives of separate but related businesses. Allows strategic planning to be done at the most relevant level within the total enterprise. Makes the task of strategic review by top executives more objective and more effective. Helps allocate corporate resources to areas with greatest growth opportunities.	It is easy for the definition and grouping of businesses into SBUs to be so arbitrary that the SBU serves no other purpose than administrative convenience. If the criteria for defining SBUs are rationalizations and have little to do with the nitty-gritty of strategy coordination, then the groupings lose real strategic significance. The SBUs can still be myopic in charting their future direction. Adds another layer to top management. The roles and authority of the CEO, the group vice-president, and the business-unit manager have to be carefully worked out or the group vice president gets trapped in the middle with ill-defined authority. Unless the SBU head is strong willed, very little strategy coordination is likely to occur across business units in the SBU. Performance recognition gets blurred; credit for successful business units tends to go to corporate CEO, then to business-unit head, last to group vice president.

Matrix Structures	
STRATEGIC ADVANTAGES	**STRATEGIC DISADVANTAGES**
Gives formal attention to each dimension of strategic priority. Creates checks and balances among competing viewpoints. Facilitates capture of functionally based strategic fits in diversified companies. Promotes making trade-off decisions on the basis of "what's best for the organization as a whole." Encourages cooperation, consensus-building, conflict resolution, and coordination of related activities.	Very complex to manage. Hard to maintain "balance" between the two lines of authority. So much shared authority can result in transactions logjam and disproportionate amounts of time being spent on communications. It is hard to move quickly and decisively without getting clearance from many other people. Promotes an organizational bureaucracy and hamstrings creative entrepreneurship.

Footnotes for Section 2.1.2 —

[1] Jay R. Galbraith. *Designing Organizations*. Jossey-Bass, 1995, p. 37–39.

[2] A. A. Thompson and A. J. Strickland. *Strategic Management, 6th Edition*. Irwin McGraw-Hill, 1995, p. 251-261.

2.1.3 STRUCTURE EVOLUTION

"At about $50 million, I felt I could run it...I could name everybody in the company. But as it grew larger, I found myself stretched. One Friday night at 11 p.m., I realized that if there wasn't a change, I'd have to stop sleeping within six months to keep up the pace."

— T. J. RODGERS

Definition

Keeping the organization structure flexible so that it can better react when emerging opportunities or dynamic events within the industry call for change.

Areas of Focus

- Structure adapts quickly to change.
- Capitalizes on key competitive advantages.
- Structure does not inhibit innovation.

Although changes in strategy may affect the strategy of an organization, outside forces can also influence the firm's overall design. No firm could change its structure in response to every one of these internal and external forces. But organizational structures do not remain static. As strategy shifts render the organization's existing structure ineffective, change becomes imperative for successful strategy implementation. Symptoms of an ineffective structure may include too many levels of management, too many meetings, too much time resolving conflicts between departments, too many people assigned to one manager, and of course, too many unrealized goals and initiatives.

Similarly, a firm's choice of structure and its responsiveness to change can and does influence strategic choices. If a strategic option were under consideration, but it required massive structural reorganization, then this would not be an attractive choice.

While it is vital to migrate to a structure that will assist with executing the new strategic paradigm for a firm, finding a structure that is flexible enough to grow and evolve with the organization is just as important.

As firms develop from small one-man shops into more complex larger organizations — with integration strategies, geographic issues, and diversification initiatives - their structures tend to evolve from one person with multiple responsibilities, to functional departments, to product or divisional specialization, to decentralized business units. Knowing when to make such changes is an organization's biggest structural challenge.

W. L. Gore and Associates, the maker of Gore-Tex fabric and other laminated materials,[1] is an organization that has remained flexible and grown. The company has no formal structure, choosing instead to enjoy a flexible lattice structure with associates, not employees, who are empowered to make critical decisions. The company has direct lines of communication, no fixed or assigned authority, sponsors rather than bosses, team leadership, and tasks and functions organized through commitments.

Its structure has evolved to include several business units that have grown organically as the market opportunities arose. The lattice structure has been put to the test several times, including a crisis when the first generation of Gore-Tex failed to keep a mountain climber warm. The company remedied the technical problems in less than a month and recalled all the existing merchandise in their distribution channels.

Other structure policies include having not more than 200 associates at any plant. These policies evolved when Bill Gore realized one day, while walking around a plant, that he did not know everyone's name. Emphasizing close-knit, flat structures that employ good communication and responsiveness is a hallmark of Gore's formal structure.

Key to Gore's success is a culture that promotes willingness to change. Today's dynamic marketplace requires an understanding of the strategic need for change, and all systems must be in place for the organization to take advantage of that changing environment.[2]

Alfred Chandler[3] describes the evolutionary process of structure as a cyclical mechanism triggered by administrative problems arising from implementation of a new strategy. As structural responses are given to ease the implementation, a new formal structure evolves.

A summary diagram (Figure 1) illustrating the evolution follows.

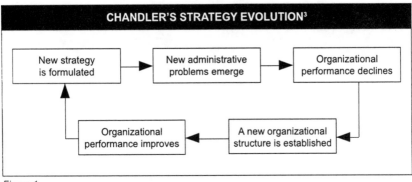

Figure 1

Footnotes for Section 2.1.3 —

1 Charles C. Manz and Henry P. Sims, Jr. *Business Without Bosses*. Wiley & Sons, 1993, p. 131-151.

2 For a more detailed discussion about adaptability to change, please see section 3.4.4.

3 Adapted from Alfred Chandler. *Strategy and Structure*. MIT Press, 1962.

2.2.0 CORE COMPETENCE

"When the external environment is in a state of flux, the firm's own resources and capabilities may be a much more stable basis on which to define its identity. Hence, a definition of a business in terms of what it is capable of doing may offer a more durable basis for strategy than a definition based upon the needs which the business seeks to satisfy." — ROBERT GRANT

Description

Core competencies are the skills, knowledge, and special abilities a company possesses that set it apart from other organizations. By effectively bundling these skills, knowledge, and special abilities, a company can create their competitive advantage, enhance customer value, and expand their market position.

Principal Elements

- Identification of Core Competence
- Application of Core Competence
- Leveraging Core Competence

One of management's most important tasks when executing strategy is to cultivate the necessary skill sets, aptitudes, and capacities that will give the organization a continued competitive advantage. Understanding the vital role that core competencies play in a firm's overall strategy is key to achieving its strategic intent.

Put simply, core competence, sometimes referred to as distinctive competence, is what a firm possesses in terms of skill sets and capabilities — qualities that enable the firm to meet the demands of its market better than its competitors.[1] It is important to distinguish between a firm's assets, environmental circumstances and core competence.

While competitive advantage can certainly arise out of these factors, (e.g., close proximity to resources, brand awareness, product quality), none could be called core competence. Certainly core competence contributes to a firm's competitive advantage, but not all competitive advantages are core competencies.

Core competencies are not to be confused with key success factors, those external and internal aspects that affect a firm's performance in the marketplace. While all core competencies should be critical to a firm's success, not all key success factors are core competencies.

Also called competencies are those basic elements, such as courteous drivers for a delivery company, that a firm may need to possess in order to do business in a particular industry. But not all of those competencies will be critical or core for a firm's success.

A firm's core competence, for example, may be its ability to process and distribute customer profiling information faster than its competitors, giving it an edge in meeting the customer's high expectations of service. Not only is this competency linked to the abilities of the IT personnel, but the skills of those in customer service, sales, marketing, product design, and manufacturing as well. It is assumed that in this particular example, quality customer service is a critical success factor of the industry.

The root of a firm's core competence rests in its people skills. These skills normally transcend traditional functional silos such as marketing, production, operations, and engineering, and involve knowledge-based activities such as product design, innovation, and customer service. These activities tend to be a big part of the value proposition in both service and manufacturing businesses.

The table on page 119 (Figure 1) shows a list of capabilities arranged by function.

Many organizations identify core competencies by reviewing specific departments or divisions for any unique or special capabilities that support that group's function. Though this method may prove to be effective, there is potential for overstated department focus, which can lead to losing sight of the organization's strategic intent. Another method of reviewing an organization's capacities and activities is through "Value Chain Analysis" (Figure 2), the sequential chain of activities that includes identifying, fulfilling, and satisfying customer needs.

The value chain normally includes the following components:
1. Defining the customer's need.
2. Conceptualizing a product or service to satisfy the need.
3. Developing the product or service.

CAPABILITIES ARRANGED BY FUNCTION [2]

Functional Area	Capability	Examples
Corporate Management	• Effective financial control systems • Expertise in strategic control of diversified corporation • Effectiveness in motivating and coordinating divisional and business unit management • Management of acquisitions • Values-driven, in-touch corporate leadership	• Hanson, Exxon • General Electric, ABB • Shell • ConAgra • Wal-Mart, Federal Express
Management Information	• Comprehensive and effective MIS network, with strong central coordination	• American Airlines, L.L. Bean
Research & Development	• Capability in basic research • Ability to develop innovative new products	• Merck, AT&T • Sony, 3M
Manufacturing	• Efficiency in volume manufacturing • Capacity for continual improvements in production processes • Flexibility and speed of response	• Briggs & Stratton • Toyota, Nucor • Benetton, Worthington Industries
Product Design	• Design capability	• Apple
Marketing	• Brand management and brand promotion • Promoting and exploiting reputation for quality • Responsiveness to market trends	• Proctor & Gamble, PepsiCo • American Express, Mercedes Benz • The Gap, Campbell Soup
Sales and Distribution	• Effectiveness in promoting and executing sales • Efficiency and speed of distribution • Quality and effectiveness of customer service	• Microsoft, Glaxo • Federal Express, The Limited • Walt Disney, Marks & Spencer

Figure 1

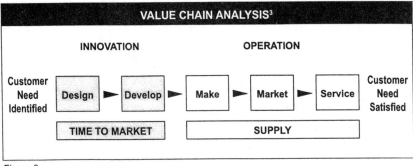

Figure 2

4. Manufacturing or producing the product or service.
5. Selling and distributing the product or service.
6. Servicing the product or service.

Since resources are limited, management should focus on those activities, capacities, and aptitudes that significantly contribute to the firm's overall strategic intent and long-term competitive success. Core competencies ought to be developed to not only sustain the current competitive advantage, but open up new opportunities for future markets.

The following matrix (Figure 3) describes the relationship between new and existing competencies and new and existing products and markets.

RELATIONSHIP BETWEEN NEW AND EXISTING COMPETENCIES[4]		
Competencies	**Current Markets**	**Future Markets**
New	What new core competencies will the firm need to build to protect and extend the firm's franchise in current markets?	What new core competencies would the firm need to build to participate in the most exciting markets of the future?
Existing	What is the opportunity to improve the firm's position in existing markets by better leveraging existing core competence?	What new products or services could the firm create by creatively redeploying or recombining the firm's current core competencies?

Figure 3

By careful identification of current and potential competencies, applying them to existing opportunities, and leveraging them for the future, an organization can enjoy sustained competitive advantages in their markets.

Footnotes for Section 2.2.0 —

[1] Gary Hamel and C. K. Prahalad. *Competing for the Future*. Harvard Business School Press, 1994, p. 199.

[2] Robert M. Grant. *Contemporary Strategy Analysis*. Blackwell, 1995, p. 76.

[3] Robert S. Kaplan and David P. Norton. *The Balanced Scorecard*. Harvard Business School Press, 1996, p. 27.

[4] Gary Hamel and C. K. Prahalad. *Competing for the Future*. Harvard Business School Press, 1994, p. 227.

2.2.1 Identification of Core Competence

"Organizations are vulnerable when they are at the peak of their success." — R. T. Lenz

Definition

Identifying a specific and unique combination of company skills and capabilities that are valued by customers and difficult to replicate by the competition. Clearly articulating these core competencies to all appropriate constituencies.

Areas of Focus

- Complete understanding of a company's distinctive skills and capabilities.
- Clearly articulating corporate core competencies.
- Viewing core competence as the foundation for strategic intent.

Recognizing the opportunities that the right set of core competencies present for an organization is part of a leader's focused purpose and future perspective for the company. One could argue that Michael Dell, of Dell Computers, identified an opportunity in the PC manufacturing industry that clearly set his company apart from competition. Dell and his team examined the traditional production and distribution process and changed their focus to marketing their products through a direct consumer delivery channel.

Not only did Dell revolutionize PC distribution, he put his organization at least one step closer to the customer. This innovative thinking resulted in more direct customer feedback and a better understanding of what their customers wanted to see in the next generation of products. This capacity to break outside the normal parameters of business and implement an innovative distribution strategy was Dell's core competency. This has been the primary driver of Dell's rapid growth and has given the company a position of industry leadership.

Hamel and Prahalad introduced an effective model, shown on page 121 (Figure 1), to identify whether a capacity is a core competence.

By utilizing this approach, a company is more likely to identify critical abilities

DEFINING CORE COMPETENCIES [1]		
Consideration	Proposition	Test
Customer Value	A core competence must make a disproportionate contribution to customer perceived value.	Readily identify a unique benefit that the firm's customers derive from its product or service that is the by-product of a specific skill, collection of skills, or capability. (The capability itself need not be identifiable by the customer – but in the benefit derived by the capability.)
Competitor Differentiation	A core competence must clearly differentiate itself among competitors.	Through benchmarking or other means, readily identify unique capability in developing, producing, or servicing the firm's product(s) from those methods deployed by its competitors.
Extendibility	While a particular competence may be core in the eyes of a single business, in that it meets the test of customer value and competitive uniqueness, it may not be a core competence from the point of view of the corporation if there is no way of imagining an array of new products or services issuing from the competence.	Readily identify any specific capability that is not only unique today both in terms of customer value and competitive differentiation, but can also form the basis for entry into new or future product markets.

Figure 1

as they relate to their long-term strategic intent. It is important to understand the relationship between identifying core competencies among the firm's human and organizational resources and not on its products or services per se.

With rare exceptions, products cannot be the source of competitive advantage. It is too easy for some intelligent producer elsewhere to clone, substitute, or improve them.[2] Therefore, it becomes necessary for an organization to align its core competencies with internal and external resources in order to advance its sustainable competitive advantage. To arrive at a sound diagnosis of a company's competitive capabilities, some managers use a value chain approach, using four steps:

1. Construct a value chain of company activities.

2. Identify the activities and competencies critical to customer satisfaction and market success.

3. Examine the linkages among internally performed activities and the linkages with supplier and customer chains.

4. Establish internal and external benchmarks to determine how well the company compares with competitors in performing activities and structuring its costs. Use this information to determine which activities represent core competencies and which ones are better outsourced.

Whatever approach is taken to identify current core competencies and opportunities for future competencies, it is vitally important that managers share a common view of the firm's current core competencies. Whereas most managers will have some sense of what the organization does best, they may have difficulty specifically linking between the competitiveness of the firm or the firm's products and the skill sets of its people.

Identifying core competencies creates a shared definition of the firm's competitive capabilities, a link between competence and customer-perceived value, and an established benchmark of current and future desired competence.

There are inherent dangers in ignoring or minimizing the importance of thinking about the firm's viability in terms of core competence. Too often, opportunities will be missed when firms focus on the here and now of current products and markets. For Richard and Maurice McDonald, it took a milkshake salesman, by the name of Ray Kroc, to recognize their expertise in their approach to fast food and its potential for replication and franchising.[3]

EMI's experience with the loss of its leadership in the CAT scan industry is a great example of a firm not identifying the core competencies required to sustain its competitive advantage. As a result of one of their scientists, who was given the Nobel Prize for his achievement, EMI enjoyed sole ownership of the CAT scan market due to their proprietary position. But failing to recognize the marketing knowledge needed to remain at the top of this industry and build for that competency, EMI was no longer in the CAT scanner business not eight years after their product's introduction. General Electric had become the market leader.[4]

Every organization has activities in which they excel or have the potential to excel. McDonald's, FedEx, Proctor & Gamble, and General Electric are excellent examples of firms who have recognized what they do best and have built their strategies around it. Recognizing what it takes to be successful in the marketplace is the first step in maintaining a competitive position.

Footnotes for Section 2.2.1 —

[1] Gary Hamel and C. K. Prahalad. *Competing for the Future.* HBS Press, 1994, p. 202-207.

[2] James Brian Quinn. *Intelligent Enterprise.* Free Press, 1992, p. 54.

[3] Robert M. Grant. *Contemporary Strategy Analysis,* 2nd Edition. Blackwell Business, 1995, p. 132.

[4] Cynthia A. Montgomery and Michael Porter. *Strategy: Seeking and Securing Competitive Advantage.* HBS Press, 1991, p. 71.

2.2.2 APPLICATION OF CORE COMPETENCE

"One defends when his strength is inadequate; he attacks when it is abundant."
— SUN TZU

Definition
Examining and evaluating core competencies in relation to creating customer value, expanding competitive advantage, or identifying new business or product opportunities.

Areas of Focus
- Applying core competence creates/sustains customer value.
- Applying core competence to support competitive differentiation.
- Applying core competence to support product or service offerings.

Maintaining a core competence perspective inside the organization is difficult. Most organizations are strategically structured to give emphasis to market activities and products. These strategic business units have, at their root, products and services targeted along customer and functional lines.

Having a core competence focus usually involves a cross-functional dialogue and the tendency to view the organization as not only a portfolio of products and services but as a portfolio of competencies as well.

Having this competency perspective makes it easier to integrate core competency building into the strategic planning process. Resting on past achievements or inherited positions cannot lead to long market leadership.

Porsche discovered this when their reputation for world-class engineering quality, normally commanding a premium price, was tarnished by their failure to sustain the advantage. It was not that their skill sets eroded; it was the fact that their nearest competitors' skill sets reached a level of parity or perhaps exceeded them in certain areas of performance. Porsche, blinded by its brand strength and the buying trends of that time, continued to ignore their relative competence and continued to raise their prices.

The savvy consumer soon discovered that paying a premium for Porsche engineering reputation did not always guarantee a superior performance. In fact, in some instances, the competitors were delivering a better performance car, for substantially less cost. The result was that Porsche's sales fell from a high of 30,741 vehicles in 1986 to only 3,738 in 1993.[1]

Building a core competency requires consistency and the adequate dedication of resources — and even then, it may still take years to achieve. Management must be stable — and even more critically — must be in agreement on what competencies to build and sustain.

Prahaled and Hamel outline several mistakes an organization may make in the process of building or not building the essential core competencies for success.[2]

1. Too firmly entrenched in current market/product silos to seize new opportunities.

2. Resources imprisoned within departmental channels; difficult to redeploy to take advantage of an emerging opportunity.

3. Fragmented and increasingly smaller business unit boundaries make cross-functional applications difficult.

4. A growing dependence on outsourced competencies.

5. A myopic focus on current end products, making future perspective dim and current competencies in danger of obsolescence.

6. Failure to understand the relationship between core competence and market success, providing an opening for new entrants with competencies developed elsewhere to compete.

Most often an organization's competencies will evolve in response to foreseen customer requirements, competitor encroachment, or the organization's effort to reinforce those skills identified as contributing to the firm's historical success.

Successful companies infuse the organization with these competencies taking a systemic approach rather than relying on specific personnel. It is important for growing companies to establish the necessary organizational systems that contain the capacity to improve the firm's durability.

This organizational capability is best sustained when it comprises skills and activities from different locations on the value chain. Because core competencies typically emerge from these combined efforts of work groups and departments, department supervisors can't be expected to shoulder the responsibility of building the overall competency on their own.

The multi-task, multi-skill nature of core competency development requires management expertise in both people skills and knowledge management, and the logistics of networking disciplines.[3] This expertise should be coupled with the necessary authority to encourage cross-discipline cooperation, as well as the senior perspective of the overall strategic intent of the organization, including the reason for the competency development.

Maintaining core competencies is a function of culture, values, structure, and organizational resource commitment. Having the necessary structure and culture to support a flexible capacity driven organization is as much a function of empowerment, motivation, values durability, and good quality information as it is a function of budget.

Finally, while it is not necessary to control all points of capacity along the value chain, it is good practice to focus on the components that add the most value and benefit to the firm's customers. Although Nike outsources all its shoe manufacturing, it keeps tight control of its core competencies in logistics, design, endorsements, distribution, and merchandising.

Footnotes for Section 2.2.2 —

[1] Gary Hamel and C. K. Prahalad. *Competing for the Future*. Harvard Business School Press, 1994, p. 208-209.

[2] Gary Hamel and C. K. Prahalad. *Competing for the Future*. Harvard Business School Press, 1994, p. 221.

[3] A. A. Thompson and A. J. Strickland. *Crafting and Implementing Strategy*. Irwin, 1995, p. 239.

2.2.3 LEVERAGING CORE COMPETENCE

"If a man takes no thought about what is distant, he will find sorrow near at hand. He who will not worry about what is far off will soon find something worse than worry." — CONFUCIUS

Definition

Implementing programs and processes to develop, strengthen, and expand core competencies.

Areas of Focus

- Expanding customer value proposition.
- Increasing competitive differentiation.
- Expanding product or service offerings.

Organizations cannot be complacent once they have identified and built their core competencies. Indeed, the visionary challenge for management in today's dynamic environment is to broaden the scope of those capacities that have led to the organization's historical success and find new applications for competition.

Once Amazon.com developed the competency to efficiently deliver books through the internet, they immediately initiated steps to expand and leverage this capacity to distribute other consumer products, such as music CDs.

Amazon.com didn't stop with music CDs; in 1999, they leveraged the same strengths to enter the on-line auction market pioneered by such firms as Ebay, and they are on course toward commanding a large share of this market as well.

Clearly, Amazon.com faces the challenge of long-term durability and achieving a level of respectable profitability. However, there is no disputing they have been relentless in their strategic pursuit to establish their core competence and leveraging that competence at every opportunity.

Other companies such as Cray, Honda, and Lotus have successfully developed and magnified their competencies by leveraging the expertise of their people by frequently reforming highly focused work teams, whose sole purpose is to bring additional value to their customers.[1]

In leveraging knowledge and skill rather than financial or market dominance, firms need a supportive culture, empowerment, values, motivation, efficient structure, short deadlines, great training programs, and efficient organizational systems.

The following is a summary of common characteristics of successfully leveraging and evolving companies:

- **Risk Orientation** – always seeking expandable opportunities; remaining flexible enough to respond to an unknown future.

- **Marketing** – Targeted messages strengthening brand image and awareness to all stakeholders and to potential markets.

- **Distribution** – Clearly defined, efficient distribution channel strategies.

- **Culture** – Motivated, talented, informed personnel with a high sense of ownership and empowerment.

- **Technology** – Investing in and aligning the appropriate technologies to leverage the quality of product, distribution, and service.

One final example of outstanding leverage of core competencies is W. L. Gore and Associates.[2] The company, founded by Bill Gore in 1958, was built upon Bill's technical expertise in working with polytetrafluoroethylene, or PTFE, which is commonly known as Teflon by consumers. Bill had gained experience with PTFE while working with DuPont.

Gore's first success came in the electronics industry, where he applied his unique method of innovation to the manufacture of PTFE-coated ribbon cable. Gore continued to build and acquire competencies needed to transfer his technology into a thriving business, thus establishing a unique culture and organizational structure, and pursuing a niche-differentiated strategy.

W. L. Gore leveraged their expertise in hiring innovative, entrepreneurial, skilled personnel. This fostered an innovative environment and supported a network of over 6,500 entrepreneurs into a flexible, responsive firm. Gore offers a fairly extensive line of high-tech products that are used in a variety of applications, including electronics, medicine, industrial filtration and seals, and fabric.

By leveraging their people skills innovation, the company has expanded their core businesses to include applications ranging from aerospace to bike cabling to arterial grafts to outdoor equipment. By 1998, the company is listed very high on *Forbes* magazine's list of the largest privately held companies, with estimated revenues exceeding $1.1 billion.

Footnotes for Section 2.2.3 —

[1] James Brian Quinn. *Intelligent Enterprise*. Free Press, 1992, p. 73.

[2] Charles C. Manz and Henry P. Sims, Jr. *Business Without Bosses*. Wiley & Sons, 1993, p. 131-151.

2.3.0 Information, Systems, and Technology

> *"To get the full benefit of technology, business leaders will streamline and modernize their processes and their organization. The goal is to make business reflex nearly instantaneous and to make strategic thought an ongoing, iterative process — not something done every 12 to 18 months, separate from the daily flow of business."*
> — Bill Gates

Description

Competitive environments require rapid and targeted information, aligned systems, and innovative and appropriate use of technology. Takes into account the quality of an organization's information, systems, and technology, and the effective alignment of these technologies with its strategic intent.

Principal Elements

- Organization Communication
- Targeted Information
- Enterprising Systems
- Applied Technology

Information is the glue that binds business operations and provides the basis for all managerial decisions. Although a traditional aim of organizational design has been to organize tasks in order to achieve the firm's strategic intent, information and information systems play an increasing role in strategic implementation. Indeed, the way an organization acquires, stores, disseminates, and applies information can be a competitive advantage.

Behind this growing dependence on information is the advent and evolution of computer technology. Because of increasing computer power and connectivity, the cost of data retrieval has fallen significantly over recent times. This data output is available quickly in a variety of formats, documents, and combinations.

To become useful to management, data must be transformed into information through filtering, screening, comparing, and other methods of analysis and interpretation. When that information is timely, accurate, and shared through an effectively managed system, it can evolve into corporate knowledge.

Knowledge management, like other popular business trends before it, has been described in as many ways as would suit those defining it. The large consulting firm, KPMG, in their "1998 Knowledge Management" report, defined knowledge management as a systematic and organized attempt to use knowledge within an organization to transform its ability to store and use knowledge to improve performance. Knowledge is defined as the information about an organization's customers, products, processes, competitors, and so on, which can be locked away in people's minds or filed on paper or in electronic form.

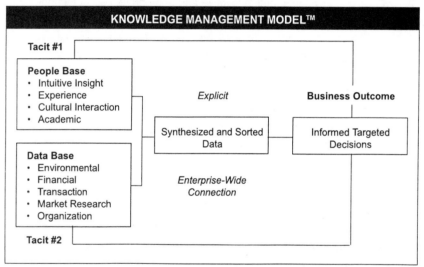

Figure 1

The model above (Figure 1) illustrates the flow of normally intangible people-based knowledge, including insights, experiences, interactions, and judgments, as well as the traditional database information about the organization, its environment, competitors, and processes.

The goals of any knowledge management system should include management commitment to sharing information, integration of the information in a meaningful way, and delivery of the right information on time to the people who need it to make effective business decisions.

The commitment to sharing information begins with an organization's recognition that collaboration between functional departments is more effective than individually hoarding data. The strategic outcome of good organizational communication is an aligned strategic train of thought synthesized from the executive team's integrated thoughts and opinions.

The information becomes useful knowledge when it is linked to the vital concerns of the organization. Systems must recognize the individual needs for knowledge within the organization and allow recombining of data in a timely fashion to support functional decision-making.

In order to retrieve the data as well as disseminate it efficiently, every vital component of the organization must participate in the system. Highly sophisticated systems link processes along the entire value chain, increasing an organization's responsiveness.

Several years ago, Frito-Lay gave each of its 10,000 route sales personnel a hand-held computer and in the process transformed them from "laborers" to "knowledge facilitators."[1] Instead of simply ordering and tracking merchandise, these employees now play a vital role in Frito-Lay's market research program. Information on sales is entered into the portables and sent to executives at Frito-Lay's Dallas headquarters. In addition to having accurate, up-to-date market share and sales information, executive response to the data was much faster.

When numbers were down in a region, careful tracking of the sales data revealed that, in one area of Texas, a local chain of stores had launched their own brand of chips. Frito-Lay was able to respond quickly with a counter-strategy, and sales returned to previous levels. To address a problem of this magnitude, what normally took several months to address was resolved in a matter of days.

Contrast this with the majority of companies with similar resources and opportunities, such as water bottle companies, delivery companies, etc., who surprisingly overlook the cost savings and potential competitive benefits of a knowledge system. It seems that how a company uses the data and information it receives is equally or more important than just obtaining it.

[1] R. H. Beeby. "How to Crunch a Bunch of Figures." The Wall Street Journal, 11 Jun 1990, p. A14.

"Without credible communication, and lots of it, the hearts and minds of others are never captured." — John P. Kotter

Definition

Implementing a system to ensure that all primary stakeholders consistently receive the necessary information to keep them well informed regarding company performance and critical activities.

Areas of Focus

- Implementing a communication system that touches all stakeholders.
- Communicating the strategic plan throughout the company.
- Providing all stakeholders with all critical business information.
- Communicating progress against key objectives.

Like personal communication, organizational communication involves the transfer of information from one source to another through the use of symbols. Successful communication is dependent on the two connecting parties' harmonious use of filters, symbols, and encoding.

Since all management functions involve communication,[1] an organization's successful strategic implementation requires understanding and commitment to be properly communicated. In fact, communication may be management's most important activity.[2]

The average manager spends 50 to 70 percent of his or her time communicating in some way.[3] Yet few managers engage in improving their own personal communication skills or the organizational inefficiencies that tend to increase as the size and complexity of the firm increases.

Analog Devices CEO Ray Strata talked about the importance of communication within the organization:[4]

> There are many impediments to organizational learning, but the most basic is communication…Only in recent years have I begun to fully understand how profoundly the words that come out of my mouth and my pen affect organizational performance both for better or for

worse. When you think about it, the only thing that a manager does that is visible to the organization is listen and speak...We can change each other by what we say and how we listen.

Formal communication within the organization can move downward, upward, and cross-functionally. A recent study by the Hay Group[5] of 250 firms showed that 54 to 67 percent of employees see top-down communication as positive, but only 30 to 42 percent see bottom-up listening programs as positive. This would imply that these companies are better at telling employees information than in listening to them. Another study[6] indicated that fewer than half of employees felt that their companies were good at letting them know what was going on.

Barriers to communication can arise when managers and other keepers of knowledge fail to share their information.[7] Such bottlenecks in information flow can hamper the organization's ability to respond quickly to outside events. This artificial scarcity of information makes knowledge very expensive in both retrieving the data that is housed internally, as well as in missing opportunities for it to benefit the organization.

Knowledge scarcity becomes expanded when those hoarding critical knowledge leave the company, taking the hard-fought data with them. The cost of replacing this knowledge becomes impossibly high as either the employee would have to be enticed to return, the data learned again within time constraints, or the information or expertise purchased from outside sources.

An unwillingness to share information (both receiving new information from others as well as guarding departmental knowledge) can stifle the information flow into and out of the company and its functional departments. Additional barriers to free-flowing information are the nature of some departments not to accept new information that is from sources of lower status in the organization, or to too willingly accept information from a higher status source within the organization.

Finally, communication can break down simply due to lack of physical infrastructure to facilitate the exchange of the desired information. Without investment in the correct technology, information simply has no place to go and can quickly become obsolete as the opportunities, and crises that demanded the information, run their course. All barriers to exchange of critical information rob the organization of its ability to respond in a timely manner.

One way to break down barriers to communication is for management to commit to sharing information vital to achieving the organization's strategic intent. This commitment must begin at the top, with the executive team leading by example. Information dissemination is vital to establishing a culture of mutual trust, openness, and active listening that will help erode barriers.

Structural approaches, such as employee action programs, grievance procedures, attitude and climate surveys, and open-door policies, along with informational approaches such as employee update meetings, bulletin boards, handbooks, policies, etc., can improve communication lines.

As information becomes more accessible, management's ability to interpret that information and use it well must also improve. Along with a potential for information distortion and data overload, management must also deal with political influences on the information it receives. Although it is impossible to resolve all inhibitors of communication, as structures and organizations develop, technology and other methods can help eliminate some of the distortions and filters so commonly associated with communication.

Footnotes for Section 2.3.1 —

[1] Fred Luthans and Janet K. Larsen. "How Managers Really Communicate." Human Relations 39, 1986, p. 161-178.

[2] Daniel R. Boyd, Stephen D. Lewis, and Grady L. Butler. "Getting Your Message Across." Management Review, Jul-Aug 1988, p. 7-10.

[3] William V. Harvey. *Communication and Interpersonal Relations*. Irwin, 1979, p. 3.

[4] Ray Strata. "Organizational Learning in Practice." McKinsey Quarterly, Winter 1992, p. 79-82.

[5] "Labor Letter, Dialogues with Workers Gained Increased Employer Attention." Wall Street Journal, 3 Jan 1989, p. A1.

[6] Walter Kiechell III. "No Word from Up High." Fortune, 6 Jan 1986, p. 125-126.

[7] Thomas H. Davenport and Laurence Prusak. *Working Knowledge*. Harvard Business School, 1998, p. 43.

2.3.2 Targeted Information

> *"To achieve nirvana, you must have perfect information about every customer order (new and old)and every asset in your business (both permanent physical assets and various inventory components). And guess what? The only way to secure, maintain, and harvest this information is through the aggressive use of technology."*
> — J. William Gurley

Definition

Using company information systems to provide managers with timely industry or competitor updates that may influence their business decisions. Providing management with current performance data, such as business unit performance, sales activity, and customer service information.

Areas of Focus

- Providing managers with the information they need to make informed decisions.
- Using a company information system to regularly disseminate important data.
- Ensuring that industry and environmental data is always current.
- Providing management with timely updates regarding performance in their area of responsibility.

Once an organization is committed to sharing information, the key to knowledge management is identifying the information that is vital to achieving its strategic intent. What is critical to an organization will vary according to key success factors, the nature of the industry, and the type of strategic choices made.

The table on page 139 (Figure 1) illustrates some of the different information needs by different levels in an organization.

Unlike data, information has meaning when applied to an organization's unique strategic situation. Organizations can transform data into useful information by adding value in different ways. The following list shows several methods:[2]

- **Contextualized** — The firm knows for what purpose the data was gathered.
- **Categorized** — The firm knows the units of analysis or key components of the data.

INFORMATION NEEDS BY LEVEL OF ORGANIZATION[1]			
Characteristic	Top Management	Middle Management	Operating Management
Planning focus	Heavy	Moderate	Minimum
Control Focus	Moderate	Heavy	Heavy
Time Frame	Long-term	Short-term	Day-to-day
Scope of Activity	Broad	Functional areas	Single focus area
Nature of Activity	Unstructured	Moderately structured	Highly structured
Level of Complexity	Many open variables, complex	Better-defined variables	Straightforward
Result of Activity	Mission, goals, objectives	Action plans	End products and services

Figure 1

- **Calculated** — The data may have been analyzed mathematically or statistically.
- **Corrected** — Errors have been removed from the data.
- **Condensed** — The data may have been summarized in a more concise form.

The key to obtaining good, targeted information is to glean knowledge from the information that can lead to corporate action. This is possible when management is trained to evaluate the information on the following:[3]

- **Comparison** — How does the information about this situation compare to other situations the firm has known?
- **Consequences** — What implications does the information have for decisions and actions?
- **Connections** — How does this bit of knowledge relate to others?
- **Conversation** — What do other people think about this organization?

Once information needs have been defined, the next step is to determine how frequently the information needs to be refreshed. Sales and production may require daily or even hourly revitalization. Competitor and environmental data may need to be reviewed weekly, monthly, or quarterly. The drivers within the firm's industry should determine the information frequency required to support its strategy.

Proctor & Gamble[4] codes more than 900,000 phone calls it receives annually on its toll-free number to obtain early signals of consumer tastes and product concerns. Mrs. Fields Cookies systems can monitor sales at 15-minute intervals and suggest product mix changes, promotional tactics, and operating changes to improve customer response.[5]

Federal Express instantly knows where any given package is in its delivery process through its tracking system. Its communications system tracks its 21,000 trucks and vans nationwide, who make over 720,000 stops per day. Its flight operations systems let a single controller direct as many as 200 FedEx aircraft simultaneously, overriding their flight plans as weather and situations develop. All of these systems are core to FedEx's strategy of next-day delivery.[6]

Accurate, timely, and targeted information is vital for functional heads and executive teams to monitor the organization's progress, taking corrective action as early as possible. Being able to quickly identify variances in expected outcomes is one of the major goals of quality information systems.

Footnotes for Section 2.3.2 —

[1] Adapted from Jerome Kanter. *Management Information Systems, 3rd Edition.* Prentice-Hall, 1984, p. 6.

[2] Thomas H. Davenport and Laurence Prusak, *Working Knowledge.* Harvard Business School, 1998, p. 4.

[3] Thomas H. Davenport and Laurence Prusak, *Working Knowledge.* Harvard Business School, 1998, p. 6.

[4] James Brian Quinn. *Intelligent Enterprise.* Free Press, 1992, p. 186.

[5] Mike Korologos. "Debbi Fields." Sky Magazine, July 1988, p. 42-50.

[6] A. A. Thompson and A. J. Strickland. *Strategic Management: Concepts and Cases*, 10th Edition. 1998, p. 675.

2.3.3 Enterprising Systems

> *"The productivity of knowledge has already become the key to productivity, competitive strength, and economic achievement. Knowledge has already become the primary industry, the industry that supplies the economy, the essential and central resource of production."* — Peter F. Drucker

Definition

Designing and implementing systems that provide synthesized information across departmental lines, which enable management to assess the organization on a holistic basis. Using these systems to provide business units with a clear understanding of the interdependencies within the company. Expediting the flow of information cross-functionally.

Areas of Focus

- Defining the specific components of a cross-functional information system.
- Information is shared across departmental lines through an integrated system.
- Facilitating the flow of information across departmental lines to maximize performance and effective decision-making.

An organization's systems are the procedures and protocols for allocating and monitoring its human, organizational, and physical resources. Effective systems should be operational through all portions of the value chain. The diagram on page 142 (Figure 1) illustrates the operational effects of a firm's enterprising systems.

Systems affect the firm's success beyond basic contribution to the firm's operational protocols. The way these processes are managed can affect the organization's ability to sustain, apply, and leverage its core competencies. Information collection, hiring practices, and capital structure practices, for example, can influence the strategic direction of an organization.

When these systems are mismanaged, or misaligned, the organization will face unnecessary obstacles to achieving their strategic intent. A classic example of systems misalignment is the organization which is strategically committed to a

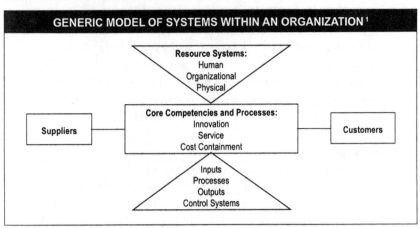

GENERIC MODEL OF SYSTEMS WITHIN AN ORGANIZATION [1]

Resource Systems:
Human
Organizational
Physical

Core Competencies and Processes:
Innovation
Service
Cost Containment

Suppliers

Customers

Inputs
Processes
Outputs
Control Systems

Figure 1

differentiated strategy in terms of offering superior customer service and high-quality products, but has an information system based on costs and a hiring protocol that focuses on entry level personnel with minimal skill sets.

It is important to point out that systemic issues for a firm do not usually stem from a lack of a significant system, but more from the way critical systems are managed. Small variances in managing these systems may have considerable impact on the company's ability to successfully implement their strategy.

A large government contractor, for example,[2] was concerned about the costs of a particular part of their operations. The engineers in charge knew of several operations overseas that were using similar processes at much lower costs. Although the potential savings to the company over the life of the government contract was several million dollars, the company refused to approve the travel budget for a benchmarking visit, since it could not contractually recover the cost of the international travel from the government agency, thereby losing the opportunity for increased profitability.

Like all design issues, in order to align better with the firm's intent, enterprise systems normally follow strategic choice. Alignment of systems can be classified in one of three levels, as shown in Figure 2.

DEGREE OF ALIGNMENT™		
Low Level of Alignment	**Medium Level of Alignment**	**High Level of Alignment**
Strong Negative Impact	*Neutral Impact*	*Strong Positive Impact*
Attributes of system work against achieving the strategic intent of the organization.	Doesn't restrain implementation, but is not suited for it, either.	Tailored to support the firm's strategy. Can deduce intent from system attributes.

Figure 2

The lowest level, illustrated above, is misalignment, where systems actually operate in opposition to the firm's strategic intent.

At the minimum or medium level of alignment, systems will neither support nor detract from a firm's strategic. Examples of this neutral impact would include systems that are driven by vague initiatives such as "people are our most valuable asset." Without a clear understanding of what constitutes a quality workforce, the company may invest in high-quality training programs without any significant return on their investment.

At the highest level, a study of an organization's systems should lead one to clearly understand the strategic intent of the firm,simply by identifying the system's attributes. Such closely aligned systems actually magnify the firm's ability to succeed.

Properly aligned information systems have two purposes: (1) connectivity, coordination, and integration, and (2) providing accurate measurements.

Ritz-Carlton[3] is the best known example of an organization which leverages its information systems into a huge competitive advantage to further the firm's intent. R-C compiles customer profiles on all of their guests. The robust data includes any formal request made during previous stays, as well as observations made by the staff during their normal course of duties. Everyone is issued a note pad for recording things such as, "Mr. Smith in Room 225 seems to enjoy tennis," after observing the tennis whites, tennis magazine, etc., in the room. The notes are quickly recorded on the enterprise-wide database.

Guest recognition coordinators receive advanced lists of incoming guests and link them to all recorded history of the guest's previous stays. Using this enterprise-wide information base, Mr. and Mrs. Smith, who preferred an early dinner and chocolate while staying in Atlanta, will find that a box of chocolates and a timely dinner reservation will be waiting for them when they check into a chain hotel in Laguna.

R-C integrates this technological system with cross-functional training in hotel services for the staff and empowers graduates with a "fix-it" budget of up to $2,000 to remedy guest problems without prior approval. R-C's guest retention rate since the start of the program has increased 25 percent.

Footnotes for Section 2.3.3 —

[1] Adapted from Alex Miller. *Strategic Management.* Irwin McGraw-Hill, 1998, p. 385.

[2] Alex Miller. *Strategic Management.* Irwin McGraw-Hill, 1998, p. 387-388.

[3] Robert Hiebler, Thomas B. Kelly, and Charles Ketteman. *Best Practices: Building Your Business with Customer-Focused Solutions.* Simon & Schuster, 1998, p. 208.

2.3.4 APPLIED TECHNOLOGY

"There really isn't any right amount to spend on information systems. Many management teams spend too much time thinking about how to beat down the information system's cost, instead of thinking about how to get more value out of the information they could have available and how to link that to strategic goals of the company."

— JOHN YOUNG

Definition

Acquiring the necessary technology to achieve strategic intent. Ensuring that there is a process or vehicle within the organization to track the role of technology within the industry.

Areas of Focus

- Strong commitment to integrating best-in-class technology.
- Effectively monitoring the role of technology within industry.
- Seeking to discover new or improved technologies.
- Ensuring that company technology needs are fully met.

Data today is available in more abundant forms and media than ever before. The rate of data availability is increasing exponentially. Technologies that drive this data access are doubling in power within shorter and shorter timeframes. Firms that efficiently and quickly acquire, interpret, and respond to information about their business can gain competitive advantage over their rivals.

Yet it remains that, while no aggressive company poised for growth would use a twenty-year-old marketing approach, many firms choose to operate with twenty-year-old computer information systems. Putting priority on maintenance and the status quo rather than innovation and opportunity will leave many of these firms far behind the pace. Many will not recover.

Technological advancement can affect entire industries in several ways. It can: (1) rejuvenate, obsolete, and create industries; (2) reconfigure industry boundaries; (3) redefine the way firms do business; (4) bring new substitute products and process innovations into a market; and (5) create new synergies across traditionally separate businesses.

Consider the following examples.

- The watch industry has been dramatically rejuvenated by the evolution of new mechanical, electronic, quartz, and digital technologies. The advent of word processing capabilities in personal computers has devastated the typewriter industry.

- Advances in information technologies have rendered old conceptions of the financial services industry obsolete: insurance firms, banks, and brokerage houses can now all be interconnected to provide new financial services, thus blurring long-held distinctions among the services offered by these industries.

- Many U.S. firms have found themselves having to reconfigure their business definitions due to the success of Japanese firms in miniaturizing products, in part, through technological advances. This is the position that Xerox found itself in, with its copier business. Because Japanese firms like Canon introduced smaller-sized copiers, Xerox soon found itself selling to different customers with different needs through different distribution channels and competing on a different basis (where price was much more important) in order to survive.[1]

- Commonly used products are often now being substituted — such as plastics replacing many uses of steel, and frozen food preparation and microwave ovens frequently being substituted for conventional ovens and cooking. In the VCR industry, firms differentiate their products through the introduction of new technological features, such as longer recording time, longer advanced time setting, sharper picture reproduction, clearer sound, and so on.

- Process innovations such as automation, robotics, and CAD/CAM (computer-aided design/computer-aided manufacturing) have bestowed cost and quality advantages on many firms. Japanese automobile manufacturers have gained a significant competitive edge on their U.S. competitors through the adroit use of this form of technology.

- Advances in telecommunications and computer technologies have made new synergies possible across businesses dealing with computers, television sets, and communications.

Technology, in its role as a critical enabler in the fulfillment of a firm's strategic intent, has often been looked at as the ultimate panacea for business performance. It is not technology per se that improves an organization, but the critical use of it. It is the responsibility of IT or IO officers to align their systems with the strategy of the company and allow the firm's intent to drive their technology use decisions.

Some minimal performance standards[2] for information systems include the following:

- They should facilitate global information consistency.
- Departments should be self-sufficient yet compatible in their information system capabilities.
- Should support cross-functional integration of the firm.
- Should integrate voice and data communications.
- Should make data and information available to anyone who demonstrates a need for it, within security and data integrity parameters.
- Design should emphasize effectiveness in the business setting over efficiency in the technical environment.

Ameritech[3] is a good example of a firm converting its information systems team from an operations function charged with reporting data to a vital link in integrating other functions through accessible information. Prior to the change, the information management system pushed out reports that no one read or used. By changing its focus, not only did the company reduce its paperwork by over 6 million pages of reports annually, it synthesized the cross-functional roles and responsibilities of the organization. By careful investment in the right type of technology for the firm, Ameritech improved its competitive position through better information utilization, while increasing profitability.

Footnotes for Section 2.3.4 —

[1] David T. Kearns and David A. Nadler. *Prophets in the Dark — How Xerox Reinvented Itself and Beat Back the Japanese.* Harper Business, 1992, p. 89.

[2] Thomas H. Davenport, Michael Hammer, and Tauno Metsisto. "How Executives Can Shape Their Company's Information Systems." Harvard Business Review 67, Mar-Apr 1989, p. 131.

[3] Brian Dumaine. "Times Are Good? Create a Crisis." Fortune, 28 Jun 1993, p. 130.

2.4.0 ORGANIZATION EFFICIENCY

"Of all the things I've done, the most vital is coordinating the talents of those who work for us and pointing them to a certain goal."

— WALT DISNEY

Description

Having the right people focused on doing the right job within an optimal performance environment. Addresses a company's approach to supervision, clarity of roles and responsibilities, organization interdependencies, and management of outsourced relationships. The objective is minimal duplication, maximum innovation, and well-managed risk.

Principal Elements

- Balanced Direction and Oversight
- Synthesized Roles and Responsibilities
- Managed Outsource and Strategic Alliances

The speed at which organizations carry out their initiatives is based partly on those responsible for implementation and understanding how their individual roles contribute to the firm's overall success. Designing an organization to optimize the firm's efficiency includes establishing supportive policies and procedures, implementing effective control systems, defining specific tasks and responsibilities, and partnering with value chain participants.

The most basic level of efficiency rests on the performance of individual tasks. These tasks are usually defined in conjunction with the organization's intent and chosen tactics for implementation. Job descriptions, policies, milestones, and evaluation criteria are part of this tactical process that promises salary increases, benefits, and promotions as rewards for individual success.

Since individuals seldom work by themselves, group effectiveness constitutes the next level of efficiency in an organization. Whether simply the sum total of individual performances, such as a group of engineers working separately on unrelated projects or the synergistic efforts of an assembly line, group effectiveness and efficiency can be influenced by dedicated, aligned support systems.

Organization efficiency and effectiveness is the synergistic effort of both groups and individuals. Through joint efforts, organization-wide communication, and systems support, the total efficiency of the organization will often exceed the collective sums of the individual and group efforts.

Management's role in improving efficiency and effectiveness can be summarized by the following diagram (Figure 1) :

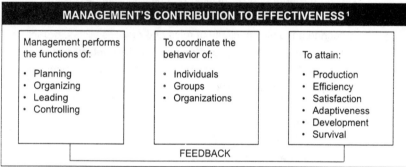

Figure 1

The purpose of management, in terms of performance and efficiency, is to coordinate behavior and to satisfy evaluators of the organization's performance. These evaluators, often stakeholders, can be concerned with any number of specific performance criteria and with either input, output, or process measures.[2] In order to satisfy these evaluators, managers must coordinate behaviors, which are closely tied to task and authority relationships through planning, organizing, leading, and controlling behavior and designing structures and processes to facilitate communication.[3] These relationships are illustrated in Figure 2 below:

SOURCES OF EFFICIENCY [4]			
Management Functions	**Individuals**	**Groups**	**Organizations**
Planning	Objectives	Goals	Missions
Organizing	Job design Delegated authority	Department bases Department size	Integrative methods and processes
Leading	Person-centered influence	Group-centered influence	Entity-centered influence
Controlling	Individual standards of performance	Group standards of performance	Organization standards of performance

Figure 2

A small bank, hoping to retain their position in a regional market, discovered through customer surveys that they ranked last in a field of twenty surveyed banks in customer service. Realizing that their effectiveness and efficiency was dependent on the individual effectiveness of their bank tellers, their primary deliverers of customer service, the bank redirected its policies to promote more customer service behavior rather than the previous "avoid errors" policies. The bank changed the status of tellers from clerical to professional and invested heavily in career development for their tellers. Recruitment tactics were changed to reflect the bank's new requirements for dedicated, self-directed, customer-oriented service providers. By offering competitive compensation, aligned with the overall intent of the bank, the company was able to retain its valuable human resources and made great improvement in the organization's performance.

Footnotes for Section 2.4.0 —

[1] James L. Gibson, John M. Ivancevich, and James H. Donnelly, Jr. *Organizations: Behavior, Structure, Processes.* Irwin, 1991, p. 40.

[2] Frank Hoy and Don Hellriegel. "The Kilmann and Herden Model of Organizational Effectiveness for Small Business Managers." Academy of Management Journal, Jun 1982, p. 308-22.

[3] Gregory H. Gaertner and S. Ramnarayan. "Organizational Effectiveness: An Alternative Perspective." Academy of Management Review, Jan 1983, p. 97-107.

[4] James L. Gibson, John M. Ivancevich, and James H. Donnelly, Jr. *Organizations: Behavior, Structure, Processes.* Irwin, 1991, p. 46.

2.4.1 BALANCED DIRECTION AND OVERSIGHT

"You cannot create prosperity by law...But you can easily destroy prosperity by law."

— THEODORE ROOSEVELT

Definition

Ensuring that, within the organization, there is clear guidance without excessive or overbearing policies. Monitoring compliance with company policies and procedures.

Areas of Focus

- Providing written policies and procedures to all divisions, departments, or units.
- Effectively monitoring compliance.
- Keeping procedures/manuals brief and to-the-point.
- Minimal "red tape."

Changes in strategic initiatives generally require some sort of adjustment in the way a firm conducts business. But asking personnel to change the way they have been doing things is often met with resistance and contempt, especially with current-trend decentralized decision-making, empowerment of individuals to act independently, and encouragement of entrepreneurship at all levels.

Having clear-cut policies and procedures as part of the change management process will aid in the accomplishment of strategic initiatives. Without effective controls in place, today's greater autonomy can result in the organization being pulled in so many conflicting directions that any progress toward the desired intent is diluted in strength or completely a random act.

Proctor & Gamble[1] pioneered empowerment and autonomy ten years before it became a popular practice. However, P&G's interpretation of autonomy deemphasized the need for personal accountability. When the firm's annual earnings growth fell from 30 percent to nearly zero, the management team realized there was still a need for controls despite all the changes that had taken place at P&G. In fact, CEO Edwin Artzt stressed measuring results and reasserted the need for individual accountability as the key for getting P&G back on track.

Other reasons for policies, procedures, and controls are:[2]

- New or freshly revised policies and procedures provide top-down guidance to operating managers, supervisory personnel, and employees regarding how certain things now need to be done and what behavior is expected, thus establishing some degree of regularity, stability, and dependability in how management has decided to execute the strategy and operate business on a daily basis.

- Policies and procedures help align actions and behavior with strategy throughout the organization, placing limits on independent action and channeling individual and group efforts along the intended path of accomplishment. Policies and procedures counteract tendencies for parts of the organization to resist or reject common approaches—most people refrain from ignoring established practices or violating company policy without first gaining clearance or else having strong justification.

- Policies and standardized operating procedures establish and help enforce needed consistency in how strategy-critical activities are performed in geographically scattered operating units. The existence of significant differences in the operating practices and procedures among organizational units performing common functions sends mixed messages to internal personnel about how to do their job and also to customers who do business with the company at multiple locations.

- Because the process of dismantling old policies and procedures and instituting new ones invariably alters the character of the internal work climate, managers charged with implementing strategy can use the policy-changing process as a powerful lever for changing the corporate culture to produce better alignment with the new strategy.

Creative, innovative policies and practices are vital to implementing a firm's strategic intent. Well-constructed policies and procedures help support the achievement of a firm's strategic intent by channeling actions, behavior, decisions, and practices in directions that improve strategy execution. When policies conflict with a firm's intent, they become obstacles to the new culture and direction the organization wants to achieve.

Nike[3] decided to focus on its core competencies of advertising, logistics, and outsourcing of its manufacturing. It developed a series of policies aimed at nurturing its relationships with its production partners. With such targeted policies in place, Nike overcame the cross-cultural barriers as well as any other long distance communication obstacles to their low-cost production strategy.

Some of their policies included:

- Having a Nike employee stationed full-time at each manufacturing site to act as liaison with Nike. They were expected to remain at site for everal years getting to know the key personnel, culture, and operating style of the factory. They matched Nike R&D efforts with factory capabilities and were responsible for keeping monthly orders in line with forecasts.

- Nike worked to minimize variances in production orders for their premium line exclusive factories. The partnership included the factories' investment in new technology and co-developing new models.

- For volume producers of Nike's low- to mid-priced line, factories were expected to balance the variances with the other five to eight buyers and stabilize their own production schedules.

- Finally, it was Nike's strictest policy to pay the factories on time and provide them with predictable cash flows. Such care led to tremendous loyalty and flexibility in production.

It is not meant to suggest that all organizations need vast amounts of policies and procedures to guarantee the achievement of their intent. Indeed, the amount of command and control should vary with the industry requirements along with the culture and expectations of the organization.

In some situations, having too many policies can stifle the creative and entrepreneurial spirit and be as costly as having no policy, or the wrong policy. Often, empowerment and encouragement of initiative and creativity is more instrumental in accomplishing the firm's overall goals than written rules and regulations. Dana Corporation's CEO Rene McPherson dramatically threw out the company's 22-1/2 inch policy manual and replaced it with a one-page statement focusing on a "productive people" philosophy.[4]

The key to supporting a firm's strategic intent is knowing the balance between giving autonomous creativity to individuals to fulfill their goals and the right amount of policies and procedures to give them structure and guidance. An audit of current policies can take place when new initiatives are generated. Management should discontinue outdated policies, revise those requiring adjustment to align with the new intent, and create new directions that would improve the implementation of the strategy.

Footnotes for Section 2.4.1 —

[1] Zachary Schiller. "No More Mr. Nice Guy at P&G." Business Week, 3 Feb 1992, p. 54-56.

[2] A. A. Thompson and A. J. Strickland. *Crafting and Implementing Strategy*. Irwin, 1995, p. 267.

[3] James Brian Quinn. *Intelligent Enterprise*. Free Press, 1992, p. 60-64.

[4] Thomas Peters and Robert Waterman, Jr. *In Search of Excellence*. Harper & Row, 1980, p. 125.

2.4.2 SYNTHESIZED ROLES AND RESPONSIBILITIES

"You want your people to run the business as if it were their own."
— WILLIAM FULMER

Definition

Ensuring that all managers and employees clearly understand their role and their role integrates with those of other departments. Continually reinforcing the need for cross-department integration and communication.

Areas of Focus

- Clearly defined management and employee roles.
- Employees/partners understand how their roles relate to strategic objectives.
- Eliminating redundancy in roles or responsibilities.

One major concern of an organization in executing a new strategy, especially one that is a significant departure from the previous course of action, is defining significant roles in executing that strategy and filling them with the most suitable personnel. Having appropriately skilled and experienced personnel occupying key positions within the firm is one of the main concerns of CEOs, venture groups, investors, and other closely tied stakeholders. Indeed, the degree of confidence that top management holds in achieving its strategic intent can be directly correlated to its confidence in the organization's leadership.[1]

The issues of whether to promote or staff these critical positions from within the firm or recruit from without is discussed in section 3.3.1. Before these key roles can be assigned, however, a strategically aligned definition of these roles should be in place. The key to successful implementation would appear not to only have the right personnel to play critical roles, but to define those roles and responsibilities in such a way as to promote cross-functional integration of efforts, and eliminate any unnecessary redundancy in the design.

All of the managerial activities required to successfully implement the strategic intent of the company should be set forth in specific structure, tasks, and authority. This organization function includes five specific activities.[2]

1. **Defining the nature and content of each job in the organization.** This activity has tangible results: job specifications, position descriptions, or task definitions. These documents describe each position's responsibilities, outcomes, and objectives. In turn, the skills, abilities, and training required to meet the defined expectations are also specified.

2. **Determining the basis for grouping the jobs together.** The essence of defining jobs is specialization, that is, dividing the work. But once the overall task has been subdivided into jobs, those jobs must be combined into groups or departments. The managerial decision involves the selection of appropriate criteria for grouping. For example, all jobs requiring similar machinery may be grouped together, or the manager may decide to group jobs according to the product or service they produce.

3. **Delegating authority to the assigned manager.** The preceding activities create groups of jobs with defined tasks. It then becomes necessary to determine to what extent managers of the groups should be able to make decisions and use the resources of the group without higher approval. This right is termed authority.

4. **Deciding the size of the group.** Jobs are grouped to facilitate supervision of the activities. Obviously, there is a limit on the number of jobs that one person can supervise; but the precise number varies, depending on the situation. For example, it is possible to supervise a greater number of similar, simple jobs than of dissimilar, complex jobs. The appropriate span of control is also affected by the group's overall task, the extent of geographic dispersion, and the availability of standardized procedures.

5. **Devising integrative methods and procedures.** An organization's structure comprises many different parts doing different things. These differences must be integrated into a coordinated whole, and it is management's responsibility to devise integrating methods and processes. If the differences among jobs and departments are not too great, then the simple exercise of authority is sufficient to integrate the differences. For example, the manager of a small yogurt shop can easily integrate the work of the order takers by issuing directives. But the manager of a multi-product, multidivisional organization will have to rely on more complex cross-functional teams, product and customer service managers, and electronic communications.

Once these roles and responsibilities are in place, management must assign these duties to appropriate personnel. Individual effectiveness requires a good fit between job requirements and individual skill sets.

Individual effectiveness can be enhanced by organizational integration activities. The more complex an organization becomes, the greater the level of integration needed to make organizational structure work effectively.[3] Federal Express, for example, needs a high level of integration mechanisms to deliver on its intent of next-day package delivery. It is famous for its customer-liaison personnel who manage transactions quickly and efficiently.

As with all increased structures, higher levels of integration are more costly. Using managers to coordinate value-chain activities is expensive. A company usually only integrates its task activities to the extent necessary to achieve its strategic intent effectively. The following table (Figure 1) lists types and examples of integrating mechanisms available to an organization, in order of complexity from the simplest to the most complex.

TYPES AND EXAMPLES OF INTEGRATING MECHANISMS [4]	
Type	Example
Direct Contact	Sales and production managers
Liaison Roles	Assistant sales and plant managers
Temporary Task Forces	Representatives from sales, production, and R&D
Teams	Organizational executive committee
Integrating Roles	Assistant vice president for strategic planning or VP without portfolio
Integrating Departments	Corporate headquarters staff
Matrix	All roles are integrating roles

Figure 1

The integration issue is for management to match the level of complexity and differentiation with the necessary level of integration in order to achieve the firm's overall strategic intent. It is readily apparent that too much complexity and not enough integration in an organization will ultimately lead to poor implementation of the intended strategy. But the reverse is also true. Too much integration for a simple organization is costly and slows down responsive decision-making. The organization becomes inflexible and overburdened. The ideal is to optimize the simplest structure needed to carry out its mission.

AT&T is a good example of an organization that adjusted its tasks and authority in response to changes within its environment. Before deregulation, AT&T cared little for the speed in which its tall, centralized structure responded to its markets. However, after the markets were forced open, AT&T found itself a poor third to the innovative, highly responsive Japanese telephone equipment manufacturers in terms of phone features and low prices. In response to these threats, AT&T bypassed its traditional functional structure and created cross-functional work teams who were given deadlines for various development phases and then left to do their work. Under this flexible structure, development time dropped by 50 percent, costs went down, and quality went up, with the company regaining some of its product prestige in the marketplace.[5]

Footnotes for Section 2.4.2 —

[1] John A. Pearce II and Richard B. Robinson. *Strategic Management: Formulation, Implementation, and Control.* Irwin, 1997, p. 355.

[2] Henry Mintzberg. "Organization Design: Fashion or Fit?" Harvard Business Review, Jan-Feb 1981, p. 103-106.

[3] P. R. Lawrence and J. Lorach. *Organization and Environment.* Harvard Business School, 1967, p. 50-55.

[4] Charles W. L. Hill and Gareth R. Jones. *Strategic Management Theory: An Integrated Approach.* Houghton Mifflin, 1995, p. 341.

[5] James L. Gibson, John M. Ivancevich, and James H. Donnelly, Jr. *Organizations: Behavior, Structure, Processes.* Irwin, 2000, p. 452.

2.4.3 Managed Outsourced and Strategic Alliances

"For most global businesses, the days of flat-out, predatory competition are over. . . . In place of predation, many multinational companies are learning that they must collaborate to compete."
— Joel Bleeke and David Ernst

Definition

Making sure that strategic alliances are carefully managed. Holding strategic partners to the same performance standards to which company employees are held.

Areas of Focus

- Outsourced activities are closely monitored.
- Strategic partner activities are closely monitored.
- Ensuring that partner performance standards are consistent with internal standards.

Managers spend a great deal of their time, energy, and resources dealing with non-strategy critical activities. These activities generally do not contribute to the firm's competitive advantage and could be best left to others to do while the firm focuses on those few vital areas that are critical to its strategic success. Companies like Nike and Liz Claiborne partner with production firms to make all of their end products, while focusing on core competencies such as design and logistics.

Critics of this growing trend of alliances and outsourcing claim the process takes the control out of the hands of management and breeds dependency on the organization's vendors and suppliers. Others would argue that globalization, limited resources, and spiraling costs make collaboration an eventual imperative. As technology and business practices blur the line between traditional internal processes and a linked value chain approach to products and services, organizations will face the challenge of managing their internal and external relationships with equal vigor and standards of control.

Kenichi Ohmae, Chairman of McKinsey & Company's Japan offices, lists twelve steps to better collaboration between firms (Figure 1).

1. Treat the collaboration as a personal commitment. It is people that make partnerships work.

2. Anticipate that it will take up management time. If you can't spare the time, don't start it.

3. Mutual respect and trust are essential. If you don't trust the people you are negotiating with, forget it.

4. Remember that both partners must get something out of it (money, eventually). Mutual benefit is vital. This will probably mean you've got to give something up. Recognize this from the outset.

5. Make sure you tie up a tight legal contract. Don't put off resolving unpleasant or contentious issues until "later." Once signed, however, the contract should be put away. If you refer to it, something is wrong with the relationship.

6. Recognize that during the course of a collaboration, circumstances and markets change. Recognize your partner's problems and be flexible.

7. Make sure that you and your partner have mutual expectations of the collaboration and its time scale. One happy and one unhappy partner is a formula for failure.

8. Get to know your opposite numbers at all levels socially. Friends take longer to fall out.

9. Appreciate that cultures — both geographic and corporate — are different. Don't expect a partner to act or respond identically to you. Find out the true reason for a particular response.

10. Recognize your partner's interests and independence.

11. Even if the arrangement is tactical in your eyes, make sure you have corporate approval. Your tactical activity may be a key piece in an overall strategic jigsaw puzzle. With corporate commitment to the partnership, you can act with the positive authority needed in these relationships.

12. Celebrate achievement together. It's a shared elation, and you'll have earned it!

Postscript
Two further things to bear in mind:

13. If you're negotiating a product original equipment manufacturer (OEM) deal, look for a quid pro quo. Remember that another product may offer more in return.

14. Joint development agreements must include joint marketing arrangements. You need the largest market possible to recover development costs and to get volume/margin benefits.

Figure 1

The key to every alliance is understanding the value of each organization's contribution to the partnership while being prepared to renegotiate the alliance as necessary. Structuring alliances that provide a win-win situation for all partners, although difficult and requiring some creative thinking, will catapult a firm to the forefront of its industry.

Strategic alliances have been a key element in Toshiba's corporate strategy since the early 1900s. Since then, Toshiba has taken advantage of partnerships, licensing agreements, and joint ventures to become one of the world's leading manufacturers of electronic products.[2]

Dartmouth professor James Brian Quinn gives several reasons for outsourcing relationships.[3]

- Intellectual and service activities now occupy the critical spots in most companies' value chains — regardless of whether the company is in the service or manufacturing sector — and if companies are not "best in the world" at these critical intellectual and service activities, then they are sacrificing competitive advantage by performing those activities internally or with their existing levels of expertise.

- Each company should focus its strategic investments and management attention on those capabilities and processes — usually intellectual or service activities — where it can achieve and maintain "best in world" status.

- The specialized capabilities and efficiency of outside service suppliers have so changed industry boundaries and supplier capabilities that they have substantially diminished the desirability of much vertical integration, and, strategically approached, outsourcing does not "hollow out" a corporation, but can decrease internal bureaucracies, flatten organizations, and give companies a heightened strategic focus, vastly improving their competitive responsiveness.

Other reasons and benefits for partnering include:

- **Improved Business Focus** — Concentrate on core competencies.

- **Access to World Class Capabilities** — The right partner can offer new technologies, tools, and techniques.

- **Accelerated Reengineering Benefits** — Having someone already versed in the new process take over saves time.

- **Shared Risks** — Become more dynamic, flexible, and adaptable to changing markets.

- **Free Resources for Other Purposes** — Redirected resources can be applied to leverage core competencies.

There are a number of examples of firms who engage in excellent strategic partnering. Microsoft's Bill Gates and Intel's Andrew Grove meet together periodically to revisit their "Wintel" strategy that has positioned Windows and Intel chips as the standard for business applications.[4] Soft-drink and beer producers work closely with their distributor/bottlers, cultivating relationships that strengthen loyalties, local market access, and commitment for cooperative marketing programs. Strategic partnerships, alliances, and close collaboration with suppliers, distributors, the makers of complementary products and services, and competitors make good strategic sense whenever the result is to enhance organizational resources and capabilities.

Footnotes for Section 2.4.3 —

[1] Kenichi Ohmae. "The Global Logic of Strategic Alliances." Harvard Business Review #89215, March/April 1998, p. 148.

[2] Richard L. Daft. *Organization Theory and Design*. Southwest Publishing, 1998, p. 102.

[3] James Brian Quinn. *Intelligent Enterprise*. Free Press, 1992, p. 32.

[4] A. A. Thompson and A. J. Strickland. *Strategic Management Concepts and Cases, 10th Edition*. Irwin McGraw-Hill, 1998, p. 443-444.

3.0 ORGANIZATION CULTURE

"Companies start with a white cloth and dye it in the colors they like." — NORITAKE KOBAYASHI

Key Components
- Values and Beliefs
- Leadership
- Human Resource Systems
- Organization Character

Every organization has its own culture. An organization's culture can be manifested in a number of ways. It can be seen as a collection of norms, systems, and practices that a company imposes on its employees. Culture can also be defined as "the values of a company in action."[1] Culture establishes company parameters for what is considered acceptable or unacceptable, right or wrong, appropriate or inappropriate. Culture teaches employees what is valued or disregarded, what is rewarded or punished. In this sense, culture becomes a major determinant for shaping employee behavior and performance.

In essence, culture is the explicit or implicit beliefs, protocols, and practices that an organization maintains for prolonged periods of time, usually much longer than the tenure of the incumbent CEO. Bill Hewlett and Dave Packard first wrote and communicated their seven *Hewlett-Packard Objectives* in 1957.[2] Thomas Watson, Jr., discussed IBM's "Respect for the Individual" in his book *A Business and its Beliefs* in the 1960s,[3] but the roots of this guiding principal date back to his father's presidency of the company in the 1920s.

Culture in an organization evolves first under the influence of the organization's founder. His or her assumptions about success form the foundation of the firm's culture.[4] For example, Ray Kroc and McDonald's, Sam Walton and Wal-Mart, and Bill Gates at Microsoft are all founders with powerful influences over the organization's culture.

The set of beliefs and assumptions the founder has about the distinctive competence of the new organization helps shape its culture and its intended strategy. These beliefs directly influence the choice of strategic response in a firm. For example, a company that prides itself on product innovation will respond to a decline in sales with new product introductions, while those firms that believe in their ability to offer a quality, low-priced product would respond by lowering costs.

However as the marketplace shifts over time, these fundamental strategic positions will change as the firm seeks to carry out its mission in a dynamic environment.

In general, the initial culture of an organization reflects the values of the founder. The culture evolves over time as the environment changes, with new elements added and others discarded to sustain the firm's strategic intent. The addition of an influential, transformational leader may also affect the firm's culture. The diagram below (Figure 1) illustrates the evolution of culture.

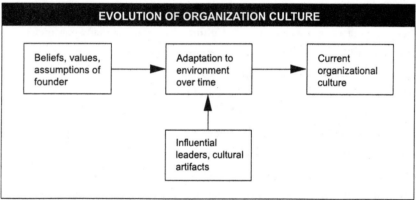

Figure 1

Although it is common to speak of an organization's culture in the singular, most companies have multiple cultures or subcultures.[5] Values, beliefs, and practice can vary by department, division, or location.

Whatever its final composition, an organization's culture can hinder or facilitate the firm's strategic initiatives. The key to sustaining competitive advantage is establishing a work environment where the culture matches well with the conditions for good strategy execution. Strategy-supportive cultures shape the mood, temperament, and motivation of the workforce. Culturally approved behavior flourishes, while disapproved behavior is discouraged. When culture and strategic direction are misaligned, strategy-supportive behavior is discouraged and criticized.

A closely-aligned culture motivates personnel to do their jobs in ways conducive to effective strategy implementation. This provides structure, standards, and a value system in which to operate, and it promotes strong employee identification with the company's vision, performance targets, and strategy.[6]

Managing the culture change required to accommodate strategic initiative can be a difficult process. Managers recognize that managing this strategy-culture relationship requires sensitivity to the interaction between the changes necessary to implement the new strategy and the compatibility or "fit" between those changes and the firm's culture. Figure 2 provides a framework for managing the strategy-culture relationship by identifying the four basic situations a firm may face.

MANAGING THE STRATEGY-CULTURE RELATIONSHIP[7]

	HIGH	LOW
MANY	Link changes to basic mission and fundamental organizational norms	Reformulate strategy or prepare carefully for long-term difficult cultural change
FEW	Synergistic — focus on reinforcing culture	Manage around the culture

Changes in key organizational factors that are necessary to implement the new strategy

Potential compatibility
of changes
with existing culture

Figure 2

Autodesk is a good example of a firm rising to the challenge of long-term cultural change. When Carol Bartz left Sun Mircrosystems, Inc., to run Autodesk, the world's sixth largest PC software company and a leader in sales of computer-aided design software, she introduced a first for the company: a management hierarchy. For the freethinkers at Autodesk, who brought their dogs to work and sent endless memos through e-mail trying to reach consensus on strategy decisions, it was a shock that sent them reeling.

But when Bartz was hired, profits were falling. Growth was continuing to slow, and stock prices were declining sharply. Bartz came in with a mandate for change and has taken a strong top-down approach to try to build a billion-dollar company in a highly competitive industry. While the company's programmers have not been happy with the new hierarchy, sales and marketing are pleased to have someone setting priorities to get the company back on track as far as sales are concerned.

Bartz knows any change, particularly one this momentous, is stressful, so she has instituted a series of "brown-bag chats" with employees to hear their side of things and try to build faith in the new structure as one that will have a positive outcome. As Bartz put it, "It's safe to say there are good ways to manage change and bad ways to manage change, and we have to get on the right side of that paradigm."[8]

Such cultural change stories are evidence that cultural climate is equally vital to the firm's strategic success as its intent and supportive structure. However, the task of aligning culture with the intended strategy of a firm is not a short-term exercise. It takes time for a new culture to evolve and take root in the organization. It is not an overnight phenomenon that can be enforced with a few tertiary workshops and lip service by leadership. The larger the organization, the longer it will take, and the more commitment will be necessary to invoke a change. It is usually more difficult to change a deeply ingrained culture that is not strategy-supportive than to evolve a supportive culture in a new organization.

It is the leaders of strategy that must consider whether or not strategies can be successful, given the unchangeable parts of the firm's culture. Clearly, proper recognition of culture as a powerful part of strategy implementation will help managers achieve their strategic intent more quickly and more effectively.

Culture by itself is not a bottom-line commodity. You won't see it itemized on a balance sheet. But a company with a healthy, adaptive culture will generally outperform a company with an unhealthy, rigid culture, sometimes in dramatic fashion.[9] Companies with strategically conducive cultures stand a better chance of achieving their goals.

Footnotes for Section 3.0 —

1   David W. Jamieson. "Aligning the Organization for Team-Based Strategy." 1995.

2   Jeffrey Abrahms. *The Mission Statement Book*. Ten Speed Press, 1995.

3   Thomas J. Peter and Robert H. Waterman. *In Search of Excellence*. Warner Books, 1982.

4   Edgar H. Schein. "The Role of the Founder in Creating Organizational Culture." Organizational Dynamics 12, Summer 1983, p. 14.

5   John P. Kotter and James L. Heskett. *Corporate Culture and Performance*. Free Press, 1992, p. 7.

6   John Alexander and Meena S. Wilson. "Leading Across Cultures: Five Verbal Capabilities" (in *The Organization of the Future*. Frances Hesselbein, Marshall Goldsmith, and Richard Beckard. Jossey-Bass, 1997, p. 291-92).

7   John A. Pearce II and Richard B. Robinson. *Strategic Management: Formulation, Implementation, and Control*. Irwin, 1997, p. 359.

8   Richard L. Daft. *Organization Theory and Design*. Southwest Publishing, 1998, p. 304.

9   John P. Kotter and James L. Heskett. *Corporate Culture and Performance*. Macmillan, 1992.

3.1.0 Values and Beliefs

> *"The basic philosophy, spirit, and desire of an organization have far more to do with its relative achievements than do technological or economic resources, organization structure, innovation, and timing. All these things weigh heavily on success. But they are, I think, transcended by how strongly the people in the organization believe in its basic precepts and how faithfully they carry them out."*
>
> — Thomas Watson, Jr.

Description

Core values and beliefs help employees understand their company's commitment to customers, to shareholders, to the community, and to themselves. Values describe the standards and ideals that a company holds in high regard. They provide a framework for implementing strategic initiatives.

Principal Elements

- Values Integration
- Values Communication
- Values Durability

In all organizations, there are two fundamental factors that impact success: *Vision,* which is the strategic component, and *Values,* which is the behavioral component. Vision (and mission) statements answer the question: What must we accomplish? Value statements answer the question: How must we behave? Optimum performance cannot be achieved without careful consideration of both factors.

At the core of an organization's culture are its values and beliefs. These shared values and beliefs shape how the work of the organization is done. In much the same way as personality influences the behavior of an individual, these shared assumptions about what is valued among a firm's employees and stakeholders influences opinions, attitudes, behaviors, and ultimately, outcomes within the organization. According to Harvard Business School professors John Kotter and James Heskett, when the beliefs and practices called for in a strategy are not compatible with a firm's culture, a company usually finds it difficult to implement the strategy successfully.[1]

Members of an organization can simply be aware of the organization's beliefs and values without necessarily sharing them in a personally significant way. However, if employees view these values as guidelines for appropriate behavior within the organization, the values tend to take on more personal meaning. Through compliance, the member of the organization is rewarded extrinsically, and the corporate goals are obtained. Real synergy, however, occurs when members of the organization derive personal satisfaction, or intrinsic rewards, from their actions being congruent with their own personal values and beliefs. Thus, aligning the internalized values of each member of the firm with the stated values of the firm leads to a stronger and strategically supportive culture.

Building a strong culture begins with identifying and defining the supporting values and beliefs of the organization. In a typical evolution, the values and beliefs of the founders have the greatest influence on establishing the culture and the initial assumption set of values and beliefs. These values can describe specific behavior towards each member of the organization, towards the customer, towards suppliers, towards the community and even towards the competition.

A strong, clearly worded values statement should be given the same status with the organization as the vision or mission statement. The mission of the company communicates what needs to be accomplished by the organization, while the values statement describes how, in terms of behavior, those achievements ought to be accomplished. Companies use many structures and processes to demonstrate its intent and assumptions to communicate the subscribed beliefs to their stakeholders. These structures and processes are also known as cultural artifacts.

Constantly reinforcing the set of values and beliefs adds credibility to the organization's culture and may be influential in committing more members of the firm to personally internalizing the firm's value system. Employees pay more attention to what is emphasized than to what is stated. Aligned with documented values and beliefs, behavior that is rewarded becomes part of the implicit value set, while stated desired behavior that is ignored loses its durability.

Hanover Insurance CEO Bill O'Brien, talking about the firm's recovery from near bankruptcy to a leader in the property and liability industry, spoke of his employee need or stated values.[2]

> Early on, we recognized that there is a burning need for people to feel part of an ennobling mission. If it is absent many will seek fulfillment only in outside interests instead of in their work...People need vision to make the purpose more concrete and tangible. We had to learn to 'paint pictures' of the type of organization we wanted to be...Core values are necessary to help people with day-to-day decision-making. Purpose is very abstract. Vision is long term. People need 'guiding stars' to navigate and make decisions day to day. But core values are only helpful if they can be translated into concrete behaviors. For example, one of our core values is 'openness,' which we worked long and hard to understand — finally recognizing that it requires the skills of reflection and inquiry within an overall context of trusting and supporting one another.

Xerox rose to legendary status as the fastest company to reach the billion-dollar mark in history. The company's success may be due in large part to the influence of founders and charter employees in establishing a benchmark set of enduring values. While rapidly developing its flagship copier, the 914, expenses were high and capital scarce. In order to save money, the company turned off the heat in the winter of 1959-60. Engineers kept bundled in jackets, with blankets draped over their machines that gave off heat, working 24 hours a day, 7 days a week in order to get the product out on time.

The successful launch of the 914 created an explosion in demand, and parts became scarce. The lack of a critical part, made in Chattanooga, threatened to shut down the entire Rochester production. The director of manufacturing and a purchasing agent decided to fly to Tennessee to get the part, but a snowstorm diverted their plane to Washington, D. C. Nonplussed, the two tried to get train tickets instead, but the railroad would not accept their plane tickets as credit. Lacking cash, the two tracked down a local Xerox employee and borrowed money to take the train. Once in Chattanooga, the two resorted to actually driving a taxi from the station to the vendor, because the regular drivers would not risk it in the storm. The parts were secured. Splitting up to increase their chances of getting back to Rochester, the two traveled a total of 72 hours nonstop, sleeping in their seats and eating peanut butter sandwiches, but the production line never stopped.[3]

Heroic efforts like this become important symbols in establishing an attitude of success in an organization. This can-do spirit was critical to Xerox's early success and no doubt contributes today to the organization's future intent some thirty years later. It is important to note that these acts were committed not by the founder or CEO. Individuals throughout an organization can exert influence on the firm's values and belief systems through their personal actions.

Employees today are generally more knowledgeable. They desire more individual autonomy than earlier generations. Companies may find it difficult to impose management methods that are based on centralized authority and control.

People have a fundamental need to belong to something they can be proud of. More than any time in the past, employees are demanding operating autonomy while also demanding that the organizations they are connected with stand for something.[4]

Footnotes for Section 3.1.0 —

[1]   John P. Kotter and James L. Heskett. *Corporate Culture and Performance*. Free Press, 1992, p. 28.

[2]   Peter M. Senge. *The Fifth Discipline*. Doubleday, 1990, p. 224.

[3]   David T. Kearns and David A. Nadler. *Prophets in the Dark — How Xerox Reinvented Itself and Beat Back the Japanese*. Harper Business, 1992.

[4]   James C. Collins and Jerry I. Porras. *Built to Last*. Harper Collins, 1994.

3.1.1 VALUES INTEGRATION

"It is the consistency of principle...that gives us direction...(Certain principles) have been characteristics of P&G ever since our founding in 1837. While Proctor & Gamble is oriented to progress and growth, it is vital that employees understand that the company is not only concerned with results, but how the results are obtained."

— ED HARNESS

Definition

The impact of core values and beliefs on a company's culture and on its bottom-line. Creating or refining core values. Addressing the unique needs of all constituencies. Aligning company systems and practices with core beliefs. Establishing consistency of culture throughout the organization.

Areas of Focus

- Values are clearly defined.
- Company practices, systems, and processes are carefully aligned with values.
- Work climates consistent throughout organization.

It is important to distinguish between an organization's core values and its practices. The artifacts of culture, those structure and processes that demonstrate a firm's intent and assumptions, are subject to many interpretations and, due to their complexity and varying origins, are difficult to decipher. The strategies, goals, and preferred methodologies are on occasion labeled values and beliefs and are used to justify behavior and align the actions of the firm's members. Core values and beliefs, however, are those underlying assumptions, perceptions, thoughts, and feelings about the way the organization views the world, its members and the nature and purpose of its existence. These assumptions often go beyond the oft-recited profit motive and enhancement of shareholder wealth.[1]

For value-driven companies, core beliefs are an integral part of strategic thinking. John Young, former CEO at Hewlett-Packard, describes the culture-strategy relationship at H-P and its commitment to its core values, as follows.

Our basic principles have endured intact since our founders conceived them. We distinguish between core values and practices; the core values don't change, but the practices might. We've also remained clear that profit — as important as it is —is not why the Hewlett-Packard Company exists; it exists for more fundamental reasons.[2]

To most of the organization core values are self-evident, timeless in their credibility, and not subject for debate or even rational explanation. Because of the deep personal nature of these ideologies, each organization should strive to identify its own set of core beliefs and not "borrow" stated values from other benchmark organizations.

The critical question to ask when identifying core values is, "What values would not be compromised, regardless of external changes in the environment, industry, or market conditions? Core values are those that are non-negotiable even when the environment punishes the firm for having them. For this reason, values should be distilled from careful consideration and not from shortcut methods of mimicking others, calculating popular positions, or assuming the most profitable short-term stances.

In response to questions regarding the most "correct" content of a company's core values, Collins and Porras,[3] in their research on core ideologies of 33 major organizations they call visionary companies, found that the authenticity of the ideology and the extent to which a company attains consistent alignment with the ideology counted more than the content of the ideology.

Johnson & Johnson has perhaps one of the most widely publicized and referenced credo or value statements. Written by founder Robert W. Johnson, and modified and expanded upon over time, the credo has played a very active role in Johnson & Johnson's culture and strategic decision making. The credo establishes the hierarchy of priorities and responsibilities, serving first the customer, then those who work with the company, then management, the community, and finally shareholders, promising them a fair return rather than the often used. "maximum profitability."

The differences in the power and influence of a firm's credo were readily apparent in 1982 when Tylenol bottles were tampered with in the Chicago area. J&J immediately responded to the crisis by pulling every bottle of product off the shelves throughout the U.S. and refitting the product with tamper-fit packaging. The recall alone cost J&J in excess of $100 million dollars. The company also organized a massive communication effort to warn the public and deal with the problem.

Contrast this response with that of Brystol-Myers who had no credo until 1987 (which now reads like a summary of J&J's credo). A few days after the Tylenol incident, bottles of Excedrin were tampered with in Colorado. The company responded by recalling only the bottle in Colorado and keeping the incident quiet. Then B-M chairman Richard Gelb was quick to emphasize that the Excedrin incident would have a negative effect on B-M's earnings.[4]

The table below (Figure 1) lists the kinds of topics that may be included in value and ethics statements. The list is not comprehensive, nor should it be construed that all of these elements ought to be included in a written statement.

TOPICS GENERALLY COVERED IN VALUES STATEMENTS AND CODES OF ETHICS [5]	
Topics Covered in Values Statements	**Topics Covered in Codes of Ethics**
• Importance of customers and customer service. • Commitment to quality. • Commitment to innovation. • Respect for the individual employee and the duty the company has to the employee. • Importance of honesty, integrity, and ethical standards. • Duty to stockholders. • Duty to suppliers. • Corporate citizenship. • Importance of protecting the environment.	• Honesty and observance of the law. • Conflicts of interest. • Fairness in selling and marketing services. • Using inside information and securities trading. • Supplier relationships and purchasing practices. • Payments to obtain business/Foreign Corrupt Practices Act. • Acquiring and using information about others. • Political activities. • Use of company assets, resources, and property. • Protection of proprietary information. • Pricing, contracting, and billing.

Figure 1

Once the values and standards have been established, integrating them into everyday action involves several steps:[6]

- Incorporating the statement of values and the code of ethics into employment orientation, training, and educational programs.
- Explicit attention to values and ethics in recruiting and hiring to screen out applicants who lack compatible character traits.
- Communication of the values and ethics code to all employees, explaining compliance procedures.

- Management involvement and oversight, from the CEO to first line supervisors.
- Strong public endorsements by the CEO.
- Word-of-mouth indoctrination.

Although core values endure, and some practices and beliefs will not, an ongoing review of shared values will promote unity of purpose and commitment not only to the organization's intent, but to its methodology as well.

Footnotes for Section 3.1.1 —

[1] Edgar H. Schein. *Organizational Culture and Leadership.* Jossey-Bass, 1992, p. 16-25.

[2] Interview with James C. Collins and Jerry I. Porra, 17 April 1992 (in James C. Collins and Jerry I. Porras' *Built to Last: Successsful Habits of Visionary Companies*). Harper, 1994, p. 48.

[3] James C. Collins and Jerry I. Porras. *Built to Last: Successful Habits of Visionary Companies.* Harper, 1994, p. 87.

[4] James Burke. "A Career in American Business." Harvard Business Review 9-389-177, Rev. July 20, 1998.

[5] A. A. Thompson and A. J. Strickland. *Crafting and Implementing Strategy.* Irwin, 1995, p. 291.

[6] A. A. Thompson and A. J. Strickland. *Strategic Management, 11th Edition.* Irwin McGraw-Hill, 1999, p. 344.

3.1.2 VALUES COMMUNICATION

"Shared values are the glue that hold this organization together."
— SHELLEY BROWN

Definition

Ensuring that company employees clearly understand the significance of company values. Using all available communication media to reinforce values and beliefs. Creating a sense of reverence and durability regarding company tenets.

Areas of Focus

- Values are consistently communicated.
- Employees understand content and spirit of values.
- Employees understand critical importance of standards.
- Consistently reinforced in company communication media.

Effectively communicating the firm's core values and beliefs can help a firm's employees understand its commitment to customers, shareholders, community, and employees. Culture can be communicated explicitly through company slogans or by placards hung on office walls; or it can be communicated implicitly through day-to-day experiences. Most employees will draw their own conclusions about their company's culture simply by observing the rewards and consequences associated with real-time situations.

At the lowest level of culture, an organization uses cultural artifacts to communicate its value system. A partial list of these cultural mechanisms is included on the next page as Figure 1.

An organization communicates its value systems through the use of artifacts, using both formal and informal channels of communication. One example of good culture communication is demonstrated by Mary Kay Ash, founder of Mary Kay cosmetics. Ash's story of not being able to find good opportunities for herself and other women led her to investing in herself and others. Communicating her concern for women's advancement and self-esteem, her success story is told over and over again by those who work for her. Such stories promote the values and

CULTURAL PRODUCTS AND ASSOCIATED DEFINITIONS [1]	
Name	**Description**
Belief	An understanding of a particular organization.
Ceremonial	A system of several rites connected with a single occasion or event.
Folktale	A completely fictional narrative.
Heroes/Heroines	Individuals whom the organization has legitimized to model behavior for others.
Language	A particular form or manner in which members of a group use sounds and written signs to convey meanings to each other.
Metaphors	Shorthand words used to capture a vision or to reinforce old or new values.
Myth	A dramatic narrative of imagined events, usually used to explain origins or transformations of something. Also, an unquestioned belief about the practical benefits of certain techniques and behaviors that is not supported by facts.
Rites	Relatively elaborate, dramatic, planned sets of activities that consolidate various forms of cultural expressions into one event, carried out through social interactions, usually for the benefit of an audience.
Ritual	A standardized, detailed set of techniques and behaviors that manage anxieties, but seldom produce intended, technical consequences of practical importance.
Saga	A historical narrative describing the unique accomplishments of a group and its leaders, usually in heroic terms.
Symbol	Any object, act, event, quality, or relation that serves as a vehicle for conveying meaning, usually by representing another thing.
Values	Life-directing attitudes that serve as behavioral guidelines.

Figure 1

norms Mary Kay seeks for its work environment — a place where women can gain self-esteem, and where high levels of motivation are desired, performance is rewarded, and management cares about its people.[2]

Disney's use of language, symbolism, ceremonies, and rituals creates a corporate culture admired worldwide. Everyone at Disney is a "cast member," job descriptions are "scripts," a work shift is a "performance," a uniform is a "costume," being on duty is "onstage," and customers are "guests." The special language reinforces the frame of mind Disney imposes on its employees. Disney's motto of never being finished as long as there is imagination in the world conveys a feeling of anticipation and innovation.[3]

Effective communication using techniques and artifacts such as these conveys not only the organization's strategic intent, but the method, atmosphere, and attitude through which the intent may be achieved. These techniques are vital to gaining the cooperation and confidence of those who would implement the strategy.

Footnotes for Section 3.1.2 —

[1] Adapted from H. M. Trice and J. M. Beyer. "Studying Organizational Cultures Through Rites and Ceremonials." Academy of Management Review 9, Number 4, Oct 1984, p. 655.

[2] A. A. Thompson and A. J. Strickland. *Strategic Management: Concepts and Cases, 8th Edition*. Irwin McGraw-Hill, 1995, p. 898.

[3] James C. Collins and Jerry Porras. *Built to Last: Successful Habits of Visionary Companies*. Harper Business, 1994.

3.1.3 Values Durability

> *"Numbers and values. We don't have the final answer here — at least I don't. People who make the numbers and share our values go onward and upward. People who miss the numbers and share our values get a second chance. People with no values and no numbers — easy call. The problem is with those who make the numbers, but don't share our values...We try to persuade them, we wrestle with them, we agonize over these people."* — Jack Welch

Definition

Establishing a process to evaluate company performance with regard to values and beliefs. Reviewing standards and ideals on a regular basis to ensure timeliness and relevance.

Areas of Focus

- Values are not compromised.
- Performance against values are tracked with the same emphasis as financial or production performance.
- No strategy adopted that might violate company standards.
- Values are reviewed periodically to maintain relevance.

In a stable corporate culture where basic values are not compromised, maintaining and renewing shared values is often difficult for an organization facing pressures to perform against increasing competitive intensity. Quarterly dividends, earnings per share, competitor encroachment, emerging technology, and the challenge of a global marketplace may affect an organization's commitment to its basic values.

Achieving the most durable level of culture, described as the internalization and alignment of the organization's values and beliefs with each member of the firm's personal value system, can only be accomplished through the consistent communication, tracking, and reviewing of artifacts and other expressions of these basic assumptions throughout the organization.

These three levels of culture (Figure 1) decrease in the amount of cultural phenomena that is visible to an observer.[1] That is, level one artifacts are clearly visible to an outside observer, yet it is difficult to interpret culture and value ramifications. Expressed values are certainly accessible, but most are practice-oriented and can change in response to the dynamics of the industry. At the core of culture are the durable core values of the organization. Some call these core values, basic values, or underlying assumptions about the world. This unwritten, underlying paradigm is often hard to observe per se, yet it commands the biggest influence on the actions of the organization.

THREE LEVELS OF CULTURE		
Artifacts Visible organizational structures and processes — hard to interpret values accurately	**Espoused Values** Strategies, goals, intent, philosophies, justifying actions; changeable in response to environment	**Underlying Core Values and Assumptions** Unconscious, taken-for-granted beliefs, perceptions, feelings, thoughts — ultimate source of values and actions

Figure 1

Whether responding to strategic change or merely formalizing the expression of core values in a credo, the process of cultural alignment can be met with resistance. Making strategic changes in an organization, even when done in order to improve its long-term viability, always threatens a culture. While this reluctance to compromise and change can be put to good use when the appropriate strategically congruent culture has been established, the initial alignment process requires commitment, patience, and leadership.

Kouzes and Posner[2] provide some practical steps for organizations attempting to clarify and renew their shared values:

1. *Participation:* Solicit feedback from everyone in the organization. An old Chinese proverb applies: "Tell me, I may learn. Teach me, I may remember. Involve me, I will do it."

2. *Build consensus:* Focus on understanding shared values. Clarify what is vital and unchangeable as well as secondary and flexible. Solicit responses to hypothetical value dilemmas. Evaluate recent decisions for alignment with agreed-upon values.

3. *Survey the climate:* The best way to know what people are thinking is to ask them. Well-designed climate surveys will illuminate which issues and values are clearly understood and which need clarifica-

tion. They will also measure commitment to established values and allow people to see areas of consistency, change, and improvement.

4. *Connect values with reasons:* The importance of certain values may be self-evident. But commitment to values is facilitated when that value is shared and is traceable to a valid rationale. It also helps people apply the "logic" of that value to new and different situations and promotes consistency in the interpretation and enactment of important principles.

5. *Structure cooperative goals:* Encourage cross-functional dialogue and interdisciplinary learning. Members should perceive that they are interconnected, interdependent, and working for the same shared goals.

6. *Communicate the business:* Solicit people's responses to the nature of the firm's business, customer profile, revenue streams, and profitability. If members of the organization don't know basic business data, how can they work together to translate shared values and purpose into achieving intent?

7. *Publicly affirm shared values:* Constituents are filled with energy and enthusiasm when their leaders speak with passion about shared beliefs. Keep people focused by constantly and enthusiastically supporting the process.

8. *Accumulate "yes's":* The key word in agreements is yes. When people say yes to one another, their relationship changes. Look for opportunities to say yes as often as possible. Acknowledge viewpoints and add your own. Don't contradict.

9. *Go slow to go fast:* Start with values and issues easily agreed upon, and move progressively toward more difficult and complex issues. Get people into the habit and role of solving things on a smaller level. Show them that consensus is possible.

10. *Establish a sunset statute:* Rethink your credo or values set periodically. Resist the temptation to rest on your success. Over time, as people leave the organization and new people enter and circumstances change, it would be good practice to review and repeat the process. The outcome may not result in any changes in core values, but the worth of involving people and reinforcing their commitment to the organization will be great.

Footnotes for Section 3.1.3 —

[1] Edgar H. Schein. *Organizational Culture and Leadership.* Jossey-Bass, 1992, p. 17.

[2] James M. Kouzes and Barry Z. Posner. *Credibility: How Leaders Gain and Lose It, Why People Demand It.* Jossey-Bass, 1993, p. 145-152.

3.2.0 LEADERSHIP

"A business short on capital can borrow money, and one with a poor location can move. But a business short on leadership has little chance of survival." — WARREN BENNIS & BURT NANUS

Description

Leaders create visions. They possess the persuasive skills and the resolve to recruit and develop followers who are committed to carrying out the vision. Leadership requires an ability to see the bigger picture and to maintain a balance between high-level strategies and front-line tactics. Research indicates that management style has a substantial impact on employee job satisfaction and performance.

Principal Elements

- Management Modeling
- Strategic/Tactical Balance
- Empowerment
- Developmental Coaching
- Building Effective Teams

Everyone agrees that leadership is essential to organizational success. No other element of an organization's culture has more immediate or regular impact on employee behavior and performance than good leadership. Yet amid this agreement of the importance of leadership, no one seems to agree on its sole definition. Most would argue that leadership involves influencing others, those who by definition would be followers.

Although seemingly obvious, unless a leader has followers, defined as those who are influenced into carrying out activities to further the intent of the organization, then the leader is not truly a leader but may be described as one in authority or a manager.

It is important to make the distinction between managers and leaders. If all leaders have followers, then some managers may not be leaders over their direct reports. Management can be defined as those processes that keep an organization running smoothly; leadership can be defined as those processes that create organizations or adapt them to changing circumstances. A leader defines what the future should look like, aligns people with that vision, and inspires them to make it happen despite the many obstacles that may intervene.[1] The following table (Figure 1) illustrates some of the differences between management and leadership.

MANAGEMENT VERSUS LEADERSHIP [2]	
Management	**Leadership**
Planning and budgeting: Establishing detailed steps and timetables for achieving needed results, then allocating the resources necessary to make it happen	**Establishing direction:** Developing a vision of the future — often the distant future — and strategies for producing the changes needed to achieve that vision
Organizing and staffing: Establishing some structure for accomplishing plan requirements, staffing that structure with individuals, delegating responsibility and authority for carrying out the plan, providing policies and procedures to help guide people, and creating methods or systems to monitor implementation	**Aligning people:** Communicating direction in words and deeds to all those whose cooperation may be needed so as to influence the creation of teams and coalitions that understand the vision and strategies and that accept their validity
Controlling and problem solving: Monitoring results, identifying deviations from plan, then planning and organizing to solve those problems	**Motivating and inspiring:** Energizing people to overcome major political, bureaucratic, and resource barriers to change by satisfying basic, but often unfulfilled, human needs
▼	▼
Produces a degree of predictability and order, and has the potential to consistently produce the short-term results expected by various stakeholders (e.g., for customers, always being on time; for shareholders, being on budget)	Produces change, often to a dramatic degree, and has the potential to produce extremely useful change (e.g., new products that customers want, new approaches to labor relations that help make a firm more competitive)

Figure 1

Managers who seek to become leaders must use their skills to balance the needs of their organization and their followers. Korzes and Posner concluded after much research that to be effective, managerial leaders rely on the following five principles of action:

- Leaders challenge the process. They are pioneers and innovators. They encourage those with ideas.

- Leaders inspire a shared vision. They are enthusiastic.

- Leaders enable others to act. They are team players.

- Leaders model the way. They show others how to behave as leaders.

- Leaders "encourage the heart." They openly and often celebrate achievements.[3]

Satisfied employees most effectively implement strategic initiatives. In a poll of 25,000 workers, conducted by the Wilson Learning Corporation, employees said their manager's leadership skills accounted for 69% of their job satisfaction.[4] According to the poll, managers get high ratings when employees are shown how their work affects the company's success, when employees are involved in decisions, when employees are offered developmental opportunities, when managers are good coaches and mentors, when employees are provided frequent performance feedback, and when managers recognize and reward achievements.[5]

Leadership can be divided into specific areas of focus. In this primer, leadership has been divided into the areas of modeling, empowerment, coaching, balance, and team building. Although there are many theories and models about leadership's role in the organization and how leadership style can impact the culture, the leadership activities selected are universal in scope and common to most organizations.

One of the best illustrations of the power and impact a leader can have is the concept of "managing by walking around." Really, "MBWA" serves a two-fold purpose — the managing function of observing, communicating, and reviewing performance, and the leadership function of inspiring and modeling behavior.[6]

Bill Hewlett made MBWA a company practice. At weekly beer busts in each division, formal structure yielded to informal socialization as employees were given the opportunity to talk freely with executives at all levels. One symbol of this leadership was the policy to have every employee called by their first name.

Roy Kroc regularly visited McDonald's franchises and conducted his own inspections on quality, service, cleanliness, and value. There are stories of his getting out of his limo to pick up litter and lecturing the staff on increased efforts on cleanliness.

Sam Walton had a long-standing reputation for visiting each store, listening to the customers, store managers, and employees. Sam insisted that the best ideas came from the stockboys and clerks.

GE's Jack Welch not only spends time personally visiting GE operations and talking with major customers, but he arranges his schedule so that he can spend time talking with GE managers taking courses at the company's leadership development center. As Welch puts it, "I'm here every day, or out into a factory, smelling it, feeling it, touching it, challenging the people."[7]

Footnotes for Section 3.2.0 —

[1] John P. Kotter. *Leading Change*. Harvard Business School, 1996, p. 25.

[2] John P. Kotter. *A Force for Change: How Leadership Differs from Management*. Free Press, 1990.

[3] James M. Kouzes and Barry Z. Posner. *The Leadership Challenge*. Jossey-Bass, 1987.

[4] "Effective Managers, Happy Employees." Small Business Reports, 18 May 1994, p. 19.

[5] "Effective Managers, Happy Employees." Small Business Reports, 18 May 1994, p. 19.

[6] Thomas Peters and Robert H. Waterman, Jr. *In Search of Excellence*. Harper & Row, 1982, p. xx, 15, 120-23, 191, 242-43, 246-47, 287-90.

[7] As quoted in Ann M. Morrison. "Trying to Bring GE to Life." Fortune, 25 Jan 1982, p. 52.

3.2.1 MANAGEMENT MODELING

"You can't be motivated by self-interests and expect to be a leader. The instant you feel exempt from the standards of the organization, you cease to be a leader. A leader galvanizes people by living their shared vision." — CHERYL BREETWOR

Definition

The effect of senior and middle managers exemplifying the company's values and beliefs through their personal behavior. The impact of management behavior on the overall credibility of the company's standards and ideals.

Areas of Focus

- Senior management "walks the talk."
- Line management "walks the talk."
- Managers are viewed as role models.
- Management styles are alkigned with values and consistent across division/departments.

Effective leaders know that their own visible behavior has great value for communicating the underlying assumptions and values to other members of the organization. In other words, the actions leaders take in demonstrating and reinforcing the type of behavior the organization is trying to develop company-wide makes leaders role models that other can follow.

This is commonly referred to as "walking the talk" — not just giving lip service to the firm's stated goals, objectives, and values, but living an organizational life every day that demonstrates a commitment to strategy through personal actions.[1]

Gayle Hamilton of Pacific Gas and Electric, a firm known for its strong culture, put it, "You can't follow someone who isn't credible, who doesn't truly believe in what they're doing — and how they are doing it."[2]

A recent survey asked employees to name characteristics of leaders they admired. Honesty was selected more often than any other trait.[3] Honesty (and its companion, integrity) are essential to leadership and establishing and maintaining trust within the organization. Nothing will establish that trust more effectively than employees observing the firm's leadership depicting and reinforcing the ideals of the organization in their personal actions.

Words are important, but as the old adage says, "Actions speak louder than words." (See Figure 1.) Unfortunately studies indicate that this obvious advice for leaders goes unheeded. As one leadership expert put it, "Ninety-five percent of American managers today say the right thing. Five percent actually do it."[4]

SOME COMMON ACTIONS THAT BUILD RESPECT, TRUST, AND A WILLINGNESS TO BE INFLUENCED	
The leader:	
Supported me	Made time for people
Had the courage to do the right thing	Shared the vision
Challenged me	Opened doors
Developed and acted as a mentor	Overcame personal hardships
Listened	Admitted mistakes
Celebrated good work	Advised others
Followed through on commitments	Solved problems creatively
Trusted me	Taught well
Empowered others	

Figure 1

A study by Booz Allen & Hamilton surveyed management teams at twenty-seven Fortune 500 manufacturing and service firms.[5] They found that although virtually all the companies surveyed paid lip service to quality, customer satisfaction, and maintaining superior service levels, virtually none of the top executives actually tracked these areas' performance on a regular basis as they did financial indicators such as profitability, costs, and stock performance.

If a leader's actions are to consistently align with his or her words, it is important that they be based on internalized convictions rather than a scripted play. Tsun-Yan Hsich, a noted leadership consultant at McKinsey & Company, explains, "Successful leaders...are not deliberately 'acting' as much as they are doing what they believe in-living it, personifying it."[6]

When leaders act contrary to their stated positions and values, in addition to creating an atmosphere of mistrust, they can directly affect the performance of the organization. A young capital equipment manufacturer that had grown to $400 million dollars in eight short years was trying to transform itself from a tightly controlled family-run shop into a fully developed corporation. While the memos and events sponsored by the firm all pushed for empowerment and lower level decision-making in customer service and sales, an area where competitor encroachment was plainly visible, the approval process on all activities still required an executive team member's signature.

The international manager expressed his frustration at missing an important proposal deadline and a subsequent chance at getting a very large order in India. The bottleneck had occurred when the CFO held up his approval of the overnight package until he had more information. The CFO waited until he could call the international manager into his office to inquire whether the response process could be streamlined to allow the packages in the future to be sent through routine US Postal Service. The international manager assured the CFO that the overnight service was required, not because of time constraints, but because of the tracking and verifying service included in the delivery. The discussion took 10 minutes and ironically interrupted a meeting the manager was having with his department on increasing the company's poor responsiveness to customer requests. The value of the invoice discussed, occupying the time of two executives and keeping five others waiting, was $12. Said the international manager, "When measured against the messages delivered that day to not only me, but to the managers at the meeting and throughout the organization, the actual cost of that savings seems a bit too high."

Building trust through management modeling, when practiced, frees up honest dialogue and holds relationships together. Lack of trust on both sides of the workforce due to inconsistent behavior prompts firms to spend as much time as possible protecting, doubting, checking, weighing and inspecting as it spends doing the real work of innovating, collaborating, and adding value.

Footnotes for Section 3.2.1 —

    [1] Alex Miller. *Strategic Management.* Irwin McGraw-Hill, 1998, p. 443.

    [2] James M. Kouzes and Barry Z. Posner. *Credibility: How Leaders Gain and Lose It, Why People Demand It.* Jossey-Bass, 1993, p. 27.

    [3] James M. Kouzes and Barry Z. Posner. *Credibility: How Leaders Gain and Lose It, Why People Demand It.* Jossey-Bass, 1993, p. 14.

    [4] John Huey. "The New Post-Heroic Leadership." Fortune, 21 Feb 1994, p. 42-56.

    [5] Ronald Henkoff. "CEOs Still Don't Walk the Talk." Fortune, 18 Apr 1994, p. 14-15.

    [6] Tsun-Yan Hsieh. "Leadership Actions." McKinsey Quarterly, Fall 1990, p. 42-58.

3.2.2 STRATEGIC/TACTICAL BALANCE

"Effective managers live in the present but concentrate on the future."
— JAMES HAYES

Definition

Establishing an organizational standard where managers are expected to see the "big picture." Ensuring that managers understand the long-term impact of their decisions. Adjusting the focus of managers from a tactical (departmental) view, to a broader, company-wide perspective.

Areas of Focus

- Tactical and strategic skills among managers are equally emphasized.
- Line managers understand the "Big Picture."
- Managers understand the broader implications of their decisions.
- Managers can effectively communicate the company's strategic plan to their staff.

Leadership and management are often an exercise in balance. Allocating limited resources such as time, personnel, budgets, and equipment always involves weighing one priority over the next. Balancing time and energy between establishing and reviewing the strategic intent of the organization with implementation is difficult. Too much attention to the day-to-day concerns causes managers to become disillusioned. Tasks in and of themselves become the focus point. If there is too much concern for people, then the jobs necessary to succeed do not seem to get done. This tradeoff most often falls to middle managers, who share responsibility for contributing to the strategic direction of their department as well as implementing the contribution to the chosen strategy.

The following model (Figure 1) illustrates the number of leadership styles available to managers, depending on concerns for people and for production. An imbalance in these concerns will tend to sway the manager to a less effective style.

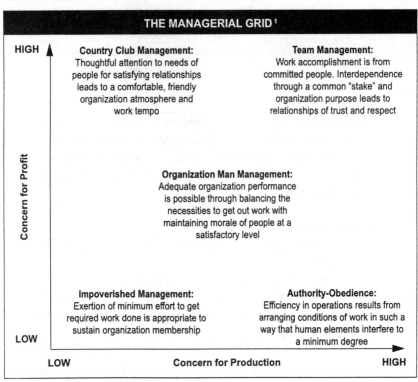

THE MANAGERIAL GRID [1]

HIGH

Country Club Management:
Thoughtful attention to needs of
people for satisfying relationships
leads to a comfortable, friendly
organization atmosphere and
work tempo

Team Management:
Work accomplishment is from
committed people. Interdependence
through a common "stake" and
organization purpose leads to
relationships of trust and respect

Organization Man Management:
Adequate organization performance
is possible through balancing the
necessities to get out work with
maintaining morale of people at a
satisfactory level

Impoverished Management:
Exertion of minimum effort to get
required work done is appropriate to
sustain organization membership

Authority-Obedience:
Efficiency in operations results from
arranging conditions of work in such a
way that human elements interfere to
a minimum degree

LOW

Concern for Profit

LOW   **Concern for Production**   HIGH

Figure 1

Leadership dichotomies and trade-offs such as task versus relationship orientation, individual versus group performance, or strategic versus tactical strategies
make it difficult to establish a single point of reference for decision-making.

Oftentimes, policies can serve as guidelines for decisions. By defining allow-
able discretion in making decisions, policies provide the strategic perspective some
employees need to keep their tactical decisions aligned with the company's strategic intent.

The following list summarizes the way policies help managers keep their strategic perspective while managing day-to-day operations:[2]

- Policies establish indirect control over independent action by clearly
  stating how things are to be done now. By defining discretion, policies in effect control decisions yet empower employee to conduct
  activities without direct intervention by top management.

- Policies promote uniform handling of similar activities. This facilitates the coordination of work tasks and helps reduce friction arising from favoritism, discrimination, and bias.

- Policies ensure quicker decisions by standardizing responses to previously encountered situations freeing management to focus on new situations.

- Policies institutionalize basic aspects of organization behavior. This minimizes conflicting practices and establishes consistent patterns of actions in implementing strategy.

- Policies reduce uncertainty in repetitive and day-to-day decision-making, providing a necessary foundation for strategically aligned efforts.

- Policies counteract resistance to or rejection of chosen strategies by organization members. When strategic change is undertaken, policies can clarify what is expected to translate intent into action.

- Policies afford managers a mechanism for avoiding hasty and ill-conceived decisions in changing operations. Strategic alignment within policies can keep firms from making emotionally charge reactive decisions and altering practices without a strategic perspective.

Well-written policies encourage all members of the organization to retain the strategic intent and reasoning behind day-to-day tasks. Policies can help maintain the balance between day-to-day performance and the strategies that give them meaning. Policies can ease communication and serve as reference points for performance.

Operating without periodic strategic reference checks has been likened to the frog that swims around a pot of lukewarm water that is slowly being brought to a boil. The frog fails to notice the gradual warming and for all his potential to take appropriate action, ends up being boiled. Too much focus on accomplishing the task, without a larger strategic view of why, will often lead to accomplishing very well the wrong things, in terms of strategic value.

Too often, complacency can play a big role in not maintaining an adequate balance between strategic and tactical imperatives. Too much success, especially when rewarded to the extent that it encourages ignoring any signals of change in the environment, can deceive a company into thinking all is well and an "if it ain't broke, don't fix it" state of being. One researcher suggested "organizations are often poisoned by their success" because they are "unable to unlearn obsolete knowledge in spite of strong disconfirmations." He concluded that "shortages are useful to prevent organizations from dying from wealth."[3]

The key to overcoming complacency and breaking out of functional silos is communicating and establishing a shared vision. With a greater understanding of the overall direction of the company, tasks will become more aligned and the work more efficient.

A shared vision has been compared to a hologram.[4] Each piece of a divided photograph can only reveal a part of the whole subject, but every piece of a hologram, whatever size, can still show the whole image intact. Combined, these pieces will actually intensify the image. Developing shared visions not only empowers the workforce, but it simplifies the task of maintaining balance between short-term actions and long-term consequences.

A group of executives from a *Fortune 500* firm visited Chaparral Steel, one of the most productive steel companies to learn how to manage its teams. One executive asked, "How do you schedule coffee breaks in the plant?" A Chaparral manager replied, "The workers decide when they want a cup of coffee." "Yes," said the executive, "But who tells them it's okay to leave the machines?" As the Chaparral manager commented later, "The guy left and still didn't get it."[5]

The Chaparral workers know when to take a break because they were trained to understand how the whole business operates. They know the "big picture." Once trained in the "Chaparral process," a worker understands how his or her job relates to the welfare of the entire organization. Financial statements are posted monthly in the mill, including a chart tracking operating profits before taxes — the key measure for profit sharing.

Footnotes for Section 3.2.2 —

[1] Robert R. Blake and Jane Srygley Mouton. *Managerial Grid III: The Key to Leadership Excellence.* Gulf Publishing, 1985, p. 15.

[2] John A. Pearce II and Richard B. Robinson. *Strategic Management: Formulation, Implementation, and Control.* Irwin, 1997, p. 322-23.

[3] B. Hedberg. "How Organizations Learn and Unlearn." In *Handbook of Organizational Design,* edited by P. C. Bystrom and W. H. Starbuck, Oxford University, 1981.

[4] Henry Mintzberg and James Brian Quinn. *The Strategy Process.* Prentice-Hall, 1996. p. 419.

[5] Brian Dumaine. "Who Needs a Boss?" Fortune, 7 May 1990, p. 52-60.

3.2.3 EMPOWERMENT

"Authority should go with knowledge, no matter if it is up the line or down the line. Emphasize 'cross-functioning' and replace vertical authority with horizontal authority."
— MARY PARKER FULLER

Definition

Utilizing localized vs. centralized authority, wherever possible. Driving decision-making responsibilities down to the lowest appropriate level in the organization. Minimizing the "red tape" in an organization.

Areas of Focus

- Decisions made without unnecessary or authoritarian approval process.
- Decisions driven to the lowest appropriate level.
- Minimal "red tape."

Many of the same organizational attributes required to develop leadership are also needed to empower employees. These facilitating factors include flatter organizational hierarchies, less bureaucracy, and a greater willingness to take risks.[1] Organizations that thrive in today's intensely competitive marketplaces usually will have flat structures, self-managing workforces, and executives that focus on providing leadership.

Leaders who adopt and utilize participative principles create motivational environments that lead to greater employee satisfaction and ultimately job performance.[2] Employees who experience a greater degree of freedom and autonomy, who are consistently recognized for their contributions, and who are involved in the decision-making process are generally more satisfied than employees who do not experience these approaches.[3]

Yet despite these outcomes many companies fail to effectively remove the barriers to employee empowerment and strategic implementations. These barriers are represented on the next page (Figure 1).

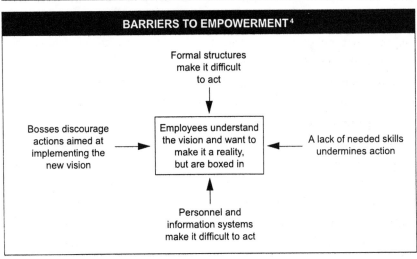

BARRIERS TO EMPOWERMENT [4]

Formal structures make it difficult to act

Bosses discourage actions aimed at implementing the new vision

Employees understand the vision and want to make it a reality, but are boxed in

A lack of needed skills undermines action

Personnel and information systems make it difficult to act

Figure 1

According to change expert John Kotter, there are four key barriers to empowerment:[4]

1. **Structural barriers** can include silos that function independently and thus inhibit communication; layers of middle-level managers who may question or second-guess employee ideas; fragmented resources that make productivity difficult; and corporate headquarters that impose centralized decision-making.

2. **Inadequate training** can inhibit empowerment. Companies must recognize that new behaviors, skills, and attitudes will be needed when major changes are initiated. Without the right skills and attitudes, people feel disempowered. The cost of training is also a deterrent.

3. **Outmoded systems** can block action. Human resource systems like recruitment programs, compensation plans, and performance management programs, as well as company information systems must be properly aligned to support empowerment.

4. **Ineffective bosses** can also undercut empowerment. With the right kind of leadership, companies are finding that they can tap into an enormous source of power to improve organizational performance.

Employees are motivated by a sense of achievement, recognition, enjoyment of the job, responsibility, and the chance for personal growth.[5] Excessive control stifles employee initiative and motivation. Implementation of a strategic plan is best served by a management style that is based on situational leadership practices, where the degree of control or empowerment is determined by the complexity of the task and the skill and maturation of the employee, and not by the personal preferences or habits of the manager. With the right structure, training, systems, and supervision in place, empowered employees can significantly contribute to improving organizational performance.

Tim Firnstahl,[7] who owns a chain of restaurants in and around Seattle, discovered the benefits of aligning systems with empowered employees. Tim's market position and overriding ethic is to provide world class customer service and to make the customer happy. The company motto, We Always Guarantee Satisfaction (WAGS), is a shared rallying cry throughout the organization and the WAGS logo appears on shirts, report forms, menus, nametags, and training manuals.

Some time after opening, however, Tim realized that although employees signed WAGS commitment pledges and were trained on their responsibility to the customer, they had not been taught to make use of their authority to please the customer. The result was finger-pointing and abdication of their role and responsibility.

Employees were given the authority to correct situations with no delay and with no paperwork. Guidelines were established. Employees were instructed to do whatever possible to ensure the guarantee was in effect. The entire tab could be picked up if necessary without penalties. Although skeptical at first, the employees' power as company representatives increased their pride in the business and increased motivation.

Creative solutions began to impress the clientele. When the customer ordered a margarita as it was made at another restaurant, the waiter informed the bartender, who called the other restaurant and got the secret recipe. When an elderly woman who had not been in for a long while ordered breakfast, which was no longer served, the crew went out and bought the required eggs and bacon and prepared the breakfast she wanted.

The end result is that profits are up, and customers always ask Tim where he found such wonderful staff. Tim's reply is that his employees are "better than most, because they have power and the obligation to solve customer problems on their own and on the spot. Giving them complete discretion about how they do it has also given them pride...The people who work for us know we take our guarantee seriously and expect them to do the same."

Footnotes for Section 3.2.3 —

[1] John P. Kotter. *Leading Change*. Harvard Business School, 1996, p. 167.

[2] Lawson K. Savery. "Attitudes to Work: The Influence of Perceived Styles of Leadership on A Group of Workers." Leadership and Development Journal, 15, 1994, p. 17.

[3] Charles C. Manz and Henry P. Sims. *Business Without Bosses*. John Wiley & Sons, 1993.

[4] John P. Kotter. *Leading Change*. Harvard Business School, 1996, p. 102.

[5] Ibid.

[6] John W. Kennish. "Motivating with a Positive, Participatory Policy." Security Management, 38, August 1994, p. 22.

[7] T. W. Firnstahl. "My Employees Are My Service Guarantee." Harvard Business Review, Jul-Aug 1989, p. 28-31, 34.

3.2.4 Developmental Coaching

"The best executive is the one who has enough sense to pick good people to do what he wants done, and self-restraint enough to keep from meddling with them while they do it."

—Theodore Roosevelt

Definition

Integrating employee personal goals with the organization's goals. Using coaching as a motivational tool rather than a punitive process. Encouraging employee initiative. Addressing performance issues in a manner that maintains employee self-esteem. Using positive reinforcement as a means to improve or sustain performance.

Areas of Focus

- Delegation is a motivational tool.
- Coaching is viewed as developmental vs. punitive.
- Managers encourage initiative.
- Employee goals/aspirations are taken into consideration.
- Managers take the time to recognize a job well done.

In leadership mythology, leaders are expected to have all the answers, to light the way for others, to balance effectively their personal world and their workload, and to do it 24 hours a day. In reality, leaders are human like those they lead, but often when the spotlight supporting these myths is placed on them too long, an atmosphere of over-dependence develops, and the entire department or unit looks toward the leader for all of its direction.

The strength of the entire group becomes limited by the human leader's abilities, skill sets, and knowledge. Creativity, innovation, and management become the sole responsibility of the leader and not the members of the group. Such abdication of stewardship by members of the group is further fueled by the leader's need to take credit for the progress of the group. The outcome most of the time is the collapse of the group when the manager leaves.[1]

Dramatic trends in empowerment and self-managing work teams are forcing managers to rethink their leadership roles. Enlightened leaders disprove the myths that they are infallible and motivate those in their stewardship to lead themselves, so when the leader departs, the system continues, buoyed up by self-directed followers.

Such empowerment can be instilled in several ways. Managers committed to developing their reports welcome initiative and support risk taking by eliminating the fear of failure. Establishing a safe haven for experimentation leads to innovation, self-reliance, and a most valuable experience.

William McKnight, CEO of the 3M Company from its beginnings in 1914 until he retired in 1966, was a strong advocate for allowing employees to develop their initiative without fear of reprisal: "Mistakes will be made (by giving the freedom and encouragement to act autonomously), but…the mistakes he or she makes are not as serious in the long run as the mistakes management will make if it is dictatorial and undertakes to tell those under its authority exactly how they must do their job. Management that is destructively critical when mistakes are made kills initiative and it's essential that we have many people with initiative if we are to continue to grow."[2]

The following are practical steps to providing people with learning opportunities to develop their capacities.[3]

- *Stop making decisions.* See to it that the people responsible for implementing decisions make them. Make sure they want to make the decisions, want to bear the consequences of them, have the necessary information to make good ones, and have the training to recognize good and bad decision criteria.

- *Stop talking at meetings.* Managers cannot listen if they are talking. One-way communication is the best way to communicate that other people's contribution isn't valuable. The best meetings are those where people are talking to one another, instead of just one person talking to the boss.

- *Set up coaching opportunities.* The chance to learn needs to be coupled with adequate training to support the learning. Putting people in situations to lead with no training and support could be disastrous. Coaching and supporting them while they lead gives people confidence and increases their appetite for more opportunities.

- *Invite people to assume responsibility.* Look for situations to ask employees, "What would you do if you were me?" This approach generates good ideas and introduces employees to the complexities of management decisions. Go one step further by inviting people to implement their workable suggestions. And back them up.

- *Give everyone a customer.* Make certain that whatever people are doing, they have another individual or group in their mind that they are serving. Having a customer focus enlarges people understanding of not only what they do, but also what the company does overall and their relationship to those goals.

- *Have an open house.* Invite your customers, suppliers, and vendors to visit your facilities. Open the guest list to include family, friends, and, neighbors. Let people feel pride and self-esteem by informing significant others about their jobs and why they're important.

- *Share the big picture.* Being given an assignment, budget, or staff without knowing exactly what to produce is like giving pieces of a 1,000-piece jigsaw puzzle to a group and telling them to put it all together since they have everything they need. Sometimes people need to see the picture on the box.

- *Enrich people's jobs.* Make certain that people's jobs are designed so that they know what is expected of them, and provide sufficient training and technical support so people can complete their assignments. Enrich their responsibilities so that they experience a variety in their task assignments and opportunities. Involve them in programs, meetings, and decisions that have direct impact on their job performance.

- *Let people teach.* Peter Drucker points out, "Knowledge workers and service workers learn most when they teach."[4] He finds the best way to improve productivity is to have people instruct their peers and others. School teachers have known this for years. They have older students tutor the younger ones. This way both are enlightened.

- *Use modeling to develop competencies.* First determine the competencies you need to develop and break them down into skill sets and sub-skills. Demonstrate the desired skill or behavior, incorporating many examples. As people perfect their skills, provide feedback, not criticism, to build confidence and fine-tune their skills. Finally, give people the opportunity to practice the new skills in situations where they are likely to produce good results.

As illustrated in Figure 1, before a company can determine which capabilities it should develop, it must first identify the "Key Success Factors" for its industry. Key success factors are fundamental proficiencies that a company must master in order to compete effectively in the market. Once these factors are identified, training programs can be created to develop the necessary skills. Over time, through repetition and continuous learning, these skills become organizational core competencies, providing the company with a distinct competitive advantage that is difficult to replicate.

DEVELOPMENT OF SKILL SETS AND CAPABILITIES			
Industry key success factors dictate required skill sets	**Skill sets and capacities** are developed through training	**Core competencies** are developed over time and continuous learning	**Distinctive competencies** give competitive advantage

Time and experience of the organization →

Figure 1

Footnotes for Section 3.2.4 —

[1] Jeffrey Sonnenfeld. *The Hero's Farewell: What Happens When CEOs Retire.* Oxford University, 1988.

[2] *Our Story So Far.* 3M Company, 1977.

[3] James M. Kouzes and Barry Z. Posner. *Credibility: How Leaders Gain and Lose It, Why People Demand It.* Jossey-Bass, 1993, p. 176-182.

[4] Peter F. Drucker. "The New Productivity Challenge." Harvard Business Review, 69(6), Nov-Dec 1991, p. 69-79.

3.2.5 BUILDING EFFECTIVE TEAMS

"In hierarchical organizations, bosses don't do much...They just preside and take all the credit. It's criminal. A lot of good...people are buried down there, and their bosses are happy to keep them buried."
—MICHAEL H. WALSH

Definition

Rewarding cooperation and collaboration. Understanding group dynamics. Leading meetings with diverse personality types. Generating team enthusiasm, loyalty, and commitment.

Areas of Focus

- Managers promote teamwork.
- Team participants are excited about and committed to their goals and objectives.
- Cross-functional communication is promoted.
- Meetings are well-planned and highly participative.

Katzenbach and Smith, consultants at McKinsey & Company, define teams as "a small number of people with complementary skills who are committed to a common purpose, performance goals, and approach for which they hold themselves accountable."[1] It is important to note that while this definition is broad, it is descriptive of teams rather than groups.

All teams are groups, but not all groups can be classified as teams. The key to differentiating a team from a group is in the unit's performance. Group performance can be defined simply as the sum of individual efforts within the group. A team's performance, however, is related to the synergistic efforts of all the individuals combined in pursuit of a common objective. In the best working groups, individuals can labor next to one another in mutual support, but the focus is always on individual accomplishments and accountability. The notion of team is reached when each individual shares the accountability and performance goals of the unit and puts the efforts and success of the team ahead of his or her own.

This esprit de corps is not established easily or quickly. Initially, team members focus on strategy or on problems, running the risk of ignoring relationship issues. By the time relationship problems begin to surface, and they almost always do, the group may be unable to deal with them effectively, and performance suffers. In order to combat these tendencies, most new groups engage in some form of team-building exercises during early formation. The following diagram (Figure 1) illustrates the evolution process of a group into a team.

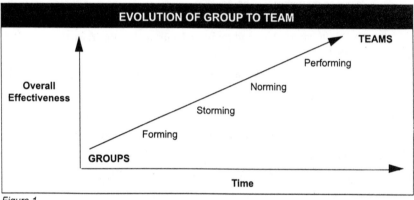

Figure 1

During the forming stage groups attempt to define their tasks and decide how to accomplish them. They also sort out how the various group members will relate to each other. During the storming stage, members begin to sense what it will take to work together as a team. Posturing and "choosing sides" goes on, eventually establishing a "pecking order" within the group. In norming, members accept the fact that they must work as a team, reconcile competing loyalties, and establish ground rules or norms by which the team members will cooperate. In the performing stage, the group has settled relationships and validated expectations and can turn to work for which they are mutually responsible. At this stage the team is capable of more work in concert than the sum of their individual efforts would have produced.[2]

The transition to self-managing teams is at least as challenging for the managers as for the team members. Managers are likely to experience four stages:[3]

1. Initial suspicion, uncertainty, and resistance. The move to teams is frequently viewed as an indication of ineffectiveness in the

manager's previous behavior. Also teams are seen as benefiting someone else (e.g. the consultant) and ultimately destined to fail.

2. Gradual realization of the positive possibilities and benefits offered by self-directed teams. Employee development of empathy for the customer, constructive peer pressure within teams, and freed up managerial time for developing key people.

3. Understanding of their new leadership role. Struggle with questions as, "What is a facilitator?" "How does self-management influence managerial behavior?"

4. Learning a new language. Managers identify and develop the verbal skills, vocabulary, and communication scripts that form the core of their new leadership role.

Building successful teams requires patience, time, and continuous effort. Training and learning opportunities need to be established for team members as well as managers to help them through the transition to their new leadership roles.

Thermos[4] used teams effectively to recover their ailing grilling products unit. The $225 million division depended largely on its grilling products for a significant portion of its sales. The markets for these products went flat and the entire industry began to cut prices to almost commodity levels.

The bureaucratic functional structure at Thermos seemed unable to respond to this crisis. CEO Monte Peterson formed a cross-functional team to develop new products and bring them to market. After the initial resistance, the team evolved to design, build, market, and sell a series of revolutionary grills. The products won four design awards and boosted Thermos' market share from 2 percent to 20 percent.

The following is a list of characteristics of effective teams:[5]

- The members of the team are loyal to its members including the leader.

- The member and leaders have a high degree of confidence and trust in each other.

- The values and goals of the team are a synergistic list of relevant values and needs of its members.

- All the interaction and problem-solving activities of the team are done in a supportive atmosphere. Suggestions, criticisms, ideas, comments are offered with a helpful orientation.

- The team is eager to help members develop to their full potential.

- Each member of the team communicates fully and frankly.
- Members of the team feel secure in making decisions that seem appropriate.

Footnotes for Section 3.2.5 —

[1] Jon R. Katzenbach and Douglas K. Smith. *The Wisdom of Teams*. Harvard Business School, 1992, p. 112.

[2] Peter R. Scholtes. *The Team Handbook*. Joiner Associates, 1988.

[3] Charles C. Manz and Henry P. Sims. *Business Without Bosses*. John Wiley & Sons, 1993, p. 40.

[4] Brian Dumaine. "Payoff from the New Management." Fortune, 13 Dec 1993, p. 103-110 — Fara Warner. "Message in a Bottle: Thermos Updates Its Image." Brandweek, 35, 31 Jan 1994, p. 32.

[5] Excerpted from Rensis Likert. *New Patterns of Management*. McGraw-Hill, 1961, p. 166-169.

3.3.0 Human Resources Systems

"For long-term success, we need to attract and retain the best people in the industry. To do that, we must create a company in which everyone can contribute his or her best, in which everyone is valued, regardless of differences." — Andrea Zintz

Description

Deals with attracting and maintaining skilled employees. Human resources systems define how a company recruits, trains, challenges, and inspires its employees in the pursuit of its strategic intent.

Principal Elements

- Selective Recruitment
- Employee Orientation
- Continuous Learning
- Performance Management
- Reward Systems

One area consistently identified as critical to an organization's success is its ability to manage its human resources.[1] Changes in the way this system is managed are both facilitated and required by changes made in other parts of the organization.[2]

The aggressive and adversarial approach to managing human resources, getting the most performance for the lowest wages and benefits, is giving way to a recognition that the workforce can be a source of competitive advantage.[3]

Texas Instruments, as part of a company-wide quality improvement effort, implemented a pilot program calling for each and every one of its employees to come up with ideas for improvement, and then to implement them.[4] They were not required to justify their ideas in terms of cost savings in order to implement them. In one plant in the program, over 60 percent of the workforce had implemented ten or more ideas for better performance.

While only half of the 7,000 ideas implemented were tied to actual cost savings, those that were provided more than $7 million of additional profits. The significance of this program was that the $7 million was for half the ideas in one plant in just one year. TI has more than 50 plants company-wide.

This new attitude towards employees is changing the way organizations manage their human resources. Some of the traditional and emerging trends are listed in Figure 1 below:

TRADITIONAL AND EMERGING IDEAS OF HUMAN RESOURCE MANAGEMENT [5]	
Traditional	*Emerging*
Emphasis solely on physical skills	Emphasis on total contribution to the firm
Expectation of predictable, repetitious behavior	Expectation of innovative and creative behavior
Comfort with stability and conformity	Tolerance of ambiguity and change
Avoidance of responsibility and decision making	Accepting responsibility for making decisions
Training covering only specific tasks	Open-ended commitment: broad, continuous development
Emphasis placed on outcomes and results	Emphasis placed on processes and means
High concern for quantity and throughput	High concern for total customer value
Concern for individual efficiency	Concern for overall effectiveness
Functional and subfunctional specialization	Cross-functional integration
Labor force seen as a necessary expense	Labor force seen as critical investment
Workforce is management's adversary	Management and workforce are partners
Evaluation and rewards focused narrowly on work output	Evaluation and rewards defined broadly, depending on strategy

Figure 1

The Human Resource value chain can be broken down into five components:

- **Selective Recruitment** is a process that screens available candidates to evaluate both their skills and compatibility with the organizational culture.

- **Employee Orientation** provides a forum to communicate the strategic intent of the company firsthand to new recruits. During the orientation, values and beliefs can be clarified and emphasized.

- **Continuous Learning** involves developing the capacity and competency of the workforce, in alignment with critical strategic goals, in order to achieve and maintain a competitive advantage. Succession planning is also a part of this process.

- **Performance Management** evaluates the quality of the skills and behaviors of the workforce relative to strategic intent. Performance standards should focus on behaviors and skills that are required for successful strategic implementation.

- **Reward Systems** must be designed to incent strategically important skills and behaviors. Rewards must be fair and impartial and must be worthy of the effort expended to achieve them.

Organizations stand little chance of success in implementing their strategies without first possessing the skill sets required to do so. Companies can accumulate talent in two ways. They can recruit it, or they can develop it. George Moore, President of Citicorp from 1959 until 1967, focused first and foremost on making Citicorp an institution built largely around procedures for finding, training, and promoting personnel. He sums up the mission and role of aligned human resource systems: "Without the capable people these procedures developed, none of our goals would have been attainable."[6]

Footnotes for Section 3.3.0 —

[1] C. A. Lengnick-Hall and M.I. Lengnick-Hall. "Strategic Human Resource Management: A Review of the Literature and a Proposed Typology." Academy of Management Review, Jul 1988, p. 454-470 — L. Baird and I. Meshoulam. "Managing Two Fits of Strategic Human Resource Management Practices." Academy of Management Executive, Aug 1987, p. 207-219.

[2] R. H. Killman. *Beyond the Quick Fix: Managing Five Tracks to Organizational Success.* Jossey-Bass, 1984.

[3] D. Ulrich and D. Lake. "Organizational Capability: Creating Competitive Advantage." Academy of Management Executive, 5, 1991, p. 77-92.

[4] A. Smith. "The 'People Factor' in Competitive Advantage." Academy of Management Executive, 5, 1991, p. 77-92.

[5] Alex Miller. *Strategic Management.* Irwin McGraw-Hill, 1998, p. 400.

[6] James C. Collins and Jerry I. Porras. *Built to Last.* Harper Collins, 1994.

3.3.1 SELECTIVE RECRUITMENT

"Eagles don't flock. You have to find them one at a time."

— ROSS PEROT

Definition

Implementing targeted recruitment and selection programs. Establishing a skills and attributes profile to help determine whether or not an individual would be conducive to the company culture. Developing manager interviewing skills. Utilizing input from boss, peers, and subordinates when considering potential candidates.

Areas of Focus

- Only high-caliber candidates are considered.
- Candidate compatibility with company culture is carefully considered.
- Interviewing skills are a company strength.
- Boss and peer input is required on critical hires.
- Managers evaluated on their ability to recruit top talent.

An organization's recruitment and hiring programs are essential for reinforcing and sustaining distinctive competencies, shared values, and strategies. Effective recruiting means more that just hiring the highest skilled talent. It means hiring the most *suitable* talent. A company must be careful to select candidates who not only possess the right technical skill sets, but who are compatible with and can flourish in the work environments created by the firm's culture, structure, and strategic intent.

Because past success is no longer a good indicator of a candidate's ability to perform in some cultures, companies must develop new criteria of choosing those most likely to succeed. In light of the technically dynamic markets of today, some of the criteria might include the ability to think critically, learn quickly and adapt to change.

Using selection criteria that emphasize soft skills as well as hard technical and analytical skills will ensure the organization has long-term resources to draw upon for future needs. Potential for teamwork, high customer service orientation, and curiosity are traits that might deserve parity in the selection process.

Some have argued that assessing these soft skills is difficult and, while agreeing that the criteria is indeed relevant, fail to give soft skills a significant role in the hiring decision. However, some companies have developed competencies in judging an applicant's potential courtesy or teamwork skills equal to their ability to assessing mathematical, accounting, or computer skills. For these companies, it has been a matter of painstakingly isolating those traits by asking pointed questions and probing inclinations and past behaviors.

Tom Melohn, co-owner of North American Tool & Die,[1] interviewed several applicants for a clerical position. Most applicants began by asking about tasks, money, hours, and other mechanics. The one he hired, however, asked questions about procedures, approaches, and the nature of the business. She was also able to handle complex tasks and seemed genuinely interested at the end of the (trial) half day.

By using selective methods to screen applicants, the dangers of asking potentially illegal or discriminatory questions (Figure 1) is greatly reduced as applicants tend to eliminate themselves from the application process.

COMMON UNLAWFUL* INTERVIEW QUESTIONS	
What is your maiden name?	Have you ever worked under another name?
Are you married?	Have you ever been refused a fidelity bond?
Where we you born?	Have you ever had your wages garnished?
Do you have proof of your age?	How tall are you?
List organizations to which you belong?	How much do you weigh?
Please supply a list of three relatives	Have you ever been arrested?
Do you have any children?	What's your wife's maiden name?
Do you own a home?	What is the lowest salary you would accept?
What kind of work does your spouse do?	What relative do we notify in case of emergency?
Are you pregnant?	What religion are you?
Do you have a photo of yourself?	

* These are typical interview questions that could be reasonably construed to be discriminatory unless the employer had a very good and statistically valid reason for asking them.

Figure 1

Before filling out an application, potential recruits at Disney are required to view a video, "Backstage," that outlines the company's dedication to its ideals of fun, fantasy, and entertainment. Grooming standards are explained along with the work ethic, attitude, and self-image. The message is strong enough that twenty percent of the applicants disqualify themselves.[2]

Southwest Airlines goes to considerable lengths to hire people who can have fun and be fun on the job. Southwest uses specially developed methods, including interviews with customers, to determine whether applicants for customer contact jobs have outgoing personality traits that match its strategy of creating a high-spirited, fun-loving, in-flight atmosphere for passengers and going all-out to make flying Southwest a pleasant experience. The company has been so selective that only about 3 percent of the candidates interviewed are offered jobs.[3]

The intense recruiting processes of these and other successful companies works for two reasons. First, a lengthy set of interviews unmistakably demonstrates that the firm cares enough about the candidate and the working environment to get people at all levels deeply involved in recruitment. Those who are hired start with key values learned from the recruiting process itself. Since these organizations live their values so completely and openly, if the candidate is uncomfortable with the culture during a lengthy courtship, he or she will drop out on his or her own.

Second, the heavy investment of time by line managers and peers puts the responsibility of matching the candidate to strategic requirements squarely on them. Their judgment, not the professionals in the human relations department, is on the line.

Having those managers who are in need of the staffing resource interview and hire their own candidate makes sense, especially for key management positions. Management's confidence level in having the right manager assigned to mission critical positions is a function of the level of management's expectation that the candidates can implement the strategic initiatives.

One practical consideration in filling key roles and assignments that have emerged from a new strategy is whether to promote candidates from within or hire new personnel. The table on the next page (Figure 2) highlights the key advantage and disadvantage of each of these alternatives.

USING EXISTING EXECUTIVES vs. BRINGING IN OUTSIDERS IN MANAGERIAL ASSIGNMENT TO IMPLEMENT A NEW STRATEGY [4]		
	Advantages	**Disadvantages**
Using existing executives to implement a strategy	Existing executives already know key people, practices, and conditions. Personal qualities of existing executives are better known and understood by associates. Existing executives have established relationships with peers, subordinates, suppliers, buyers, et al. Use of existing executives symbolizes organizational commitment to individual careers.	Existing executives are less adaptable to major strategic changes because of their knowledge, attitudes, and values. Past commitments of existing executives hamper the hard decisions required in executing a new strategy. Existing executives have less ability to become inspired and credibly convey the need for change.
Bringing in outsiders to implement a new strategy	Outsiders may already believe in and have "lived" the new strategy. Outsiders are unencumbered by internal commitments to people. Outsiders come to new assignment with heightened commitment and enthusiasm. Bringing in outsiders can send powerful signals throughout the organization that change is expected.	Bringing in outsiders often is costly in terms of both compensation and "learning –to-work-together" time. Candidates suitable in all respects may not be available, leading to compromise choices. Uncertainty exists in selecting the right outsiders to bring in. "Morale costs" are incurred when an outsider takes a job that several insiders want. The "what to do with poor ol' fred" problem arises when outsiders are brought in.

Figure 2

Finally, the new trends in empowerment and self-managed work teams give managers new challenges in workloads and leadership. Skill sets such as coaching, electronic data communication, and having a results orientation should be part of the selection criteria.

Footnotes for Section 3.3.1 —

[1] Tom Peters. *Thriving on Chaos*. Knopf, 1988, p. 316.

[2] "Selecting the Best: Casting for a Role in Our Show." Walt Disney World workshop in interviewing, p. 35.

[3] James L. Gibson, John M. Ivancevich, and James H. Donnelly, Jr. *Organizations: Behavior, Structure, Processes*. Irwin, 2000, p. 84.

[4] John A. Pearce II and Richard B. Robinson. *Strategic Management: Formulation, Implementation, and Control*. Irwin, 1997, p. 356.

3.3.2 Employee Orientation

> *"Yesterday's idea of the boss, who became the boss because he or she knew one more fact than the person working for them, is yesterday's manager. Tomorrow's person needs to envision a shared set of values, a shared objective."* — Jack Welsh

Definition

Getting new employees off to a good start. Designing orientation programs that create enthusiasm and excitement. The impact of senior management involvement. Establishing follow-up and support activities, particularly during the employee's first year.

Areas of Focus

- Company provides a comprehensive orientation program.
- Values and beliefs are underscored.
- Senior managers participate in the process.

Once a recruit is hired, an organization must effectively acclimate the new employee to the organization's culture. Since each employee is hired to contribute specifically to the achievement of the company's strategic intent, orientation should include an overview of the firm's vision, an explanation of each major division's contributes to the intent of the firm, and how each employee will participate in the organization's success.

The two-day orientation at Disney is often celebrated as a case study in establishing shared values from the beginning of an employees career. At Disney, every new hire, including the summer "ninety-day" employee goes to "Disney Traditions." The list of attendees includes vice presidents, popcorn vendors, and housekeepers, who all share seats in the classroom.

Class size is held to forty and rank is unrecognized at the Disney Institute. Everyone wears a nametag with only their first name on it. The only special people, they are told, are the guests. Split into smaller groups, the rookies are taken into the Magic Kingdom to observe veterans working at their posts. Occasionally one of the veterans will give a scenario to a rookie and ask how they would respond. The goal is to get their people connected and comfortable as soon as possible.[1]

During this process, new hires learn Disney's four cardinal principles of guest relations — safety, courtesy, show, and efficiency — which together provide a framework for all decisions made in the operating areas. Faced with a dilemma of conflicting values safety always comes first.

After their orientation, new hires begin to work at their assigned locations. They meet their supervisors as well as their Disney Qualified Trainer, a veteran at the same job always available to answer questions. With an outline and a checklist, new employees start training programs of various lengths, monitored by human resources managers to ensure a smooth transition.

Disney is perhaps mentioned most often when discussing employee orientation, because they pay attention to the culture symbols and artifacts that communicate the high ideals that Walt Disney, himself, established when he opened for business.

Another case study in employee orientation is General Electric's Crotonville Management Development Institute in Ossining, New York. The thirty-one-year-old institute spreads Chairman Jack Welch's vision of the company to over 2,500 new MBA recruits per year, who stay for a two-and-a- half day orientation.

The institute offers continuous learning to senior and middle management in such areas as team building and leadership. The institute's motto reads, "To make GE managers more action-oriented, more risk-oriented, more people-oriented."

It is through intensive orientation programs such as these two examples that employees get acquainted with the core values of the firm. In addition to gaining insight into the overall strategic intent of the organization, the new hires are taught their personal role and responsibility and, just as important as the tactical to-do list, the relationship between their duties and the company's overall success.

It is important to note that in successful orientation programs, senior management communicates their support of the things being taught by their personal presence and or endorsement.

Some guiding principles of a good orientation program:

- Invest in human capital as much as in hardware.[2]
- Use orientation as a vehicle for building trust.

- Train everyone in problem-solving techniques to contribute to quality, however defined, and performance improvement.

- Connect the individual's role and responsibility with the success of the organization.

- Train new hires in specific skills that are needed for strategic implementation.

Finally, a Stanford MBA who spent a summer at Disney doing financial analysis, strategic planning, and other similar work described his experience at the Disney Traditions class:[3]

> I recognized the magic of Walt's vision on my first day at the Walt Disney Company…At Disney University, through videos and "pixie dust," Walt shared his dream and the magic of Disney's "world." Disney archives treasure Walt's history for cast members to enjoy. After orientation, I stopped at the corner of Mickey Avenue and Dopey Drive — I felt the magic, the sentimentality, the history. I believed in Walt's dream and shared this belief with others in the organization.

Footnotes for Section 3.3.2 —

[1] Robert Hiebler, Thomas B. Kelly, and Charles Ketteman. *Best Practices: Building Your Business with Customer-Focused Solutions*. Simon & Schuster, 1998, p. 195.

[2] Tom Peters. *Thriving on Chaos*. Knopf, 1988, p. 322.

[3] Student paper on Walt Disney, Stanford University.

3.3.3 CONTINUOUS LEARNING

"How can your company grow if your people don't?"
— JOHAN BEECKMANS

Definition

Providing training and development opportunities to managers and employees. Ensuring that educational programs are high-quality and that they are aligned with the company's strategy and key objectives. Establishing educational policies and standards. Succession planning criteria and process are fully developed.

Areas of Focus

- Training is a company priority.
- Employees are provided with necessary training to perform at optimum levels.
- Training programs aligned with strategic goals.
- Training programs are well designed and structured.
- Company spends strategically proportionate amount of money on training.
- Succession planning is carefully designed.

Organizations have a two-fold training mission — first, to train employees in specific skill sets required for the effective performance of their duties, and second, to develop employees over the long-term to qualify for advancement along their careers.

The most successful development efforts have a three-part mission that extends beyond ordinary skill set enhancement into the management fields of shared vision, capability nurturing, and developing contacts and shape management relationships.[1]

In Matsushita's management development program, called "cultural and spiritual training," trainees study the company credo, the "Seven Spirits of Matsushita" and the founding philosophy of Konosuke Matsushita. Then they learn to translate these internalized lessons into daily behavior and even operational decisions.

The second objective, broadening management perspective, opens up the possibilities to managers of nontraditional structures, strategies, and an adaptive cultures.

The third aim of good development is often accomplished as a by-product of meeting together for training. Managers not only get the vision and values indoctrination, they can develop personal relationships and informal contacts that often are more powerful than formal systems and structure within the organization.

Most successful companies invest aggressively in employee training and professional development programs. Merck, 3M, P&G, Motorola, GE, Disney, Marriott, and IBM all made significant investments in company "universities" and "educational centers". Motorola, for example, targets forty hours of training per employee per year and requires that every division spend 1.5 percent of payroll on training.[2] By the early 1970s, Marriott was spending up to 5 percent of pretax profits on management development.

Such formalized training program requires a firm commitment from management. Training can not only be expensive in terms of dollars spent but also in time. Training classes may require employees to be off the job for days, weeks, or more. Organizations must see the long-term value in educating its people when planning regular training opportunities in light of these obstacles. Sometimes a critical strategic initiative can provide the impetus for that commitment.

From 1976 to 1982, Xerox saw their market share in the copier business shrink from 80% to 13%, due in part to the encroachment of higher quality, lower cost machines from Japan. The company implemented a now-famous quality improvement program that eventually won them the Malcolm Baldridge Award.

This program provided six full days of training for each of the company's more than one hundred thousand employees, took four years to complete, and cost millions of dollars. Why did Xerox decide to make this huge investment in time and money? They estimated that the problems associated with the lack of quality were costing the company $1.4 billion dollars a year.[3]

Training is developmental when employee career goals are taken into consideration. Stephen Covey asserts that employees want to make a meaningful contribution. He contends that companies who want to get the highest level of performance from their employees must first see them as more than just resources or assets. Covey maintains that employees are "spiritual beings," not just economic or social beings, and that they want meaning, a sense of doing something that matters.[4] For these reasons, both corporate needs and employee aspirations should be considered when designing training programs (Figure 1).

ELEMENTS OF A SUCCESSFUL TRAINING PROGRAM [5]
1. Extensive entry-level training that focuses on exactly the skills the firm wants to be distinctive.
2. All employees are treated as potential career employees.
3. Regular retraining is required.
4. Both time and money are generously expanded.
5. On-the-job training counts too.
6. There are no limits to the skills that can profitably be taught to everyone.
7. Training is used to herald a commitment to a new strategic intent.
8. Training is emphasized at a time of crisis.
9. All training is line-driven,
10. Training is used to teach the organization's vision and values.

Figure 1

Footnotes for Section 3.3.3 —

[1] Henry Mintzberg and James Brian Quinn. *The Strategy Process*. Prentice-Hall, 1996. p. 379.

[2] James C. Collins and Jerry I. Porras. *Built to Last*. Harper Collins, 1994, p. 197.

[3] David T. Kearns and David A. Nadler. *Prophets in the Dark — How Xerox Reinvented Itself and Beat Back the Japanese*. Harper-Collins, 1992.

[4] Stephen R. Covey. *Principle-Centered Leadership*. Simon and Schuster, 1991.

[5] Tom Peters. *Thriving on Chaos*. Knopf, 1988, p. 326.

3.3.4 PERFORMANCE MANAGEMENT

"Good management consists in showing average people how to do the work of superior people."

— JOHN D. ROCKEFELLER

Definition

Having a well-designed performance management system. Establishing clear, results-oriented goals. Using a participative goal-setting approach. Establishing rewards and consequences. Using performance tracking and feedback methods. Conducting comprehensive, well-substantiated performance reviews. Using interim performance review sessions to maintain/correct performance.

Areas of Focus

- Performance management system is results-oriented.
- Goals are challenging, but realistic.
- Accountabilities and timelines are clear.
- Interim performance reviews are standard practice.
- Performance evaluations are comprehensive and well-substantiated.

The glue that holds all human resource systems together is the performance management process that is used to gauge a company's incremental progress towards achieving its strategic intent. Through this process, managers take accountability for their contribution to the strategic intent.

The first step in creating a strategy-supportive system of rewards and incentives is to define jobs and assignments in terms of the desired outcomes and not the duties and functions to be performed. Placing emphasis on deliverables rather than time spent or resources used increases the chance of achieving the strategic intent of the position and the subsequent organization.

It is foolish to expect task performance to automatically achieve established goals and objectives. Working hard, staying busy, and diligently performing assigned tasks does not guarantee results. Stressing what to accomplish instead of what to do, performance management systems focus the attention of the worker on intended outcomes rather than just showing up for work.

By regularly tracking actual outcomes against targeted performance, managers can proactively concentrate on making the right things happen rather than on closely supervising people in hopes that the right outcomes will materialize, simply by doing everything according to the employee handbook.

The danger of assessing duty, actions, and hoping for desired outcomes is that unintended consequences may result from some otherwise proactive intents and actions. Figure 1 below lists some of these unintended outcomes:

EXAMPLES OF UNINTENDED CONSEQUENCES [1]		
Intended Consequence	**Measure**	**Potential Unintended Consequence**
Sustained levels of innovation and growth	Sales of new products	Lack of attention to and early abandonment of older products leads to sales decline
Focused attention to market standing relative to the competition	Growth in market share	Increasingly narrow definition of the market, leading the organizations to ignore valuable market segments
Lowering labor costs	Employee turnover	Workforce ages, and this drives up health care costs
Improved level of stockholder value	Cash flow from operations	Managers consistently underinvest in order to conserve cash in the short run, weakening the value of the company
Improved working capital productivity and cash flow	Accounts receivable turnover	Heavy-handed collections techniques drive off customers and lower future sales, limiting future cash flow
Improved competitiveness through speed	Cycle time for new product development	Corners are cut, leading to massive returns, huge warranty costs
Increased earning potential	Sales growth	Sales force accepts orders at levels too low to allow a profit
Expansion of quality improvement efforts	Number of active quality improvement teams	Numerous shell teams are created, making a mockery out of the quality program and damaging morale
Performance of the order fulfillment process	Number of inventory stock outs	Overstocking drives up inventory costs, making the order fulfillment process less competitive
Lowered production costs	Cost variance reports	Fear of not meeting standard costs limits experimentation, and costs fail to improve significantly

Figure 1

Aligning the achievement of the strategic intent of the organization with work assignments requires identifying the strategic and financial goals of the firm as a basis for incentive compensation.[2] If the details of the strategic intent have been integrated from the top layer down to the operating level, appropriate performance measures can be developed. These become targets that implementers focus on and the basis for allocating resources such as jobs, skills, funding, and a timeframe to achieve them.

Usually a number of performance measures should be in place at each level, as shown in Figure 2:

SOME PERFORMANCE MEASURES AT DIFFERENT LEVELS OF THE ORGANIZATION	
Level	**Measures**
Corporate	Profitability measures Sales and earnings growth Market share Product quality Customer satisfaction Improved market position
Manufacturing	Unit manufacturing costs Employee productivity Production and shipping schedules Defect rates Number or extent of work stoppages
Marketing	Unit selling costs Dollar sales and unit volume Sales penetration of each target segment Market share New product success Customer complaints Advertising effectiveness
Subjective	Employee morale Customer satisfaction Advertising success Relative position on quality, service and technological capability

Figure 2

In summary, the steps to establishing a performance measurement system are as follows:

1. Determine key outcomes.

2. Identify the cross-functional processes that produce the key outcomes.

3. Identify the critical activities and capabilities required to carry out the processes.

4. Develop a means of tracking performance on the activities and capability.

Footnotes for Section 3.3.4 —

[1] Alex Miller. *Strategic Management*. Irwin McGraw-Hill, 1998, p. 414.

[2] A. A. Thompson and A. J. Strickland. *Crafting and Implementing Strategy*. Irwin, 1995, p. 278.

3.3.5 REWARD SYSTEMS

"If you talk about change but don't change the reward and recognition system, nothing changes." — PAUL ALLAIRE

Definition

Effectively rewarding the skills and contributions that advance a company's strategic intent. Ensuring that rewards are fair and proportionate to employee effort. Team performance is rewarded at a level that is equal to or greater than individual performance.

Areas of Focus

- Appropriate skills and behaviors are being rewarded.
- Rewards are fair and equitable.
- Rewards are worth the effort.
- Promotions are deserved.
- Team performance is rewarded (greater than or equal to individual performance).
- No reward for achievement at the expense of others.
- Reward programs are monitored for effectiveness.

The execution of strategy ultimately depends on individuals within an organization. Organizations strive to control employee behavior by linking rewards to their performance management system. An organization must decide which behaviors it wishes to reward, adopt a control system to measure those behaviors, and link the rewards to them. The incentive structure is a vital element in an organization's strategic process, because, properly designed, it will positively affect the norms, values, culture, as well as the performance behavior of everyone in the organization.

For example, top managers that are rewarded with stock options may be more entrepreneurial and more concerned with increasing efficiency, quality, and innovation than those who lack this reward.

On the other hand, rewarding the wrong behavior while hoping for a positive outcome is shortsighted and foolish. A large furniture company learned this lesson the hard way. After establishing a good customer base, the company desired to increase its sales revenues. Rewarding the sales staff for every increased sales transaction soon led the firm to higher sales, but drove the company into bankruptcy. With rewards based on sales, all efforts had focused on the transaction. Sales staff were quick to finance sales transactions in the quest for numbers. Little attention was paid to cash flow and profitability. The overriding assumption was more sales, more money. However, after a few months of loaning short and offering long-term financing, the firm's cash reserves dried up and they were out of business.

So identifying, motivating, and rewarding strategically aligned behavior by individuals and groups is key to successful strategy implementation. If the achievement of the firm's strategic intent is top priority, then the reward system should reflect it.

Designers of the firm's reward system utilize many reward mechanisms - compensation, raises, bonuses, stock options, incentives, benefits, promotions, demotions, recognition, praise and criticism, group norms, performance appraisal, tension and fear.

The challenge for reward system designers is to create one that energizes every person in the organization. Managers at every level can improve the effectiveness of their reward system by following these nine guidelines:[1]

1. **Link rewards tightly to the strategic plan.** Rewards linked to the accomplishment of strategic objectives, milestones, completion of key projects, or actions that sustain competitive advantage keep people energized and focused on the right things and on doing them right.

2. **Use variable incentives and make them a major part of everyone's compensation.** If a significant portion of a person's compensation (20 to 60 percent) varies with performance, then a person should be inclined to perform well. This guideline can backfire if the reward system is not fair, not understood, or not consistent with the next guideline.

3. **Rewards and incentives must be linked to an individual's job and the outcomes the individual can personally effect.** People are more accepting of incentive programs when they feel that they control those things being measured.

4. **Reward performance and link value to success, rather than to a position in the organizational hierarchy.** While seniority has its

place, and positions of responsibility often correlate with contribution to results, progressive managers are focusing on the skill sets and expertise essential for success.

5. **Reward everyone and be sensitive to discrepancies between the top and bottom of the organization.** Incentive-based systems should include programs wherein every member of the firm participates in some fashion. And while varying skill sets, responsibilities, and roles must be recognized with different rewards, extremely high rewards out of sync with everyone else can erode confidence and commitment.

6. **Be scrupulously fair, accurate, and informative.** Reward systems that are perceived to be fair work better than those that are not. Accurate measurements of the outcomes triggering the rewards play a key role in perceived fairness.

7. **Reward generously when successful; minimally when not.** Reward systems that reinforce success do just that. Systems that reward with no link to performance can send a message that effort does not matter.

8. **Don't underestimate the value of a rewarding and motivational environment.** While cash, stock, and perks get people's attention, a motivating environment is a very important part of any effective reward system. Increased responsibility, autonomy, recognition, and opportunity for growth are all proven "rewards" that motivate people.

9. **Be open to changing the reward systems.** Strategies and tactics change. Situations change. Organization members encounter different needs. Certain aspects of a reward system may no longer be appropriate. Managers should regard reward systems as evolving, rather than permanent. Avoid confusion and unfairness when changing the rules.

Footnote for Section 3.3.5 —

[1] John A. Pearce II and Richard B. Robinson. *Strategic Management: Formulation, Implementation, and Control.* Irwin, 1997, p. 362.

3.4.0 ORGANIZATION CHARACTER

"There is a gap between what the organization says it wants and what it feels like to work there. Those gaps between what you say and what you do erode trust in the enterprise and in the leadership, and they inhibit action. The more you can narrow that gap, the more people's energies can be released toward company purposes."

— ROBERT HASS

Description

Refers to the "behind the scenes personality" of a company. Deals with the explicit or implicit protocols that become apparent to all employees. Takes into account how an individual's perception of his or her company is shaped to a large extent by day-to-day experiences.

Principal Elements

- Informal Communication
- Organization Feedback
- Organizational Credibility
- Adaptability to Change

Organizational character is defined by the familiar routines that employees experience on a daily basis. The character of the organization extends to include the informal organization and the implicit protocols of communication and work processes. These conditions of the environment influence the climate in which employees work.

Organizations that are open in structure and facilitate communication between traditional function silos and between hierarchal levels seem more appealing than those with top-down communication policy and distant inaccessible management.

An organization's character is made up of four major components: informal communication protocols, organizational feedback systems, credibility and trust, and adaptability to change.

Informal communication refers to the way managers and peers communicate outside the formal structure of the organization. It occurs continuously within the organization and includes impromptu discussions of new work procedures, new initiatives, and any change management issues or ambiguous policies. When formal communication is congruent or consistent with the way the organization behaves, then the informal communication network should align itself as well to reinforce the organization's intent. When the character of the organization is less than noble, the informal network will rapidly communicate the less-than-desirable work conditions and the discrepancies between what is expected on the part of the organization and what actually transpires.

Feedback systems work in a similar fashion. Sharing information is critical in developing people's capacities. Leaders have learned that unless people see and experience the effects of their behavior, they won't care. When people have the same information and understand that they are part of a community, with common values and shared interests, the results flow. Leaders soliciting feedback on their own performance are much more in touch with the climate and character of their unit and can respond in a more proactive manner.

Credibility and trust are also important components in the free flow of information throughout an organization. Members of the firm should not fear the free exchange of ideas, constructive feedback, and suggestions for new objectives. The atmosphere and climate of the organization should support this informal exchange to prevent fear of reprisals. An organization that deals with violation in a swift and just manner will provide a more stable work environment for its employees. Without worry about inconsistent responses, employees will be more willing to invest in long-term behavioral changes and commitment to the organization's strategic initiatives.

Finally, the character of the organization is expressed in its adaptability and willingness to change. With open channels of communication, both formal and informal, along with employee trust and consistent behavior on the part of management, change issues are more easily accepted and acted upon than in atmospheres of mistrust, closed minds, and constant criticism.

An organization that has a poor character will commit many of the mistakes firms make when faced with change imperatives.[1]

- The organization that cannot communicate feedback, good or bad, will sink into complacency. Without feedback, it is perceived that all is well, therefore urgency is lost and change cannot happen.

- Without strong respected champions leading the way, any change initiative will fail due to the amount of inertia to overcome.

- Lack of good communication will dampen efforts to communicate the new corporate vision, rendering change impossible.

- People will not make sacrifices for an organization to change if they do not trust the organization to recognize that sacrifice and to respond in kind.

- Changing is difficult with little or no feedback or trust.

- Real change or transformation takes time.

- Without clear communication and trust in leadership and systems, change may only be temporary.

- Without proper communication of the company's strategy and how it fits with the organizational culture, employees may misinterpret the strategy and credibility and performance will be affected further.

In a fast, highly-competitive environment, poor organizational character and the issues of poor communication, leadership, and consistency of purpose can adversely effect total organizational performance. Mishandling new initiatives, due to frustrated employees creating unnecessary resistance, can slow progress to the point of not being able to meet the customer's emerging need. Sales can fall, budgets get pinched, and the organization is left to struggle.

These errors are not inevitable; they can be avoided by supporting issues of character within the organization.

Footnote for Section 3.4.0 —

[1] John P. Kotter. *Leading Change*. Harvard Business School, 1996, p. 4-14.

3.4.1 Informal Communications

> *"Nobody tells you to be a customer service hero; it's just sort of expected."* — Nordstrom Employee

Definition

Establishing general communication norms, one-on-one and group interactions. The impact of position power on communication. Establishing conflict resolution techniques. Having "open door" vs. hierarchical cultures. Ensuring a balance of technology and face-to-face communication.

Areas of Focus

- Open exchange of ideas without fear of reprisal.
- Using conflict or disagreement constructively.
- Cross-functional communication encouraged.
- "Open-door" policy; non-hierarchical.
- Balance of technology and face-to-face communication.

Informal communications are those dialogues, emails, memos, and messages that pass between members of the organization through informal channels. An informal channel could be a work group on break, conversations at lunch, or observations of management or organizational behavior.

Managers should be tuned to the "grapevine" and its capacity to handle free-flowing information. Of concern to management is that, although the information on an informal network is most often accurate, the more emotionally charged the information, the more likely it will be inaccurate. Since inaccurate information can lead to mistrust and loss of credibility, all attempts should be made to correct disinformation.

Keith Davis has studied the organizational grapevine for more than 30 years. "With the rapidity of a burning powder train," Davis claims, "information flows out of the woodwork, past the manager's door and the janitor's closet, through the steel walls or construction glass partitions." The messages are often "symbolic expressions of feelings." For example, if a rumor says the boss may quit, and he or she is not going to, it may be that the employees wish it were true.

Among Davis' findings are the following:[1]

- Grapevines are accurate 75 to 95 percent of the time.

- There are only a few sources that supply the entire formal network. There are not many other channels of communication as capable of supplying the entire formal network.

- Admittedly, the grapevine can have some dramatic failures in accuracy.

- The grapevine is a psychological reflection of employee interest in the organization or its members.

- Levels of activity in the informal network parallel those in the formal network.

- Troublemakers sometimes use the grapevine. All untrue rumors, whether started by troublemakers or not, are best countered by truth and told directly by management to employees early in the situation in question.

Davis concludes that wise managers "feed, water, cultivate the grapevine," because it "cannot be abolished, rubbed out, hidden under a basket, chopped down, tied up, or stopped. It is as hard to kill as the mythical glass snake which when struck, broke into fragments and grew a new snake out of each piece."[2]

The grapevine can be nurtured by the manager through developing friendships, relationships with the key people in it, and by providing useful information from time to time.

Other aspects of informal communications include the communication styles of management in nurturing their interpersonal relationships with members of the organization. These style issues include having an "open door" policy where employees, peers, and senior managers can communicate ideas, feedback, and information in a non-hierarchical atmosphere without fear of reprisal. These "off the record" conversations keep managers' fingers on the pulse of the organization. Information can be clarified, the grapevine can be accessed, and positive information can filter out in a non-threatening manner.

Within this atmosphere of open dialogue, cross-functional conversations are encouraged. Workers can participate in decisions regarding organizational issues that span traditional silos. By first establishing an atmosphere of friendship, teamwork, and trust, good informal communications can open the way for more structured, team-based decision-making.

Footnotes for Section 3.4.1 —

[1] Keith David. "Cut Those Rumors Down to Size." Supervisory Management, June 1975, p. 2-6 — "The Care and Cultivation of the Corporate Grapevine." Dun's Review, July 1973, p. 44-47 — "Management Communication and the Grapevine." Harvard Business Review, Sep-Oct 1953, p. 43-49.

[2] Ibid.

3.4.2 Organization Feedback

"There's a big difference between showing interest and really taking interest." — Michael P. Nichols

Definition

Implementing methods or forums to solicit employee feedback. Encouraging employees to offer their input regarding important operational elements of the company. Acting on the feedback and communicating the result.

Areas of Focus

- Establishing methods for internal feedback.
- Recognizing the value of employee input.
- Encouraging employees to offer their ideas and opinions.
- Communicating the outcomes of the feedback.

Organizational feedback systems provide a channel of communication that enables each member of the organization to understand the interdependencies of each person, group, and department in terms of organizational performance. As CEO Jack Stack points out, at most companies, "No one explains how one person's actions affect another's, how each department depends on the others, what impact they all have on the company as a whole. Most important, no one tells people how to make money and generate cash. Nine times out of ten, employees don't even know the difference between the two."[1]

Jack's people are taught how to read financial statements and shown the results weekly to track the company's progress. Within thirty-six hours of posting, every employee knows what he or she needs to do to improve the company's performance. To back this up, a complete detailed financial statement is published monthly. Sharing information rather than guarding it facilitates dialogue and lets everyone understand how decisions are made and how they are linked to shared values and common purpose.

People's inclination to improve their productivity on a task increases only when they have a challenging goal and receive feedback on their progress.[2] Goals without feedback and feedback without goals have little effect on motivation.

With detailed information that includes factors such as quality, quantity, timeliness, and customer service, people can self-correct and more easily understand the big picture. They can also determine what help they need from others and who might be able to benefit from their help.[3]

Leaders can encourage employees to voice their concerns, ideas, and suggestions. Sam Goldwyn had a philosophy about feedback. After a series of box office losers, Mr. Goldwyn called his brain trust together and told them, "I want you to tell me exactly what's wrong with MGM, even if it means losing your job." Goldwyn was looking for some strong opinions, not "yes men."[4]

Giving an honest opinion is vital if the work unit is going to learn to improve. This is accomplished only through accurate information given by people who, with the best interests of the unit in mind, speak up and tell it like it is.

There is a story about Nikita Khrushchev[5] meeting in Washington at a Press Club gathering. He was asked a question, "Today, you talked about the hideous rule of your predecessor, Stalin. You were one of his closest aides and colleagues during those years. What were you doing all that time?" Khrushchev's face grew bright red. "Who asked that?" he shouted, but no one answered. "Who asked that?" he repeated firmly. Again, there was silence. "That's what I was doing," Khrushchev said. Silence will not help a leader improve.

Footnotes for Section 3.4.2 —

[1] J. Stack. *The Great Game of Business.* Doubleday, 1992, p. 5.

[2] A. Bandura and D. Cervone. "Self-Evaluative and Self-Efficacy Mechanisms Governing the Motivational Effects of Goal Systems." Journal of Personality and Social Psychology, 45 , 1983, p. 1017-1028.

[3] James M. Kouzes and Barry Z. Posner. *Credibility: How Leaders Gain and Lose It, Why People Demand It.* Jossey-Bass, 1993, p. 173.

[4] Warren Bennis. "Followers Make Good Leaders Good." New York Times, 31 Dec 1989, p. 3.

[5] Warren Bennis. "Followers Make Good Leaders Good." New York Times, 31 Dec 1989, p. 3.

3.4.3 ORGANIZATION CREDIBILITY

"A vision not consistent with values that people live by day by day will not only fail to inspire genuine enthusiasm, it will often foster outright cynicism." — PETER M. SENGE

Definition

Creating work environments that are aligned with, and conducive to, the core values and beliefs of the company. Using rewards or consequences to emphasize the importance of these beliefs. Assessing the day-to-day experiences of managers and employees relative to company ideals and standards. Taking steps to deal with violations of company values.

Areas of Focus

- Employee day-to-day experiences consistent with values.
- Quick to rectify inconsistencies or deal with violations.
- Rewarding behaviors that are consistent with values/standards.
- Confronting behaviors that violate values/standards.
- Cynicism virtually absent.

Social cognition research shows that individuals pick up on all the signals in their work environment — big and small — as cues for how they should behave. Employees notice little things. They want to believe in their company's expressed vision and values, but they are always watchful for those inconsistencies that destroy the credibility of the core ideology.[1]

When people were asked to define credibility in terms of believability of a leader, the two components of almost every definition were what leaders say and what they do.[2] Credibility is about consistency between action and words. People tend to hear the words, observe the actions, and measure the gaps. The speaker is deemed credible when the gaps are too small to worry about.

When the credibility test is put to an organization by its members, the test expands beyond just words and actions. People want a leader who is competent, has a vision, and is dynamic, but when speaking for the organization, the leader should speak for everyone. "This is what we say we are going to do."

To lead people through change requires a shared vision. The organization gains credibility when it does what its members have expected it to do, sticks to its strategic agenda, and takes effective steps when its values are violated.

Cynicism, born from consistent disappointment, is virtually nonexistent in a credible organization. Everyone has a voice and acts on behalf of the unit. Credible leaders in credible organizations find unity among diverse interests, points of view, and beliefs. Strengthening the firm's credibility requires clarity, unity, and intensity from its leadership. By clarifying meaning, unifying members of the firm, and intensifying actions (Figure 1), leaders demonstrate their own commitment to a consistent set of expectations. This process, repeatedly followed, earns the organization credibility and sustains it over time.

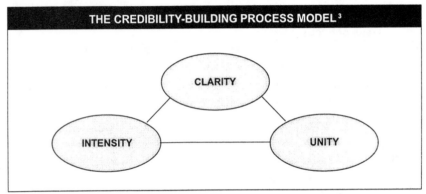

THE CREDIBILITY-BUILDING PROCESS MODEL [3]

Figure 1

Credibility begins with leaders clarifying their own values and mirroring the values of the other members of the team. When clarity exists, everyone knows the guiding principles and core competencies that most directly contribute to the organization's success.

With that clarity, organizations build a community of shared vision and values. Unity exists when people widely share, support, and endorse the intent of the organization. They understand that shared vision and values are important to the future success of the organization.

People will feel so strongly about the common purpose for the organization that they will be anxiously engaged in executing the strategy. Sound execution leads to better understanding, reevaluation, and clarifying of the next intent.

The end result is an organization that lacks cynicism, where employees are engaged in their day-to-day tasks without surprise or frustration, and the organization is quick to respond to any variations or violations of the expected norm.

Footnotes for Section 3.4.3 —

[1] James C. Collins and Jerry I. Porras. *Built to Last*. Harper Collins, 1994.

[2] James M. Kouzes and Barry Z. Posner. *Credibility: How Leaders Gain and Lose It, Why People Demand It*. Jossey-Bass, 1993, p. 47.

[3] James M. Kouzes and Barry Z. Posner. *Credibility: How Leaders Gain and Lose It, Why People Demand It*. Jossey-Bass, 1993, p. 49.

3.4.4 ADAPTABILITY TO CHANGE

"Changing the structure is only part of it. We are also changing the process by which we manage, the rewards and other mechanisms that shape those processes, and the kind of people we place in the key management positions. Finally, we are trying to change our informal culture — the ways we do things, the behaviors that drive the business. In fact, the term 'reorganization' doesn't really capture what we are trying to do at Xerox. We are redesigning the 'organizational architecture' of the entire company." — PAUL ALLAIRE

Definition

Designing and implementing change management processes. Selecting appropriate change management styles. Effectively communicating the need or rationale for change. Determining organizational tolerance for change. Evaluating the overall level of employee acceptance or resistance to change. Assessing a company's ability to quickly respond to threats or opportunities.

Areas of Focus

- Company is proficient at change management.
- Ensuring that all employees understand the reasons for the change.
- Ensuring that all employees understand the process and methods that will be used to implement the change.
- Employees expect change.
- Company able to respond and adapt to change effectively.

Ralph Kilmann describes an adaptive culture as:[1]

...an adaptive culture that entails a risk-taking, trusting, and proactive approach to organizational as well as individual life. Members actively support one another's efforts to identify all problems and implement workable solutions. There is a shared feeling of confidence: the members believe, without a doubt, that they can effectively manage whatever new problems and opportunities will come their way. There is widespread enthusiasm, a spirit of doing whatever it takes to achieve organizational success. The members are receptive to change and innovation.

Rosabeth Kanter[2] argues that adaptive cultures favor entrepreneurship, which can help a firm adapt to a changing environment by allowing it to identify and exploit new opportunities.

Digital Equipment Corporation is one example of an adaptive culture. They have promoted risk-taking innovation, candid discussions, entrepreneurship, and leadership at multiple levels in the hierarchy. This culture has helped the firm adapt more successfully to a rapidly changing environment than such companies as Honeywell, whose cultures have not encouraged risk taking or entrepreneurship. Superior adaptability is key for DEC's continued success.

If the adaptive culture is so appealing, why do firms resist change and cling to a culture of stability? McDonald's is one of the largest restaurant chains in the world and enjoys some tremendous business strengths. Yet despite all of its strengths, McDonald's share is declining, its stock performance is lagging, and its industry is experiencing shifts in customer tastes. What has gone wrong at McDonald's? First and foremost is top management's failure to recognize the need for change. In the face of these industry shifts and competitor encroachment, McDonald's chairman was quoted as saying, "Do we have to change? No, we don't have to change. We have the most successful brand in the world."[3] As the company's performance deteriorated, top executives tended to blame others. They have publicly blasted dissident franchises and negative news accounts are chalked up to misperceptions by the media. One particular reporter was barred from the biennial briefing.[4]

The table on the following page (Figure 1) compares adaptive cultures with unadaptive ones.

Deal and Kennedy emphasized that making strategic changes in an organization always threatens a culture: "People form strong attachments to heroes, legends, the rituals of daily life, the hoopla extravaganza and ceremonies, and all the symbols of the workplace. Change strips relationships and leaves employees confused, insecure, and often angry. Unless something can be done to provide support for transitions from old to new, the force of a culture can neutralize and emasculate strategy changes."[5]

ADAPTIVE vs. UNADAPTIVE CULTURES [6]		
	Adaptive Corporate Cultures	**Unadaptive Corporate Cultures**
Core Values	Most managers care deeply about customers, stockholders, and employees. They also strongly value people and processes that can create useful change (e.g., leadership up and down the management hierarchy).	Most managers care mainly about themselves, their immediate workgroup, or some product (or technology) associated with that work group. They value the orderly and risk-reducing management process much more highly than leadership initiatives.
Common Behavior	Managers pay close attention to all their constituencies, especially customers, and initiate change when needed to serve their legitimate interests, even if that entails taking some risks.	Managers tend to behave somewhat insularly, politically, and bureaucratically. As a result, they do not change their strategies quickly or adjust to or take advantage of changes in their business environments.

Figure 1

To successfully adapt to change, leaders follow these simple and distinct steps, as shown in Figure 2:

STEPS IN IMPLEMENTING CHANGE [7]			
Determining the need for change	Determining the obstacles to change	Implementing change	Evaluating change

Figure 2

Sometimes the need for change is obvious; yet often enough, the need is more subtle and often overlooked. Recognition occurs when the gap between the expected performance becomes too great when compared to actual performance.

Determining the obstacles to change can take some focus. Obstacles can exist in any level of the organization.[8] Corporate-level obstacles include its strategy, structure, and anything that may affect the organization as a whole. Divisions that are interrelated and trade resource pose big problems for change. Resistance is greatest where the biggest impact will be.

Generally a company can adapt to change in two ways: either top-down or bottom-up. In top-down change, the change is led by a strong CEO; bottom-up change is more gradual.

Finally, evaluating the effects of the change on organizational performance involves comparing the previous performance with the current one.

The following table (Figure 3) lists several change approaches that can be taken to reduce resistance to change and establish a more adaptive culture:

APPROACHES TO LESSENING RESISTANCE TO CHANGE [8]			
Approach	**Commonly used when...**	**Advantages**	**Disadvantages**
Education + communication	There is a lack of information or inaccurate information and analysis.	Once persuaded, people will often help implement the change.	Can be very time-consuming if many people are involved.
Participation + involvement	The initiators do not have all the information they need to design the change, and others have considerable power to resist.	People who participate will be committed to implementing change, and any relevant information they have will be integrated into the change plan.	Can be very time-consuming if participants'design an inappropriate change.
Facilitation + support	People are resisting because of adjustment problems.	No other approach works as well with adjustment problems.	Can be time-consuming, expensive, and still fail.
Negotiation + agreement	Some person or group with considerable power to resist will clearly lose out in a change.	Sometimes it is a relatively quick and inexpensive solution to resistance problems.	Can be too expensive if it alerts others to negotiate for compliance.
Manipulation + co-optation	Other tactics will not work, or are too expensive.	It can be a relatively quick and inexpensive solution to resistance problems.	Can lead to future problems if people feel manipulated.
Explicit + implicit coercion	Speed is essential, and the change initiators possess considerable power.	It is speedy and can overcome any kind of resistance.	Can be risky if it leaves people angry with the initiators.

Figure 3

Footnotes for Section 3.4.4 —

[1] Ralph H. Killman, Mary J. Saxton, and Roy Serpa, editors. *Gaining Control of the Corporate Culture*. Jossey-Bass, 1986, p. 356.

[2] Rosabeth Kanter. *The Change Masters*. Simon & Schuster, 1983.

[3] Joseph P. Quinlan, quoted in David Leonhardt. "McDonald's: Can It Regain Its Golden Touch?" Business Week, 9 Mar 1998, p. 71.

[4] David Leonhardt. "McDonald's: Can It Regain Its Golden Touch?" Business Week, 9 Mar 1998, p. 72.

[5] T. Deal and A. Kennedy. *Corporate Cultures: The Rites and Rituals of Corporate Life*. Addison-Wesley, 1982.

[6] John Kotter and James Heskett. *Corporate Culture and Performance*. Free Press, 1982.

[7] Charles W. L. Hill and Gareth R. Jones. *Strategic Management Theory: An Integrated Approach*. Houghton Mifflin, 1995, p. 428.

[8] L. C. Coch and R. P. French, Jr. "Overcoming Resistance to Change." Human Relations, Aug 1948, p. 512-532 — P. R. Lawrence. "How to Deal with Resistance to Change." Harvard Business Review, Jan-Feb 1969, p. 4-12.

[9] John P. Kotter and Leonard Schlesinger. "Choosing Strategies for Change." Harvard Business Review, Mar-Apr 1979.

GLOSSARY OF VIRTUAL CEO™ TERMS AND AREAS OF FOCUS

The following glossary of terms has been arranged according to the order they have been discussed in this book. The glossary contains definitions and descriptions of the numbered terms and principal elements discussed, along with the areas of focus which apply to each.

1.0 Organization Strategy

1.1.0 Mission, Vision, and Competitive Advantage

Description — A company's mission, vision, and competitive advantage describe the business it is in, its short- and long-term market position, and the manner in which it will differentiate itself from the competition.

1.1.1	Definition	Areas of Focus
Mission: The Focused Purpose	Effectively mapping a course of action for the near term. Understanding the needs of a company's primary stakeholders. Stating a clear point of differentiation from the competition.	• Clearly defined purpose short-term purpose. • Realistic approach. • Serves the best interests of all stakeholders. • Clearly defined point of differentiation.
1.1.2 Vision: The Future Perspective	Having a clear long-term vision for the organization. Having a clear projection of the company's market position for the future. The long-term needs of stakeholders are respected. Evolutionary in nature, responsive to evolving opportunities.	• Clearly defined long-term outlook. • Appeals to the long-term interests of the company's stakeholders. • Provides foundation for all decisions. • Flexible; allows for meeting evolving opportunities. • Clear understanding of long-term financial requirements.
1.1.3 Strategic Advantage	Identifying what a company perceives to be its competitive advantage. Initiating specific activities that support the company's point of differentiation within their industry. Employees understand how their performance supports the strategic advantage.	• Competitive advantage is the key driver to forming strategy. • Competitive advantage is clearly understood by all stakeholders. • Employees clearly understand how their role supports the company's strategy.

1.1.4	Definition	Areas of Focus
Strategic Integration	Synthesizing the strategic formulation process and the implementation planning process. Ensuring that managers who are responsible for implementation plans participate in or receive detailed information relating to the company's strategy. Making sure that implementation plans are uniform and that they reflect the company's strategic intent.	• Strategy and tactics aligned. • Implementers participate in the strategic formulation process. • Units and divisions effectively plan together. • Plans specify how divisions, departments, or groups will contribute. • Plans reflect a universal approach.

1.2.0   External Assessment

Description — Reflects an organization's approach to gathering and analyzing essential market data. Included in this data are competition profiles, macro and micro economic studies, industry opportunities and threats, and key success factors.

1.2.1	Definition	Areas of Focus
Customer Profile	A company's efforts to fully explore the multiple dimensions of its customers. Having a clear understanding of the needs of its customers, including specific benefits sought by the customer, their resistance points to purchase, shifts in habit, bargaining power, specific buying characteristics, and choice of distribution channels.	• Clearly defined reasons why customers buy company products/ services, and why they do not. • Clearly defined benefits that customers seek. • Clearly defined reasons why customers would not buy company products or services. • Assessed customer bargaining power. • Knowing customer-preferred choice of distribution channel.
1.2.2 Industry and Competitive Analysis	Applying the necessary resources to put critical industry and competitive data at a company's disposal. Assessing the outlook for industry growth, the rising sales of substitute products, the entrants into the marketplace, and the industry's key market drivers. Maintaining sufficient data relating to specific direct and indirect competitors; their strengths, weaknesses, and strategic intent.	• Clearly identified primary competitors. • Identified potential or indirect competitors. • Clearly defined strengths, weaknesses, and strategies of direct/ indirect competitors. • Assessing the threat of substitute products or services and new entrants into the marketplace. • Defined key market drivers. • Ongoing market evaluation process.

1.2.3	Definition	Areas of Focus

Environ-mental Assess-ment	Assessing and understanding the critical environmental conditions that face a company's industry. This includes assessing economic conditions, technology shifts, demographic shifts, socio-cultural values and institutions, regulatory infringement, and vulnerability to unidentified business cycle influences.	• Defined and clarified regulatory requirements.
		• Assessing vulnerability to adverse business cycles.
		• Summarized opportunities and threats due to:
		  - Economic conditions
		  - New technology
		  - Demographic structure
		  - Legal or political events
		  - The natural environment
		  - Socio-cultural conditions

1.2.4 Key Success Factors	Applying a critical thinking process when evaluating market data. Determining which factors drive success and influence business within a particular sector of commerce. Utilizing a "key success factor" approach to identify opportunities within a given industry.	• Implementing critical thinking process. • Clearly measured competitive intensity. • Clearly defined product or service demand within our markets. • Clearly defined key drivers to success within our industry. • Having a system that consistently monitors key influences within the industry.

1.3.0   Internal Assessment

Description — Reflects the company's ability to objectively evaluate its strengths and weaknesses. This would include defining its market position, its management processes, and how effectively it utilizes a "value-chain" analysis approach.

1.3.1	Definition	Areas of Focus

Market Position	Maintaining a consistent awareness of a company's specific market position. Understanding its proprietary position, market share, and the outlook for a growing customer base.	• Maintaining or sharing a dominant role within company markets.
		• Competitors viewing company as a market leader.
		• Possessing a proprietary position in:
		  - Patents
		  - Technology
		  - Innovations
		  - Distribution
		• Growing at a rate that meets or exceeds the industry.
		• Having a higher degree of customer retention than main competitors.

	Definition	Areas of Focus
1.3.2 Finance	Effective alignment of financial resources. Adequate funding of key initiatives. Utilizing cost/benefit models. Employing "if/then" scenario techniques. Ensuring accurate financial and economic forecasting as well as long-term financial planning. Overseeing effective financial controls.	• Consistently performing within a range of financial goals. • Adequate funding of key initiatives. • Employing a "cost/benefit" approach to resource allocation. • Having a targeted long-term financial plan. • Employing an "if/then" model when forming strategy. • Establishing realistic goals based on past performance. • Resources are well-aligned. • Financial plan allows for economic or environmental disruption.
1.3.3 Research, Development, and Design	Maintaining an aggressive attitude toward discovery and innovation. Resource allocation reflects a commitment to the R&D function.	• R&D has all required resources to successfully fulfill its function. • Maintaining a creative and innovative process. • Performance reflects robust R&D contribution.
1.3.4 Production	The ability to manufacture goods and provide services to the marketplace. Consistently demonstrating operating efficiency, speed, flexibility, and a capacity for continual improvement.	• Fully integrating all departments to support production. • Production process is fast and cost-efficient. • Evolves to reflect changes within company and within industry. • Process contributes to competitive advantage. • Strategic partners consistently fulfill production commitments.
1.3.5 Marketing	Creating a targeted marketing plan. Maintaining a constant awareness of the company's branding approach or competitive advantage when developing promotional strategies. Using available targeted information to support marketing decisions. Clearly determining the "return-on-investment" on all marketing campaigns.	• Having a clearly defined marketing plan. • Coordinating all departments to support marketing. • Monitoring the ROI of all marketing campaigns. • Branding plays a critical role. • Utilizing a marketing system or database to track customer and market information. • Marketing department contributes to product or service development. • "Competitive advantage" is a key driver for all marketing decisions.

	Definition	Areas of Focus
1.3.6 Sales and Distribution	Developing and executing an effective sales management process. Achieving sales goals. Rewarding the sales organization for the correct skills and behaviors. Consistently demonstrating efficiency or speed of distribution. Having the means to track sales activity from lead generation through close.	• Employing a fully-integrated sales management process. • Coordinating all departments to support the sales process. • Consistently achieve sales goals. • Sales teams/channels possess all required skills to achieve plan. • Sales teams/channels are provided with the necessary information to achieve their goals. • Sales channels are quick and responsive. • Tracking sales activity from lead generation through close. • Competitors recognize sales process as "Best-in-Class".
1.3.7 Customer Service	Clearly defining service standards and maintaining an effective customer service management system. Ensuring that customer expectations are consistently met or exceeded. Tracking and measuring service strengths such as customer loyalty, repeat business, and minimal complaints.	• Meeting or exceeding customer expectations. • Measuring customer satisfaction by routinely obtaining direct customer feedback. • Managers and employees share a high commitment to achieving customer loyalty. • Maintaining a customer relationship management system that provides critical service information to make the best decision.

1.4.0   Objectives, Initiatives, and Goals

Description — Reflects the company's ability to articulate what it wants to accomplish, how it will do it, and when it will be achieved. The company's process of defining its direction, aligning financial and human resources, while instilling accountability and critical measurements.

	Definition	Areas of Focus
1.4.1 Vital Direction	Effectively converting strategic intent into clearly defined, actionable activities. Prioritizing critical objectives by their strategic importance, aligning these objectives with the company's values and beliefs, and remaining poised to integrate dynamic emerging opportunities.	• Identifying key strategic objectives. • Actions fully integrated into values and beliefs. • Action items clearly prioritized by importance and magnitude. • Having quantifiable and measurable actions. • Remaining flexible to respond to new opportunities.

1.4.2	Definition	Areas of Focus
Resource Alignment	Committing the necessary capital, human, or technological resources to achieve key strategic objectives. Evaluating individual or group capacity when planning resource allocations.	• Resources are clearly defined for each action. • Resource alignment is linked to competitive advantage. • Individual or group capacity plays a critical role in assigned workload.
1.4.3 Organization Account-abilities	Ensuring that individuals and groups within the company have a clear understanding of management's expectations, and that they understand their specific roles in accomplishing critical objectives, initiatives, and goals. Communicating progress against key objectives.	• Ensuring that employees understand how their roles and responsibilities relate to strategic objectives. • Employing a standardized vehicle and format to track and report performance. • Having an internal system that routinely communicates status of key objectives.

1.4.4
 	
Measure-ment
	Demonstrating consistency when tracking or reporting performance. Using an effective and uniform measurement process for financial reporting, project management, third party performance, and operating standards.	• Effectively measuring key performance indicators, such as:
		  - Financial ratios
		  - Project phases and milestones
		  - Qualitative processes
		  - Individual, group, or partner performance
		  - Technology

2.0   Organization Design

2.1.0   Basic Structure

Description — Evaluates an organization's hierarchy and design in relation to the "Demand Criteria" indicated in the strategic plan. Evaluates whether or not the company is structurally poised to achieve its strategic intent. Basic structure also pertains to an organization's ability to adjust to an evolving environment.

2.1.1	Definition	Areas of Focus
Strategic "Demand Criteria"	Assessing the organization structure prior to making a strategic commitment. Being willing to reorganize to advance a strategy. Not allowing political or departmental influence to shape design decisions.	• Structure reflects strategy. • Company willing to reorganize, if necessary. • Structure is based on strategic need, not "in-house" politics.
2.1.2 Formal Structure	Ensuring that the current structure optimizes the company's value-chain (Research, Development, Design, Production, Marketing, Sales, Distribution, and Service). Creating a structure that provides for interaction across departmental lines. Designing sensible and effective reporting relationships and lines of authority.	• Structure optimizes execution of the "value-chain." • Structure facilitates inter-department collaboration. • Current structure is optimal for current strategy.
2.1.3 Structure Evolution	Keeping the organization structure flexible so that it can better react when emerging opportunities or dynamic events within the industry call for change.	• Structure adapts quickly to change. • Capitalizes on key competitive advantages. • Structure does not inhibit innovation.

2.2.0   Core Competence

Description — Core competencies are the skills, knowledge, and special abilities a company possesses that set it apart from other organizations. By effectively bundling these skills, knowledge, and special abilities, a company can create their competitive advantage, enhance customer value, and expand their market position.

2.2.1	Definition	Areas of Focus
Identification of Core Competence	Identifying a specific and unique combination of company skills and capabilities that are valued by customers and difficult to replicate by the competition. Clearly articulating core competencies to all appropriate constituencies.	• Complete understanding of a company's distinctive skills and capabilities. • Clearly articulating core competencies. • Viewing core competence as the foundation for strategic intent
2.2.2 Application of Core Competence	Examining and evaluating core competencies in relation to creating customer value, expanding competitive advantage, or identifying new business or product opportunities.	• Applying core competence to create/sustain customer value. • Applying core competence to support competitive differentiation. • Applying core competence to support product or service offerings.
2.2.3 Leveraging Core Competence	Implementing programs and processes to develop, strengthen, and expand core competencies.	• Expanding customer value proposition. • Increasing competitive differentiation. • Expanding product or service offerings.

2.3.0   Information, Systems, and Technology

Description — Competitive environments require rapid and targeted information, aligned systems, and innovative and appropriate use of technology. Takes into account the quality of an organization's information, systems, and technology, and the effective alignment of these technologies with its strategic intent.

2.3.1	Definition	Areas of Focus
Organization Communication	Implementing a system to ensure that all primary stakeholders consistently receive the necessary information to keep them well informed regarding company performance and critical activities.	• Implementing a communication system that touches all stakeholders. • Communicating the strategic plan throughout the company. • Providing all stakeholders with all critical business information. • Communicating progress against key objectives.

2.3.2	Definition	Areas of Focus
Targeted Information	Using company information systems to provide managers with timely competitor updates or environmental data that may influence their business decisions. Providing management with current performance data, such as business unit performance, sales activity, and customer service information.	• Providing managers with the information they need to make informed decisions. • Using a company information system to regularly disseminate important data. • Ensuring that industry and environmental data is always current. • Providing management with timely updates regarding performance in their area of responsibility.
2.3.3 Enterprising Systems	Designing and implementing systems that provide synthesized information across departmental lines, which enable management to assess the organization on a holistic basis. Using these systems to provide business units with a clear understanding of the interdependencies within the company. Expediting the flow of information cross-functionally.	• Defining the specific components of a cross-functional information system. • Information is shared across department lines through an integrated system. • Facilitating the flow of information across departmental lines to maximize performance and effective decision-making.
2.3.4 Applied Technology	Acquiring the necessary technology to achieve strategic intent. Ensuring that there is a process or vehicle within the organization to track the role of technology within the industry.	• Strong commitment to integrating best-in-class technology. • Effectively monitoring the role of technology within industry. • Seeking to discover new or improved technologies. • Ensuring that company technology needs are fully met.

2.4.0   Organization Efficiency

Description — Deals with having the right people focused on doing the right job within an optimal performance environment. Addresses a company's approach to supervision, clarity of roles and responsibilities, organization interdependencies, and management of outsourced relationships. The objective is minimal duplication, maximum innovation, and well-managed risk.

2.4.1	Definition	Areas of Focus
Balanced Direction and Oversight	Ensuring that, within the organization, there is clear guidance without excessive or overbearing policies. Monitoring compliance with company policies and procedures.	• Providing written policies and procedures to all divisions, departments, or units. • Effectively monitoring compliance. • Keeping procedures/manuals brief and to-the-point. • Minimal "red-tape."
2.4.2 Synthesized Roles and Responsibilities	Ensuring that all managers and employees clearly understand their role and their role integrates with those of other departments. Continually reinforcing the need for cross-department integration and communication.	• Clearly defined management and employee roles. • Employees/partners understand how their roles relate to strategic objectives. • Eliminating redundancy in roles or responsibilities.
2.4.3 Managed Outsourced and Strategic Alliances	Making sure that strategic alliances are carefully managed. Holding strategic partners to the same performance standards to which company employees are held.	• Outsourced activities are closely monitored. • Strategic partner activities are closely monitored. • Ensuring that partner performance standards are consistent with internal standards.

3.1.0   Values and Beliefs

Description — Describes a company's commitment to its constituencies: customers, shareholders, employees, the community, vendors, etc. Values describe the standards and ideals that a company holds in high regard. They provide a framework for implementing strategic initiatives.

3.1.1	Definition	Areas of Focus
Values Integration	The impact of core values and beliefs on a company's culture and on its bottom-line. Creating or refining core values. Addressing the unique needs of all constituencies. Aligning company systems and practices with core beliefs. Establishing consistency of culture throughout the organization.	• Values are clearly defined. • Company practices, systems, and processes are carefully aligned with values. • Work climates consistent throughout organization.
3.1.2 Values Communication	Ensuring that company employees clearly understand the significance of company values. Using all available communication media to reinforce values and beliefs. Creating a sense of reverence and durability regarding company tenets.	• Values are consistently communicated. • Employees understand content and spirit of values. • Employees understand critical importance of standards. • Consistently reinforced in company communication media.
3.1.3 Values Durability	Establishing a process to evaluate company performance with regard to values and beliefs. Reviewing standards and ideals on a regular basis to ensure timeliness and relevance.	• Values are not compromised. • Performance against values are tracked with the same emphasis as financial or production performance. • No strategy adopted that might violate company standards. • Values are reviewed periodically to maintain relevance.

3.2.0   Leadership

Description — Deals with creating a clearly-articulated vision and possessing the skills and resolve to recruit and develop followers who are committed to carrying out the vision. Having the ability to see the bigger picture and to maintain a balance between high-level strategies and front-line tactics.

3.2.1	Definition	Areas of Focus
Management Modeling	The effect of senior and middle managers exemplifying the company's values and beliefs through their personal behavior. The impact of management behavior on the overall credibility of the company's standards and ideals.	• Senior management "walks the talk." • Line management "walks the talk." • Managers are viewed as role models. • Management styles are aligned with values and consistent across divisions/departments.
3.2.2 Strategic/ Tactical Balance	Establishing an organizational standard where managers are expected to see the "big picture." Ensuring that managers understand the long-term impact of their decisions. Adjusting the focus of managers from a tactical (departmental) approach, to a broader, company-wide perspective.	• Tactical and strategic skills among managers are equally emphasized. • Line managers get understand the "big picture." • Managers understand the broader implications of their decisions. • Managers can effectively communicate the company's strategic plan to their staff.
3.2.3 Empowerment	Utilizing localized vs. centralized control, wherever possible. Driving decision-making responsibilities down to the lowest appropriate level in the organization. Minimizing the "red tape" in an organization.	• Decisions made without unnecessary or authoritarian approval process. • Decisions driven to the lowest appropriate level. • Minimal "red tape."
3.2.4 Developmental Coaching	Integrating employee personal goals with the organization's goals. Using coaching as a motivational tool rather than a punitive process. Encouraging employee initiative. Addressing performance issues in a manner than maintains employee self-esteem. Using positive reinforcement as a means to improve or sustain performance.	• Delegation is a motivational tool. • Coaching is viewed as developmental vs. punitive. • Managers encourage initiative. • Employee goals/aspirations are taken into consideration. • Managers take the time to recognize a job well done.
3.2.5 Building Effective Teams	Generating team enthusiasm, loyalty, and commitment. Encouraging cooperation among team members. Understanding group dynamics. Leading meetings with diverse personality types.	• Managers promote team work. • Team participants are excited about and committed to their goals and objectives. • Cross-functional communication is promoted. • Meetings are well-planned and highly participative.

3.3.0 Human Resources Systems

Description — Deals with attracting and maintaining skilled employees. Human Resources systems define how a company recruits, trains, challenges, and inspires its employees in the pursuit of its strategic intent.

3.3.1	Definition	Areas of Focus
Selective Recruitment	Implementing targeted recruitment and selection programs. Establishing a skills and attributes profile to help determine whether or not an individual would be conducive to the company culture. Developing manager interviewing skills. Utilizing input from boss, peers, and subordinates when considering potential candidates.	• Only high-caliber candidates are considered. • Candidate compatibility with company culture is carefully considered. • Interviewing skills are a company strength. • Boss and peer input is required on critical hires. • Managers evaluated on their ability to recruit top talent.
3.3.2 Employee Orientation	Getting new employees off to a good start. Designing orientation programs that create enthusiasm and excitement. The impact of senior management involvement. Establishing follow-up and support activities, particularly during the employee's first year.	• Company provides a comprehensive orientation program. • Values and beliefs are underscored. • Senior managers participate.
3.3.3 Continuous Learning	Providing training and development opportunities to managers and employees. Ensuring that educational programs are high-quality and that they are aligned with the company's strategy and key objectives. Establishing educational policies and standards. Succession planning criteria and process are fully developed.	• Training is a company priority. • Employees are provided with necessary training to perform at optimum levels. • Training programs aligned with strategic goals. • Training programs are well designed and structured. • Company spends strategically proportionate amount of money on training. • Succession planning is carefully designed.

3.3.4	Definition	Areas of Focus
Perform-ance Manage-ment	Having a well-designed performance management system. Establishing clear, results-oriented goals. Using a participative goal-setting approach. Establishing rewards and consequences. Using performance tracking and feedback methods. Conducting comprehensive, well-substanti-ated performance reviews. Using interim performance review sessions to maintain/correct performance.	• Performance management system is results-oriented. • Goals are challenging, but realistic. • Accountabilities and timelines are clear. • Interim performance reviews are standard practice. • Performance evaluations are comprehensive and well-substanti-ated.
3.3.5 Reward Systems	Effectively rewarding the skills and contributions that advance a company's strategic intent. Ensuring that rewards are fair, equitable, and proportionate to employee effort. Team perfor-mance is rewarded at a level that is equal to or greater than individual performance.	• Appropriate skills and behaviors are being rewarded. • Rewards are fair and equitable. • Rewards are worth the effort. • Promotions are deserved. • Team performance is rewarded (greater than or equal to individual performance). • No reward for achievement at the expense of others. • Reward programs are monitored for effectiveness.

3.4.0 Organization Character

Description — Refers to the "behind the scenes personality" of a company. Deals with the explicit or implicit protocols that soon become apparent to all employees. Takes into account how an individual's perception of his or her company is shaped to a large extent by day-to-day experiences.

3.4.1	Definition	Areas of Focus
Informal Communi-cation	Establishing general communi-cation norms, one-on-one and group interactions. The impact of position power on communi-cation. Establishing conflict resolution techniques. Having "open door" vs. hierarchical cultures. Ensuring a balance of technology and face-to-face communication.	• Open exchange of ideas without fear of reprisal. • Using conflict or disagreement constructively. • Cross-functional communication encouraged. • "Open-door" policy; non-hierarchi-cal. • Balance of technology and face-to-face communication.

3.4.2	Definition	Areas of Focus
Organization Feedback	Implementing methods or forums to solicit employee feedback. Encouraging employees to offer their input regarding important operational elements of the company. Acting on the feedback and communicating the result.	• Establishing methods for internal feedback. • Recognizing the value of employee input. • Encouraging employees to offer their ideas and opinions. • Communicating the outcomes of the feedback.
3.4.3 Organizational Credibility	Creating work environments that are aligned with, and conducive to, the core values and beliefs of the company. Using rewards or consequences to emphasize the importance of these beliefs. Assessing the day-to-day experiences of managers and employees relative to company ideals and standards. Taking steps to deal with violations of company values.	• Employee day-to-day experiences consistent with values. • Quick to rectify inconsistencies or deal with violations. • Rewarding behaviors that are consistent with values/standards. • Confronting behaviors that violate values/standards. • Cynicism virtually absent.
3.4.4 Adaptability to Change	Designing and implementing change management processes. Selecting appropriate change management styles. Effectively communicating the need or rationale for change. Determining organizational tolerance for change. Evaluating the overall level of employee acceptance or resistance to change. Assessing a company's ability to quickly respond to threats or opportunities.	• Company is proficient at change management. • Ensuring that all employees understand the reasons for the change. • Ensuring that all employees understand the process and methods that will be used to implement the change. • Employees expect change. • Company able to respond and adapt to change effectively.

BIBLIOGRAPHY

Derek F. Abell. *Defining the Business: The Starting Point of Strategic Planning*. Prentice-Hall, 1980.

Fred C. Allvine. *Marketing: Principles and Practices*. Harcourt Brace Jovanovich, 1987.

Vincent P. Barabba. *Meeting of the Minds*. Harvard Business School Press, 1995.

Robert R. Blake and Jane Srygley Mouton. *Managerial Grid III: The Key to Leadership Excellence*. Gulf Publishing, 1985.

A. B. Blankenship and George E. Breen. *State of the Art Marketing Research*. American Marketing Association, 1995.

L. J. Bourgeois, Irene M. Duhaime, and J. L. Stimpert. *Strategic Management: A Managerial Perspective*. Dryden, 1999.

Eugene F. Brigham and Louis C. Gapenski. *Financial Management — Theory and Practice*, Dryden, 1994.

Alfred Chandler. *Strategy and Structure*. MIT Press, 1962.

James C. Collins and Jerry Porras. *Built to Last: Successful Habits of Visionary Companies*. Harper Collins, 1994.

Stephen R. Covey. *Principle-Centered Leadership*. Simon and Schuster, 1991.

Richard L. Daft. *Organization Theory and Design*. Southwest Publishing, 1998.

Thomas H. Davenport and Laurence Prusak. *Working Knowledge*. Harvard Business School, 1998.

Fred R. David. *Strategic Management, 7th Edition*. Prentice-Hall, 1998.

T. Deal and A. Kennedy. *Corporate Cultures: The Rites and Rituals of Corporate Life*. Addison-Wesley, 1982.

Peter Drucker. *Management: Tasks, Responsibilities and Practices*. Harper & Row, 1974.

Liam Fahey and V. K. Narayanan. *Macroenvironmental Analysis for Strategic Management*. West, 1986.

Jay R. Galbraith. *Designing Organizations*. Jossey-Bass, 1995.

Bill Gates. *Business at the Speed of Thought*. Warner Books, 1999.

Bill Gates. *The Road Ahead*. Penguin, 1996.

James L. Gibson, John M. Ivancevich, and James H. Donnelly, Jr. *Organizations: Behavior, Structure, Processes*. Irwin, 1991 and 2000 editions.

Robert M. Grant. *Contemporary Strategy Analysis*. Blackwell, 1995.

Gary Hamel and C. K. Prahalad. *Competing for the Future*. Harvard Business School Press, 1994.

William V. Harvey. *Communication and Interpersonal Relations*. Irwin, 1979.

Robert Hiebler, Thomas B. Kelly, and Charles Ketteman. *Best Practices: Building Your Business with Customer-Focused Solutions.* Simon & Schuster, 1998.

Charles W. L. Hill and Gareth R. Jones. *Strategic Management Theory: An Integrated Approach.* Houghton Mifflin, 1995.

Robert Jolles. *Customer Centered Selling.* Free Press, 1998.

Jerome Kanter. *Management Information Systems, 3rd Edition.* Prentice-Hall, 1984.

Rosabeth Kanter. *The Change Masters.* Simon & Schuster, 1983.

Robert S. Kaplan and David P. Norton. *The Balanced Scorecard.* Harvard Business School Press, 1996.

Jon R. Katzenbach and Douglas K. Smith. *The Wisdom of Teams.* Harvard Business School, 1992.

David T. Kearns and David A. Nadler. *Prophets in the Dark — How Xerox Reinvented Itself and Beat Back the Japanese.* Harper Business, 1992.

R. H. Killman. *Beyond the Quick Fix: Managing Five Tracks to Organizational Success.* Jossey-Bass, 1984.

Ralph H. Killman, Mary J. Saxton, and Roy Serpa, editors. *Gaining Control of the Corporate Culture.* Jossey-Bass, 1986.

W. R. King and D. I. Cleland. *Strategic Planning and Policy.* McGraw-Hill, 1979.

Philip Kotler. *Marketing Management.* Prentice-Hall, 1984.

John P. Kotter. *A Force for Change: How Leadership Differs from Management.* Free Press, 1990.

John P. Kotter. *Leading Change.* Harvard Business School Press, 1996.

John P. Kotter and James L. Heskett. *Corporate Culture and Performance.* Free Press, 1982 and 1992 editions.

James M. Kouzes and Barry Z. Posner. *Credibility: How Leaders Gain and Lose It, Why People Demand It.* Jossey-Bass, 1993.

James M. Kouzes and Barry Z. Posner. *The Leadership Challenge.* Jossey-Bass, 1987.

P. R. Lawrence and J. Lorach. *Organization and Environment.* Harvard Business School, 1967.

Rensis Likert. *New Patterns of Management.* McGraw-Hill, 1961.

Charles C. Manz and Henry P. Sims, Jr. *Business Without Bosses.* Wiley & Sons, 1993.

Michael E. McGrath. *Setting the PACE in Product Development.* Butterworth-Heinemann, 1996.

Alex Miller. *Strategic Management.* Irwin McGraw-Hill, 1998.

Henry Mintzberg. *The Fall and Rise of Strategic Planning.* The Free Press, 1994, p. 324.

Henry Mintzberg and James Brian Quinn. *The Strategy Process.* Prentice-Hall, 1996.

Henry Mintzberg, James Brian Quinn, and John Voyer. *The Strategy Process.* Prentice Hall, 1995.

Cynthia A. Montgomery and Michael Porter. *Strategy: Seeking and Securing Competitive Advantage.* Harvard Business School Press, 1991.

John A. Pearce II and Richard B. Robinson. *Strategic Management: Formulation, Implementation, and Control*. Irwin, 1997.

John J. Peter and James H. Donnelly, Jr. *A Preface to Marketing Management, 6th Edition*. Irwin, 1994.

Thomas Peters and Robert H. Waterman, Jr. *In Search of Excellence*. Harper & Row, 1980 and 1982 editions.

Tom Peters. *Thriving on Chaos*. Knopf, 1988.

Michael E. Porter. *Competitive Strategy*. Free Press, 1980.

James Brian Quinn. *Intelligent Enterprise*. Free Press, 1992.

V. Kasturi Rangan, Benson P. Shapiro, and Rowland T. Moriarty. *Business Marketing Strategy: Cases, Concepts and Application*. Irwin, 1995, p. 244.

Edgar H. Schein. *Organizational Culture and Leadership*. Jossey-Bass, 1992.

Peter R. Scholtes. *The Team Handbook*. Joiner Associates, 1988.

R. Schroeder. *Operations Management*. McGraw-Hill, 1981.

Peter M. Senge. *The Fifth Discipline*. Doubleday, 1990.

Jeffrey Sonnenfeld. *The Hero's Farewell: What Happens When CEOs Retire*. Oxford University, 1988.

J. Stack. *The Great Game of Business*. Doubleday, 1992.

A. A. Thompson, Kem Pinegar, and Tracy Robertson Kramer. *Wal-Mart Stores*, Irwin McGraw-Hill, 1994.

A. A. Thompson and A. J. Strickland. *Crafting and Implementing Strategy*. Irwin, 1995.

A. A. Thompson and A. J. Strickland. *Strategic Management: Concepts and Cases*. Irwin McGraw-Hill, (6th/8th? edition, 1995; 10th edition, 1998; 11th edition, 1999).

Michael Treacy and Frederik D. Wiersema. *Disciplines of Market Leaders*. Addison-Wesley, 1995.

Fredrick E. Webster. *Marketing for Managers*. 1974.

Steven C. Wheelwright and Kim B. Clark. *Leading Product Development*. Free Press, 1995.

Peter Wright, Mark J. Kroll, and John Parnell. *Strategic Management, 4th Edition*. Prentice-Hall, 1998.

What Is Virtual CEO™?

VIRTUAL CEO™
INCORPORATED

- **A rapid, convenient, real-time performance management system.**

Virtual CEO™ radically transforms an organization's ability to evaluate and improve performance. The program enables senior executives to quickly and conveniently evaluate their organization's performance against over 200 best practices tied to 49 important business disciplines. VCEO dramatically reduces the time it normally takes to **identify needs, develop solutions, plan actions, and support execution.** In fact, using Virtual CEO™, executives can assess the performance of their entire organization in just two hours. Action-planning sessions are reduced to as little as one day.

Virtual CEO™ has been designed as a multi-media platform. Participants can access the VCEO program by CD-ROM, local server, or via the internet. The *Executive Version* is a very comprehensive tool designed for busy senior executives. The *Organization Version* is a direct subset of the *Executive Version*, intended for the general workforce.

- **An ROI-driven program.**

Virtual CEO™ challenges management to link return-on-investment (ROI) to every objective developed as part of the VCEO process. Using VCEO, senior managers quickly identify business disciplines that are considered to be both *high-impact* and *low-performing*. A key benefit of the VCEO program is that it allows executives to rapidly develop and implement results-oriented solutions to resolve critical performance problems.

- **A fully researched, fact-based, best practices tool.**

  The 200+ best practice statements contained within the Virtual CEO™ program are drawn from the works of internationally recognized experts in the fields of strategy, sales, marketing, core competence, economics, corporate culture, leadership, and several other disciplines required to run a successful organization. Every statement can be linked back to best practices.

- **A revolutionary action-planning process.**

  The Virtual CEO™ Validation and Action Planning software enables a consultant (internal or external) to electronically facilitate an action-planning workshop. This action-planning software literally **eliminates the need for flipcharts**. Objectives, resource allocation, ownership, milestones, and measurements are all entered into the software program while being projected on a big screen. At the end of the session, the summary report is printed and distributed to the group immediately. Consultants or facilitators no longer have to take dozens of flipcharts back to their office to manually produce an action plan report.

- **An enterprise-wide application.**

  VCEO can radically accelerate the process of mapping organization alignment. There is no restriction on how deep or how many managers and employees can participate. Going deeper into the organization provides a richer profile and maximizes the information base used to make informed decisions.

Why Do Executives Use Virtual CEO™?

VIRTUAL CEO™
INCORPORATED

- **They need an ROI-based performance management system.**

  Whether organizations are publicly or privately held, the pressure is growing to increase profits and revenue while reducing costs and increasing efficiency. There is increasing pressure to demonstrate quantifiable return on investment.

  Virtual CEO™ provides an ideal solution. All VCEO outcomes are tied to ROI. Action plans are produced immediately and include quantifiable results. Managers can readily integrate VCEO-generated objectives into their existing strategic initiatives.

- **They prefer a process that respects their time.**

  Virtual CEO™ rapidly evaluates organizational performance and accurately targets strategic and tactical opportunities. Our diagnostic process is completely non-invasive. With Virtual CEO™, executives can avoid making time during their workday to be interviewed by a consultant. Instead, they can complete the performance assessment, in just one or two hours, in the privacy of their offices, their homes, or on an airplane or via the internet, completely on their own schedule.

  The VCEO **Results and Key Findings** report quickly identifies a company's **high impact/low performance** areas. Executive teams then use this information to develop and implement targeted and measurable solutions. This sensible approach is ultimately better for both executives *and* consultants.

- **They recognize the need to operate in alignment with each other.**

  Virtual CEO™ provides a forum for senior executives to share their perspectives regarding critical performance issues facing their organization. This process encourages executives to take a cross-functional view of their organization. Before VCEO, the means by which this information was shared usually meant a brainstorming session, resulting in several flipcharts taped around a room. With VCEO, consultants don't begin an offsite by *asking* executives how they perceive the performance of their company…they begin by *telling* executives how they perceive their company, based on the information in the VCEO reports. This information creates immediate focus, which then facilitates targeted dialogue and debate, leading to more rapid agreement and alignment at the top.

- **They must compete successfully with other organizations.**

  Virtual CEO™ equips senior executives with the information they need to position themselves to take on the most formidable competitors. VCEO outcomes focus on problem areas that diminish an organization's ability to respond quickly to market or industry events. The action-planning software revolutionizes the execution and turnaround time associated with implementing business solutions. **All phases of the Virtual CEO™ program are geared to radically accelerate an organization's ability to achieve business excellence.**

VIRTUAL CEO™
INCORPORATED

1-949-248-2404   or   1-877-FOR-VCEO
www.virtualceo.com